BEYOND THEISM AND ATHEISM

STUDIES IN PHILOSOPHY AND RELIGION

1. FREUND, E.R. *Franz Rosenzweig's Philosophy of Existence: An Analysis of* The Star of Redemption. 1979. ISBN 90 247 2091 5.

2. OLSON, A.M. *Transcendence and Hermeneutics: An Interpretation of the Philosophy of Karl Jaspers.* 1979. ISBN 90 247 2092 3.

3. VERDU, A. *The Philosophy of Buddhism.* 1981. ISBN 90 247 2224 1.

4. OLIVER, H.H. *A Relational Metaphysic.* 1981. ISBN 90 247 2457 0.

5. ARAPURA, J.G. *Gnosis and the Question of Thought in Vedānta.* 1985. ISBN 90 247 3061 9.

6. HOROSZ, W. and CLEMENTS, T. (eds.) *Religion and Human Purpose.* 1987. ISBN 90 247 3000 7.

7. SIA, S. *God in Process Thought.* 1985. ISBN 90 247 3103 8.

8. KOBLER, J.F. *Vatican II and Phenomenology.* 1985. ISBN 90 247 3193 3.

9. GODFREY, J.J. *A Philosophy of Human Hope.* 1987. ISBN 90 247 3353 7.

10. PERRETT, R.W. *Death and Immortality.* 1987. ISBN 90 247 3440 1.

11. GALL, R.S. *Beyond Theism and Atheism: Heidegger's Significance for Religious Thinking.* 1987. ISBN 90 247 3623 4.

BEYOND THEISM AND ATHEISM: HEIDEGGER'S SIGNIFICANCE FOR RELIGIOUS THINKING

ROBERT S. GALL

American Academy of Religion

1987 **MARTINUS NIJHOFF PUBLISHERS**
a member of the KLUWER ACADEMIC PUBLISHERS GROUP
DORDRECHT / BOSTON / LANCASTER

Distributors

for the United States and Canada: Kluwer Academic Publishers, P.O. Box 358, Accord Station, Hingham, MA 02018-0358, USA
for the UK and Ireland: Kluwer Academic Publishers, MTP Press Limited, Falcon House, Queen Square, Lancaster LA1 1RN, UK
for all other countries: Kluwer Academic Publishers Group, Distribution Center, P.O. Box 322, 3300 AH Dordrecht, The Netherlands

Library of Congress Cataloging in Publication Data

```
Gall, Robert S.
   Beyond theism and atheism.

   (Studies in philosophy and religion ; v. 11)
   Bibliography: p.
   Includes index.
   1. Heidegger, Martin, 1889-1976--Contributions in
religious thought.  2. Religious thought--19th century.
3. Religious thought--20th century.  I. Title.
II. Series.
B3279.H49G27   1987     200'.1      87-24836
```

ISBN 90-247-3623-4 (hardback)

Copyright

PRINTED IN THE NETHERLANDS

To My Parents

CONTENTS

PREFACE

My first year in graduate school marked by initial expo-
sure to Heidegger and some of his important early essays. At
that time, disenchanted with the state in which "religious
thought" lay, I was quickly struck by the potential Heidegger
presented for breaking new ground in a field that had seemingly exhausted itself by reworking the same old issues and
answers. That insight, along with the conviction that Heidegger had been misused and misunderstood by theologians and
religious thinkers ever since he burst upon the intellectual
scene with the publication of *Sein und Zeit*, grew throughout
my graduate career and resulted in a dissertation on Heidegger
and religious thinking, of which the present text is a revised
and updated version. This text reflects my belief that Heidegger, when "properly" understood on such matters as truth,
God (and gods), and "faith", presents us with a unique voice
and vision that cannot be co-opted into any sort of theology
-- be it negative, existential, dialectical or Thomistic --
and indeed seriously challenges the viability of any "theology". Herein I have tried to "lay the foundation" (if we may
even talk of foundations in this post-modern, deconstructive
age) for a radical rethinking of religious thought by working
from the "ground" up, interpreting Heidegger on a variety of
issues with an eye toward the application of Heidegger's
thinking to various conflicts and problems in religious
thought. My hope is that I have managed -- in some small way,
at least -- to clear away the misuse and misunderstanding of
Heidegger in the field of religious thought and pointed the
way toward areas in which Heidegger's thought may make an even
greater and more fruitful impact than has been realized previously.

I have had help, of course, in my journey. I wish to
thank the two readers on my dissertation committee, Gerhard
Spiegler and Charles Wei-hsun Fu, for their helpful sugges-
tions and criticisms while this work was in progress. A
special note of thanks also goes to my graduate advisor,
Thomas J. Dean, for his encouragement and helpful insights
along the way toward the development of this thesis, and his
meticulous review of the work in progress that helped avoid
any number of problems.

Finally, I also wish to thank Aun-Khuan Tan and Terry
Levan of the Computer Center at Blackburn College, Carlinville, Illinois, for their help in the preparation of this
text.

Carlinville, Illinois   *Robert S. Gall*

ABBREVIATIONS

AED	*Aus der Erfahrung des Denkens*
EM	*Einführung in die Metaphysik*
EHD	*Erläuterungen zu Hölderlins Dichtung*
FD	*Die Frage nach dem Ding*
G	*Gelassenheit*
GP	*Die Grundprobleme der Phänomenologie*
GR	*Hölderlins Hymen >>Germanien<< und >>Der Rhein<<*
HW	*Holzwege*
ID	*Identität und Differenz*
KM	*Kant und das Problem der Metaphysik*
N I, II	*Nietzsche I, II*
Sp	*Spiegel*-Gespräch
PT	*Phänomenologie und Theologie*
Preface	in *Heidegger: From Phenomenology to Thought*
SG	*Der Satz vom Grund*
SZ	*Sein und Zeit*
TK	*Die Technik und die Kehre*
US	*Unterwegs zur Sprache*
VA	*Vorträge und Aufsätze*
WD	*Was Heisst Denken?*
WP	*Was ist das -- die Philosophie?*
WM	*Wegmarken*
ZD	*Zur Sprache des Denkens*

CHAPTER   1

INTRODUCTION

> *Had they deceived us*
> *Or deceived themselves, the quiet voiced elders,*
> *Bequeathing us merely a receipt for deceit?*
> *The serenity only a deliberate hebetude,*
> *The wisdom only the knowledge of dead secrets*
> *Useless in the darkness into which they peered*
> *Or from which they turned their eyes.*
>   T.S. Eliot[1]

How do things stand with religious thinking today?   To some, confident of the genius of modern science and technology, the question is strange. In this day and age, what need have we of religious thinking and its talk of God, of faith and belief, myth, rite, ritual, and church? The self-correcting rationality of modern scientific thought seems more than sufficient for our needs. In the natural sciences it has produced an impressive, objective, ever-expanding picture of our universe that reaches from the peculiarities of sub-atomic particles to those of massive stars and galaxies hundreds of light years away. In the medical, social, and human sciences it has probed our tissues, our psyches and our social relationships and given us often remarkably successful answers for curing what ails us. What is more, it has produced technologies that provide us with vast powers of information, communication, and physical strength that allow man to literally change the world. What need have we of gods and superstition if we can be as gods ourselves, or create our own gods (e.g., the computer), and thereby become content amidst the brilliant logical dazzle of science and technology?

There may be no "need", at least as science defines it, yet the religious questions -- of meaning, purpose, of the right and the true -- still haunt us. One reason may be that the joys of science and the joys of human life do not always converge as nicely as the picture above would have us believe. The exhiliration of discovering how to unlock the vast powers of the atom or the intricacies of the genetic code does not coincide with the agony of the problems such discoveries have created (e.g., nuclear weapons and waste, genetic engineering). Another reason we are haunted may be the sort of man "scientific" thinking often breeds: like the gods descending from Olympus, they often seem inhuman, almost bestial, treating men as numbers and statistics and devices to be used, and reducing everything to wants and needs, drives and chemical reactions. Such an occurrence is strange when we consider that thinking is usually considered to be what is peculiarly

human. Finally, the peculiar single-mindedness in pursuit of
an answer to a problem or in defense of a theory in "scientific" thought often tends, ironically, to take on "religious"
forms. Recent philosophers of science, with some controversy,
have pointed this out,[2] and we merely have to point to the
cultism of psychoanalytic schools, the undying faith in Marx-
ism or the promise of technology on the part of some, for
three examples in which there seem to be manifest more faith
and hope than thought. All this suggests that we are not as
sure of what constitutes "thinking" and "religious thinking"
as we might first suppose.
     Others would find our question strange for other reasons.
Do we not only have to look around us to see that religion is
thriving and religious questions openly debated? There is the
fundamentalist fervor animating Islam, a "revival" of sorts in
Catholicism brought about by Pope John Paul II's mobile papa-
cy, and the increased profile of evangelical and fundamentalist Protestants in the United States. All this indicates a
vitality in religious thinking. Or does it only seem so? If
modern scientific thought and consciousness are questionable,
these various neo-Orthodoxies (and others like them) are no
less questionable as we ask about religious thinking. For
instance, is there not more desperate nostalgia and reaction
than reanimation and regeneration through thinking in all
these examples? Indeed, there seem to be fundamental denials
of the way things are in all these examples of religious
"vitality" -- fundamental denials of the changes that time,
history, and science have wrought in our world that demand new
ways of thinking rather than willful and unconvincing reasser-
tions of the way things were. Attempts to cloak Medieval
formulations of Christian doctrine in a modern idiom which
thereby overlook the critical social, political, and "worldly"
issues that have arisen since the Middle Ages in both indus-
trialized and underdeveloped nations, preachers who decry
modern science on television -- none of this makes any sense.
Too many questions are left unasked; people do not think, they
"believe". One answer is assumed as given and obvious when in
fact we move within a transformed, pluralized context with a
wide range of questions and answers both "secular" and "religious". Hence even if we were to grant the plausibility of
simply reaffirming the tradition over against science and
secularization, we would still have to ask: "Which tradition?" Here again neo-Orthodoxy is left to question-begging
and ad hoc answers (e.g., the uniqueness of Christian faith as
given for Karl Barth) that are less than convincing.
     There are yet "liberal" attempts at religious thinking
apparently thriving about us and taking up the social, moral,
and ecumenical questions of the day. Such attempts, through
some sort of "method of correlation", undertake a kind of
"cognitive bargaining" between a particular religion and the
present situation with its modern scientific sensibilities and

plurality of choices.   Such attempts by and large begin with
"ordinary" human experience, i.e., with the experience of
modern secular man and the secular standards he understands.
Religion, since it can no longer make larger claims on the
world and the culture around it according to such secular
standards, is "saved" by drawing it into the realm of human
subjectivity, consciousness, and experience and asserting it
as a unique kind of human experience with some sort of value
or utility (e.g., it serves to maintain morality).   Religion
is thereby made over into a technique for orienting and transforming the self -- a leap of faith, an existential decision,
a moral commitment, an expression of ultimate concern -- that
saves man from anxiety and lostness in the world.   Religion
thereby becomes privatized and secured against any "outside"
criticism of the "outward" manifestations of religious experience in time and place.   Indeed, a common move here is to
investigate the religious experiences of other cultures (e.g.,
as in phenomenology of religion, misnamed the "history of
religions") to determine the core experience -- the basic human experience of the transcendent -- that is "religious" experience. One thereby closes ranks and defends religion a-
gainst the outside, secular world by bringing other religions
up in defense of one's own assertion of the essentiality of
religious experience to humanity, and therefore trying to make
it invulnerable to criticisms of its "accidental", historical
aspects.   Yet in reducing religion to some core experience and
thereby sheltering it, it retreats into practical irrelevance.
One passes from the metaphysical to the psychological, from
thought to emotion, from publicly debatable truth to "subjective" truth.   One becomes interested in the idea of the holy
or the consciousness of God and what that expresses, rather
than the truth of God's existence (which is more or less
assumed because of our consciousness of him [Him]).   Indeed,
the divine becomes a utilitarian construct and representation.[3]   But now there is little difference between theists and
atheists (whereby there can even be a "death of God" theology,
of all things) except that the theist claims some sort of
special importance or utility for his use of traditional language.   Ironically, present-day "liberal" theology all but
accedes to Feuerbach and Freud in seeing religion as a projection, but then does what is surely incredible: it believes in
the projection.   Theology literally becomes belief in belief,
for the sake of soothing our anxiety.   There is obviously no
less desperation here than in neo-Orthodoxy; one clings to
traditional language and concepts at all costs, even when such
concepts have been emptied of all belief-content (or, more
accurately, receive their content via the belief in belief).
There is no less degradation of time and history here than in
neo-Orthodoxy, except that where neo-Orthodoxy retreats to a
religion of will, "liberalism" retreats to the passivity of
"experience".   In all of this, one conveniently fails to ask

questions -- e.g., whether my consciousness of God is not
perhaps delusionary, or whether other religious "experiences"
are not in fact very different from and indeed critical of
one's own "experience". Instead one rests secure in the
indubitability of experience and subjectivity and irrelevance,
an irrelevance revealed by the reactionariness of neo-Orthodoxy or the indifference of modern secular man, who has so
many "techniques" more stylish than religion for orienting
himself.

In the end, to ask about religious thinking is strange
because it seems it is all too often a question *not* asked
despite the fact that what thinking and religious thinking are
is far from decided. Between those for and against religion,
for and against God, we find all too many questions, questions
not stilled by the lifeless compromises of those who would
have it both ways (i.e., "liberals"). We stand at an impasse.
It seems, if we are to continue, we would do well to reconsider our starting point, to undertake some radical rethinking of
how we are to conceive of thinking and, beyond that, religious
thinking. It seems we should ask about the possibilities of
thinking and religious thinking, and attempt to understand
them in ways that help us make sense of our past, our present,
and our future endeavors along these lines.

Such is the subject of this study, and for such a quest we
turn for help to the 20th century thinker Martin Heidegger.
At first, this may seem to be a strange choice, for Heidegger
did not appear to make religious matters a central issue in
his thinking, though they were of some concern to him prior to
his writing *Being and Time*.[4] Indeed, it often seems that
Heidegger tries to make a very clear distinction between faith
and/or theology and his pursuit, philosophy (cf. EM 9; PT 14-
15, 40; WM 379). Yet despite such examples (which we will
have to examine later), our turn to Heidegger in quest for
possibilities of religious thinking does seem sound for a
number of reasons. First, even the most vociferous critic of
Heidegger would probably have to admit that he is the first,
and perhaps only, great thinker of this century to evade the
Cartesian alternative in thinking,[5] and thereby provides possibilities for overcoming the problems of religious thinking.
Heidegger therefore provides us with a starting point for the
radically different direction in thinking that would seem to
be necessary for any reorientation and reanimation of religious thinking. It might be objected that another (e.g.,
Eastern) tradition might provide us with a radically different
direction for religious thinking -- indeed, might even be
better in such provision. However, turning to another tradition poses problems of correlating and translating issues
between traditions -- correlation and translation that cannot
be done without first thinking through our own tradition.
Turning to Heidegger solves that problem insofar as Heidegger
provides a radically different direction for thinking from

within and out of the Western tradition in which our puzzlement about religious thinking has arisen. Turning to Heidegger therefore seems to hold an advantage over what could,
without great care, end up being a romantic flight to other
traditions.
     Another reason for turning to Heidegger is that, in stak-
ing out an alternative to Cartesianism and the whole order of
thinking up till now, he has dealt with the general philosophical problems that bear on religious thinking to an extent
and in a way unmatched by others in this century. Compared to
Wittgestein, for instance, who has been about as influential
as Heidegger but has left us mostly incomplete and unedited
notes (including *Philosophical Investigations,* which were
edited and published posthumously), Heidegger has provided us
with a generous supply of carefully considered and edited
books, lectures, and essays which give us a good many hints as
to what directions our thinking might take on such matters as
language, truth, the gods, art, science, and the nature of
man. And again, these reflections are carried out with a
sense of history and tradition that Wittgenstein, for instance, seemed to lack, yet with that decisive step away from
traditional modes of thinking intact. Thus, instead of losing
touch with the questions and answers about religious thinking
that have emerged from the Western tradition, Heidegger provides us with the opportunity to assimilate and transform the
traditional puzzles in a fashion that does not sacrifice our
adherence to the new directions called for by our situation.
     However, the most important reason for turning to
Heidegger might be that his thinking contains an elusive
element and dimension that strikes many -- for better or for
worse -- as "religious."[6] It is a dimension that goes beyond
his willingness to deal with such topics as the holy, the gods
and divinity, or his willingness to talk with theologians; it
seems to well up from the very depths of his thinking to
concern the whole bearing and attitude of his thinking. Of
course, any attempt to characterize even a dimension or element in Heidegger's thinking as "religious" seems suspect, for
the exact meaning of "religion" and what is "religious" thereby becomes questionable and vague. Indeed, it might be advised that we either provide a precise definition of what is
meant by "religion" and the "religious", or drop the term
altogether. Heidegger in fact might have advised the latter
option, given his observation that the term "religion" has a
definite history and is tied to the matter of the Roman interpretation of the relation between man and gods (EHD 114). Yet
to use some precise definition of what is "religious" would
seem to close out our quest -- for the *possibilities* of religious thinking -- before it has even begun, and to throw out
any use of the term "religious" seems, at best, premature,
since we wish to focus on phenomena generally recognized as
religious. It seems best to abide in the ambiguity of the

term, for that is how things stand in our thinking. Indeed,
that ambiguity in our understanding and in the application of
the term "religious" to Heidegger's thinking seems to be the
reason we turn to Heidegger; in showing a "religious" dimension, Heidegger's thinking seems to embody the very puzzlement
we have concerning what "religious" thinking could possibly
entail.   If we could somehow open up that ever-elusive dimension in his thinking that strikes one as "religious" and
uncover what bearing that has on the issues he takes up in his
thinking in general (e.g., truth, world, meaning, language),
it seems we would go a long way toward uncovering the possibilities available for "religious" thinking.

     Of course, in pursuing an investigation of the "religious"
dimension in the thinking of Heidegger in the hope of uncovering possibilities for religious thinking, we also hope to make
a   significant   contribution   to   the   interpretation   of
Heidegger's thinking.   For one thing, we should be able to
arrive at a position where some sort of decision regarding the
theological appropriation of Heidegger can be made.   This
appropriation has   haunted all too long not only the way
Heidegger is seen with regard to religion, but also how he is
interpreted in general.   Hence devotees are often a bit uneasy
when they see talk of the gods and the holy and "piety", for
it seems to be a retrenchment and retreat from the promise of
new things from Heidegger.   And, of course, the theological
appropriation has helped make Heidegger an easy target of
criticism and suspicion regarding his real intentions.   Some
of the shadow of doubt concerning Heidegger's thinking might
then be lifted if we are able to clarify his "religious"
significance.   In addition, our interpretation, mindful of
this "religious" dimension and therefore having to weave it
into the entire fabric of his thinking, should hold out the
promise of showing Heidegger's thinking as more meaning-full
as a whole.

     One thing, though, should be made clear from the start:
our concern in trying to open up this elusive "religious"
dimension in the thinking of Heidegger in order to bring forth
possibilities for "religious" thinking does not include a
search for Heidegger's "philosophy of religion".   Such a
search would entail a radical misunderstanding of Heidegger,
for it would take Heidegger's thinking as thought, as a set of
doctrines which we could point to as "Heideggerian" and then
dissect, criticize, or use.   But Heidegger did not "have" a
"philosophy", let alone a "philosophy of religion".   To interpret him so is to interpret him in terms of the metaphysical
tradition from which he is emerging and stepping away.   It is
an interpretation which overlooks him as a thinker and overlooks the radical and original character of his thinking for
which we have sought him out in the first place.   What is
essential to interpreting Heidegger is seeing his thinking as
a way (US 98-99), a way or path which his thinking both builds

and follows as it unfolds; it is an enactment or performance of what it is about. What is essential is that we pay heed to the ever-shifting gradient and direction of that way of thinking, not as an outline to be followed but as a path that opens up before us and must be explored on our own responsibility.[7]

The above point highlights one of the problems of wrestling with Heidegger's thinking. If we approach his thinking from the tradition (e.g., as "having" a "philosophy of religion"), we obscure how he moves away from the tradition. Retranslating his thinking back into the language of the tradition and the (artificial) problems it has set up simply will not do. We must approach his thinking from "within" and see what insight his revelations provide for future attempts at thinking. Of course, in so approaching Heidegger we face another problem: we risk being and appearing uncritical, of being "in thrall" of Heidegger and his thinking. This is especially true if one spends a good deal of time "simply" expounding Heidegger's thinking and using a good deal of his "jargon". However, despite appearances, it should be made plain to the reader that what is going on in the text below is far from uncritical. To begin with, an interpretation is already a critical stance toward the thinking laid out, if only in its realization that a thinking is in need of interpretation and clarification. In addition, the extensiveness of the interpretations in the following chapters, far from being uncritical "expositions", serve two critical purposes. First, there are enough misunderstandings and ambiguities in the burgeoning literature on Heidegger that his thinking needs to be laid out in detail in order to "clear the air" and get ourselves on track in terms of the matter Heidegger would have us think. This is especially true in some of the areas in which we are most interested (e.g., the gods and the holy, the "thankful" and "poetic" aspects of thinking). Second, thorough interpretations of the thinking of Heidegger in each of our chapters helps us avoid, as much as possible, overleaping his path of thinking and, with that, the trouble and labor of his thinking. A short, unobtrusive "exposition" of Heidegger's thinking on a matter risks presuming too much -- about the hidden assumptions in our thinking, about what to expect of Heidegger, and about the matters with which Heidegger is dealing. We are likely to deem certain matters obvious if we do not take the time to see how Heidegger works in, through, and out of traditional contexts and problems. Thus, in short, if we are to bring forth possibilities of religious thinking from the thinking of Heidegger, we must first come to understand Heidegger, and we can only come to understand Heidegger by taking the time to thoroughly investigate and lay out his thinking.

As to the extensive and perhaps uncritical use of Heideggerian "jargon", we should take note of a few points. First, since we are moving in a different language than that through

which Heidegger moved, rendering his thinking intelligble
requires that we think on our own, finding the correct word or
phrases that will show what Heidegger was trying to show.
Hence we are not really simply mimicking Heidegger's language
and thinking. There is of course still a problem insofar as
the English translation of Heidegger itself has had a tendency
to take on the look and feel of "jargon". It is hoped that
this will be allayed by our own translations and explanations
of terminology at the proper places. Secondly, Heidegger's
linguistic peculiarities are, to a large extent, inseparable
from his thinking and any attempt to explain that thinking.
His language is part of his "phenomenology", part of his
attempt to *show* important connections and *reveal* hidden possibilities (which is one reason why the reader will find
extensive notations of the original German in the text). To
avoid these peculiarities is to avoid what is shown to us by
his language. Thus excessive concern over the use of Heideggerian "jargon" risks both a misunderstanding of Heidegger and
the function of his language. Heidegger's language aims to
reorient our thinking by knocking us out of the ruts along
which our thinking tends to move. His language, and our
attempts to render them into English, therefore aim at being
strange to a certain extent, in order to show new ways of
approaching problems and to get the reader to think about what
is going on in one's own thinking and in the thinking of the
tradition. To clamor too loudly for an explication, justification, and rendition of Heidegger's thinking according to
traditional categories -- as some think we are bound to do --
is to wish away the labor of trying to understand a new form
of thinking that is indeed strange, and should be experienced
as such.
     Finally, it should be pointed out that our primary purpose
here is to first understand Heidegger and the impact he could
and should have on religious thinking. Only if we understand
a thinker can we then "think against" him, i.e., be "critical"
of him, and it is a central issue of this work that Heidegger
has all too often been misunderstood and thereby criticized
regarding religious thought. To that end, each of our chapters will "expound" on Heidegger's approach to particular
issues, and then apply those expositions -- sometimes extensively, sometimes tentatively -- to issues in religious
thought. This, it is hoped, will lay the "foundation", as it
were, for further, more fruitful study of Heidegger within the
context of religious thought than has been done before.
     There is one more observation we may make on the way in
which we will approach Heidegger's thinking which is sigifi-
cant both for our study and the interpretation of Heidegger in
general. If we are to attend to the way of Heidegger's thinking, it seems incumbent upon us to consider the whole of his
thinking and, beyond that, to see his thinking as a whole, as
a unity that is loyal to its own thinking and what it has to

think about. In other words, it seems necessary to resist
chopping up Heidegger's thinking into sections, or focusing
too much attention on any one publication or set of publica-
tions that he has "presented" to us. This is because all talk
of "early" and "later" Heidegger and the infamous *Kehre* in
between, of Heidegger I, II, and even Heidegger III -- all
this is based once again on a doctrinal reading of Heidegger's
thinking that disrupts its flow and its immanent self-criti-
cism as it assimilates and transforms what has gone before.
One attends to what is said rather than to what he is speaking
to and about, what he is trying to show and reveal in his
thinking. One becomes entangled in formulations (e.g., the
meaning or "house" of being, the very use of the word "being")
which results in misunderstandings and criticisms that further
lose their way and the matter at stake. One begins to read
"early" Heidegger (notably *Sein und Zeit*) as a traditional
philosophical treatise on man, and thus perhaps as the realization of a Nietzschean philosophy of the overman who wills
his own destiny; one begins to read the "later" Heidegger as
"mystical" and "cryptic" and therefore to be vilified or
praised depending on whether one delights in clear logical
thinking or deep, murky mutterings. One even begins to look
for events in Heidegger's life that would "explain" the apparently phenomenal change between his early and late periods.
None of this, however, makes much sense if Heidegger's thinking is taken as a whole and attention is paid to his thinking
and what it has to think about, as he hoped and continually
stressed.[8] Of course at times it will seem as if such an
interpretation is nevertheless slanted in one direction or the
other, particularly toward the "later" Heidegger (to those who
still insist on thinking that way). This is due, by and
large, to the process of assimilation and transmutation taking
place in Heidegger's thinking whereby early attempts at thinking are later re-called in ways sometimes more significant for
our interpretation (in the sense that they more clearly point
out what is going on in the thinking). Despite this, it is
hoped that enough will be done in earlier chapters to show the
"completeness" of the interpretation of Heidegger so that a
few references here and there in later chapters will direct
the reader back to the full significance of how Heidegger's
thinking is being laid out. Again, what must be kept in mind
throughout is the way of thinking, and what it is trying to
show.

     In the end, it is not an easy interpretation we are at-
tempting; we have to think through changes in language and
emphasis and try to bring forth Heidegger's thinking in all
its strangeness and meaningfulness. It is not meant as an
introductory exposition that reduces the thinking of Heidegger
to easily manipulated, familiar formulations. Yet, despite
all the difficulties, the task will be more rewarding in that

Heidegger is understood as more meaningful and therefore richer in possibilities for (religious) thinking.

                              * * *

    As for the way of that interpretation, it will begin by
trying to dismantle the principal obstacle to any reconsideration of the significance of the thinking of Heidegger for
religious thinking: the theological appropriation (and rejec-
tion) of his thinking.   Central to our task in Chapter 2,
then, will be an examination of the significance of two key
figures in Heidegger's thinking -- Nietzsche (predominantly)
and Hölderlin.   By correlating the death or lack of God as
proclaimed by these two with the key issues and themes of
Heidegger's thinking -- e.g., the oblivion of being, nihilism,
death, anxiety, the nothing -- we will make a provisional
attempt to point out the radical difference between what is at
stake in the thinking of Heidegger and what is at issue in any
sort of theology.   Sighting that difference provides not only
an opportunity to criticize the particular theological appro-
priations of Rudolf Bultman and Heinrich Ott, but also provides us with the opportunity to show how Heidegger's thinking
stands in critical opposition to theology and yet appropriates
its "religious" task.   Thus we will try to show that the
thinking of Heidegger should be taken on its own terms for
opening up *new* vistas in religious thinking.
    Chapter 2, as we have said, will be provisional, meaning
both that it will "run ahead" (cf. German *vor-laufen*) and give
us a pre-view of nearly all the themes and issues that arise
throughout the remainder of the thesis, and that it is an
effort provided for the time being, a "leap", so to speak,
into the circle of thinking that will expand and unfold and,
it is hoped, gain greater clarity along the way.   Hence the
reader will find the argument against theological thinking
continued and amplified in Chapter 3 with an analysis of how
truth, meaning, and world are understood by Heidegger, and how
that understanding provides an alternative to the transcendent-transcendental interpretation of those themes in onto-
theo-logical thought.   By bringing this alternative thinking
to bear on what we have noted as a central issue for religious
thinking today -- plurality -- we will also get a first indication of what sigificance the thinking of Heidegger can have
for "religious" thinking.   This insight will be expanded and
deepened along more traditionally religious lines in Chapter 4
by exploring the twofold matter of the holy and the gods as
it arises in the thinking of Heidegger.   This, of course, will
give us further insight into the extent to which Heidegger
takes us away from theological thinking and yet is able to
deal with such religious issues as the gods and the holy.
Thus we will have further hints of the extent to which religious thinking is possible today.
    With the reflections of the two preceding chapters com-
pleted, we will then be able to turn in Chapter 5 to a consid-

eration of thinking itself as Heidegger sees it.   Special
attention will be paid here to the call and response motifs
Heidegger uses, as well as the "poetic" and "thankful" character of thinking.   These issues, joined with those of the
preceding chapters, will provide us with an outline of the
"piety of thinking" -- i.e., the religious dimension in thinking -- and of how that might change the way we see any number
of religious phenomena (e.g., language, myth, time and eternity, the comportment of the "man of faith").   Chapter 6 will
solidify this transformation of our understanding of "religious" thinking by taking up the spectre of nostalgia and
hopefulness that seems to loom over Heidegger's understanding
of thinking. The issue of nostalgia will allow us, 1) to take
up the very important issue of science and technology *vis à
vis* religion and religious thinking, 2) to clarify once and
for all the difference between traditional, onto-theo-logical
thinking (with its search for security and origins) and
Heidegger's thinking, and 3) to further develop the role of
the divine and God in the thinking of Heidegger and how
Heideggerian religious thinking differs from "faith".   This
will be followed by concluding remarks in Chapter 7 where we
will try to summarize what has been accomplished and what yet
still needs to be thought.

NOTES

1. "Four Quartets" in *The Complete Poems and Plays: 1909-1950* (New York: Harcourt, Brace and World, 1971), p. 125.

2. See Thomas Kuhn, *The Structure of Scientific Revolutions*, 2nd, enlarged ed. (Chicago: University of Chicago Press, 1970); Paul Feyerabend, *Against Method* (1975; rpt. London: Verso, 1978).

3. E.g., a recent article by the theologian Gordon D. Kaufmann entitled "Theology as Imaginative Construction," *The Journal of the American Academy of Religion* 50 (1982), pp. 73ff, is typical of the emphasis placed on symbols and "imperfect" representations of the divine in theology.

4. E.g., see John Caputo, *Heidegger and Aquinas: An Essay on Overcoming Metaphysics* (Bronx, N.Y.: Fordham University Press, 1982), pp. 15-61, and Thomas Sheehan, "Heidegger's 'Introduction to the Phenomenology of Religion' 1920-21," *The Personalist* 60 (1979), pp. 312-324.

5. E.g., Marjorie Grene, certainly no devotee of Heidegger, saying that "for this reason if no other it is fair to say that any contemporary philosophy ought to proceed from the foundation established once and for all in *Being and Time*." *Philosophy In and Out of Europe* (Berkeley: University of California Press, 1976), p. 29.

6. See William Barrett, *The Illusion of Technique* (Garden City, N.Y.: Anchor Press/Doubleday, 1979), p. 251; H.J. Blackham, *Six Existentialist Thinkers* (New York: Harper Torchbooks, 1959), p. 103; Annemarie Gethmann-Siefert, *Das Verhältnis von Philosophie und Theologie im Denken Martin Heideggers* (Freiburg/München: Karl Alber, 1974), pp. 96-98; Karl Löwith, *Heidegger: Denker in dürftiger Zeit*, 2nd, expanded ed. (Gottingen: Vandenhoeck and Ruprecht, 1960), pp. 10, 72, 111. Of course, those with definite conceptions of what religion is (e.g., theologians) are less inclined to so characterize Heidegger's thinking; see John Caputo, "The Poverty of Thought: A Reflection on Heidegger and Eckhart" in *Heidegger: The Man and the Thinker*, ed. Thomas Sheehan (Chicago: Precedent, 1981), p. 125; Heinrich Ott, "Die Bedeutung von Martin Heideggers Denken für die Methode der Theologie" in *Durchblicke: Martin Heidegger zum 80. Geburtstage* (Frankfurt: Klostermann, 1970), p. 27; John R. Williams, *Martin Heidegger's Philosophy of Religion* (Waterloo, Ontario: Wilfrid Laurier University Press, 1977), p. 4.

7. Cf. J.L. Mehta, *Martin Heidegger: The Way and the Vision* (Honolulu: University Press of Hawaii, 1976), pp. 5-6, 79n, 467; Zygmunt Adamczewski, "On the Way to Being: Reflecting on Conversations with Martin Heidegger" in *Heidegger and the Path of Thinking*, ed. John Sallis (Pittsburgh: Duquesne University Press, 1970), pp. 21-22.

8. David Farrell Krell has been the most forceful in arguing against the preoccupation with the *Kehre* and the division of Heidegger's thinking into various phases; see "Nietzsche and the Task of Thinking: Heidegger's Reading of Nietzsche" (Diss. Duquesne University, 1971), pp. 261, 262n; "Nietzsche in Heidegger's *Kehre*," *Southern Journal of Philosophy* 13 (1975), pp. 197-204; and "Death and Interpretation" in *Heidegger's Existential Analytic*, ed. Frederick Elliston (The Hague: Mouton, 1978), pp. 247-255. See also William J. Richardson, *Heidegger: Through Phenomenology to Thought* (The Hague: Martinus Nijhoff, 1963), pp. 625-26, where Richardson cites parallel themes between "Heidegger I" and "Heidegger II" such

that he says the latter is a "re-trieve", a self-interpretation, of the former. Our only problem with Richardson is his insistence on continuing the division (e.g., pp. 243ff) and then trying to piece the two together.

For Heidegger's comments on the *Kehre*, see his Preface to Richardson's book, pp. xviii, xx, xxii, and David Farrell Krell, "Work Sessions With Heidegger," *Philosophy Today* 26 (1982), pp. 133-34.

See Michael Zimmerman, *The Eclipse of the Self* (Athens: Ohio University Press, 1981) for an example of the tendency toward a psychologistic and biographical interpretation of Heidegger's thinking that results from dividing it up into sections.

CHAPTER 2

GOD IS DEAD:
THE DESTRUCTION OF ONTO-THEO-LOGY

I said to my soul, be still, and let the dark come upon you
Which shall be the darkness of God.

T.S. Eliot

1. THE PROBLEM -- THE THEOLOGICAL USE OF HEIDEGGER

If we are to understand Heidegger's sigificance for religious
thinking and explore whatever religious dimension there is in
his thinking, we must first consider what animates his thinking; we need to find out what matters to Heidegger, i.e., what
is the matter [*Sache*] of thinking for him. Heidegger tells us
the matter on the very first page of his epoch-making *Sein und
Zeit*:   what matters for him and concerns his thinking is what
he would later call the oblivion [*Vergessenheit*] of being,
i.e., that the question of the meaning of being, of what it
means to be, has been forgotten. We no longer ask about
being, or understand what it would be to ask such a question,
though this question enlivened the thinking of Plato and
Aristotle and thereby provided the impetus for the whole of
Western thinking. In the trivialization and forgetfulness of
such a momentous questioning, Heidegger senses a darkening of
our world, a creeping destitution and nihilism that pervades
our thinking and thus lays claim to his thinking as what he
has to think about. In this sense of foreboding Heidegger
finds two kindred spirits in the most recent history of the
West -- Friedrich Nietzsche, and Friedrich Hölderlin.

   Nietzsche and Hölderlin, Hölderlin and Nietzsche; their
words and thoughts ring out throughout Heidegger's writings as
do no other two figures in the history of the West.[1] They
are much alike, these two, from their fragmentary styles
(asyntactical in the case of Hölderlin, aphoristic in the case
of Nietzsche), to their awareness of man's plight in a God-
foresaken world, to the prophetic fervor of their response to
that plight.[2] For Heidegger, both demand thinking, and decision -- Hölderlin, because he talks of the essence (and that
means being) of poetry for our time, and therefore how we may
speak -- Nietzsche, because he overturns the whole of Western
philosophy by thinking the essence (and that means being) of
thought hitherto, and therefore how we may think. What is
more, they both fortunately (for us) say this being and its
claim in similarly religious terms, i.e., in terms of the
death or lack [*Fehl*] of God. Hence to follow Heidegger's
considerations of these two would give us not only a insight
into the matter of thinking for Heidegger,[3] but it would

provide us with a starting point for gauging the propriety of
the theological uses of Heidegger that have hitherto determined in what ways Heidegger's thinking bears on religious
thinking. Such is the plan of this chapter. We will first
concern ourselves with Heidegger's interpretation of Nietzsche
and the death of God, and how this is connected with what he
is trying to do in his thinking. This leads us to a point at
which we may question the suitability of using Heidegger's
thinking as a prolegomenon to any sort of (Christian) theology. Finally, we round out the discussion by briefly (but by
no means completely) considering the part Hölderlin plays in
this line of thought and what directions are thereby opened
up.

2. THE DEATH OF GOD AND THE MATTER TO BE THOUGHT

Nietzsche's word "God is dead" -- what does that mean, what
does that signify? Heidegger notes that of course, first and
foremost, it is a declaration of the death of the Christian
god, the moral god, the "father" in heaven who metes out
punishments and rewards according to our account of virtues --
i.e., "that God with which one did business" (N I 321). Beyond this, however, it is clear that the word "God" for
Nietzsche designates the whole supersensory realm of ideas and
ideals, purposes and norms, that have determined the essence
of man since the late Greek and Christian interpretation of
Plato (i.e., Platonism). Hence "God is dead" indicates that
this whole realm no longer quickens and sustains life; the
ground of everything real, the working reality of everything
real, has become unreal (HW 216-17, 254).
   We could of course try to avoid all account of this word
of Nietzsche by pointing out that it is merely the "moral"
God who is dead and not "God in himself".[4] However, beyond
the fact that such an evasion resurrects the supersensible
realm (the "in itself") that is being challenged here by
Nietzsche, it overlooks the fundamental experience of an event
of Western history -- the destiny of two millenia of Western
history -- that Heidegger finds in the word "God is dead".
That destiny is: nihilism. Nihilism is that historical movement and process "already ruling throughout the preceding
centuries and determining the next century" through which the
supersensible realm "above" has lost its worth and meaning.
Nihilism is that history whereby the death of the Christian
god comes to light slowly but irresistibly, a "long-lasting
event in which the truth about beings as a whole essentially
changes and is impelled through to its determined end" (N II
32-33; cf. HW 218).
   What is noteworthy about all this, and what is captured in
the word "God is dead", is that nihilism is not determined by
unbelief. Nietzsche's word is not an atheistic pronouncement;

it does not declare that God does not exist. Indeed, the
Christian god is so far from being the measure of godlessness
that Nietzsche has found him dead, in the sense indicated (N I
322). That God is dead suggests that he has been killed, and
what is more, killed by man. Man has killed God! How is that
possible? It is possible because man has risen up into the
subjectivity of the *ego cogito*, whereby being is posited as
constant presence, constantly available to our thinking, and
all beings are transformed into object, brought to stand
through re-presenting (i.e., by being presented again, "done
over") for the sake of man's security and dominion over
beings. Beings are swallowed up in the immanence of subjectivity; their horizon is now nothing more than the point of
view posited in the value-positing of the will to power,
whereby even God is posited as the highest good, the highest
value, and thus placed at man's disposal (to be done away
with, or invoked, as the case may be). Man has risen up into
the bright clarity of modern metaphysics, wherein everything
is secured unconditionally (HW 257-62).

In this way, man has his revenge on the earth, the revenge
that characterizes Platonism and Christianity in their setting
up a supersensible, "real" world "above" the sensible world.
Re-presenting [*Vor-stellen*], *re*-presentation -- presenting
what is present, *again*, through reflection -- is that setting
something down *before* one which determines what has being,
makes it secure, and thereby secures man (HW 108; N II 464)
and gives him power over beings (will to power). Such representing is offended by the past (the 'It was') -- i.e., by
time, and its transience, which vanquishes and injures a will
that would will its security, because it takes away into the
past whatever was secured. Time is repellent to the will,
which thus wills the cessation of the suffering time brings.
In such willing, all things which emerge, come to stand and
endure out of a coming-to-be -- i.e., all things which exist
-- are pursued in order to depose and ultimately decompose
them (so that they may be re-presented). Willing wills the
disappearance of all things, degrades the transient, the
earthly, and all that is part of it, calling it *me on*, non-
being. Such degradation is the revenge. It is complete when
reflection (representation) posits ideas as absolute, i.e.,
with the arrival of Platonism and Christianity and the formation of the true and apparent worlds (VA 111-17; WD 36-40).
In Platonism (and Christianity as Platonism for the people)
comes "the primordial and determining grounds of the possibility of the upsurgence of nihilism and the rise of life-nega-
tion" (N I 186-87). In other words, nihilism begins, not with
the dissolution of the "true" world, but with the erection of
that world, at the beginning of the history of Western philosophy.

What is the result? The result is what Nietzsche calls
"the last man".

'What is love? What is creation? What is longing? What
is a star?' Thus asks the last man, and he blinks.
   The earth has become small, and on it hops the last man,
who makes everything small. His race is as ineradicable as
the flea-beetle; the last man lives the longest.
   'We have invented happiness,' say the last men, and they
blink . . . Becoming sick and harboring suspicion are harmful
to them: one proceeds carefully. A fool, whoever still
stumbles over stones or human beings![5]

In-sisting (standing unmoved *in* the present) rather than ex-
-isting (standing-*out* in time),the man who is the center of
,the world, the last man who wills and represents, makes things
small (i.e., harmless and mediocre) so that he need not worry
about a threat to his security and happiness. He no longer
has great aims, for his only aim is establishing and securing
his subjective happiness. What is not subordinate to him
(e.g., a star) is not really there, for then it would be a
threat to his secure dominion. He cannot even see the star,
for he has risen up into "the great noon", that dazzling
brilliance of his that makes everything so bright and clear
and self-evident to him. He is so dazzled, he blinks.

   To blink -- that means: to play into and set up an appearing and seeming, to which one agrees as something valid,
   and, indeed, with the mutual consent, which is not expressly
   disputed, to further everything thus set up. Blinking: the
   setting up, agreed upon and finally no longer in need of
   agreement, of the objective and static surfaces and fore-
   ground facets of all things as alone valid and valuable, with
   whose help man carries on and degrades everything (WD 30).

   The last man, dazzled by his representing, is no longer
able to look beyond himself, to rise above himself, up to the
level of his own task in which he will be asked to take
dominion over the earth.   He is incapable of such a task
because he has not yet entered into his essence.   Man hitherto, the last man, the *animal rationale* as he has been called
so far, created in God's image and therefore 'transcendent'
(SZ 65-66), this last man is as yet undetermined, for he has
not yet entered into his *own* essence; he is inauthentic
[*uneigentlich*].[6]   This is the danger that both Nietzsche and
Heidegger see: this last man, the necessary consequence of
unsubdued nihilism, degenerating because he has lost his essence, will be the end, the *last* man; and he will last the
longest, perhaps eternally (WD 24-25, 27, 30; N I 241).
   Strangely enough, Nietzsche, who gives us our insight into
the last man and his danger, also succumbs to the last man and
his thinking; Nietzsche too gets "dragged down" to the level
of metaphysics (Platonism) and its revenge. His entire "system" of thought depends on the metaphysical notion of the will

to power which, as the essence of everything real, consummates
the modern metaphysics of subjectness, for it secures its own
constancy and stability as a necessary value (will to will)
and sets up beings as steadily constant, at the disposal of
the will. His philosophy impresses the character of being (as
constant presence) on becoming with the notion of the eternal
return óf the same. Nietzsche's thinking becomes value-positing thinking that, initiating a "revaluation of all values",
erects goals and ideals once again (HW 238-40; VA 120-22).
Hence Nietzsche too, brought to the edge of the abyss, flees,
taking refuge in a new principle of valuative thinking that
exhausts representational thinking. He takes truth as a kind
of error, an illusion necessary for life. With this the
essence of truth is now valuation, for truth as adequation
becomes justification [Gerechtigkeit], i.e., what is justified
by the will to power to will its own constant presence. He
thereby steers metaphysics into that dimension where truth and
beauty, art and thought engage in vicious battle (for they all
enhance life) and abandons it there, condemned to a nameless
dimension of suspicion (for one can no longer clearly distinguish the true and apparent worlds when truth is error) where
metaphysical permanence [Beständigkeit] is exposed as human
securing-permanence [Bestandsicherung] and the fictitious but
necessary character of the Platonic world of permanence is
brought to light.[7] Nietzsche thus overturns Platonism, but in
so doing, he remains entangled in Platonism. Yet such over-
turning exhausts the essential possibilities of such metaphysical (Platonic) thinking by realizing the goal of such thinking, whereby there is nothing left for metaphysics but to turn
aside into its own inessentiality and disarray (HW 209, 217; N
II 201; VA 83).

    In other words -- and this is where Nietzsche's importance
lies for Heidegger and for us -- it is important to realize
that Nietzsche is not just a metaphysician, but that he is the
last metaphysician, differing from his predecessors in exhaus-
ting the possibility of metaphysical Grundstellung (setting up
of first principles) and making clearer than any other Grundstellung the full essence of nihilism.[8] As our latest thinker, taking metaphysics in its most extreme possibility,
Nietzsche thus gathers up and completes the whole of Western
thinking; all the themes of Western thought, though trans-
muted, fatefully gather in Nietzsche's thought (WD 21; N I
13). He is the eschaton of the history of being -- end here
signifying place, "the place in which the whole of philosophy's history is gathered in its most extreme possibility.
End as completion thus means this gathering" (ZD 63). In this
most extreme possibility, being has come to nothing; it is a
"vapor and a fallacy", as Nietzsche puts it in Götzendämmerung, to be forgotten. Such a saying, however, bears witness
to a new necessity (EM 32), for it makes being questionable,
questionworthy [frag-würdig], and hence demands a new ques-

tioning of being. Such a questioning is concretized in a
"destruction" of ancient ontology (SZ 36) -- that is, in a
deconstruction of the rigid and secure metaphysical systems
that are founded on some transcendental characterization of
beings in general (onto-logy) or on some highest being (theology) -- wherein what is sought are the original experiences
of (i.e., the possibilities of thinking about) being that have
been covered up, concealed, and abandoned in metaphysics (N II
415; WM 417). Since Nietzsche is the *eschaton* of being, to
interpret him is to carry out this destruction, to interpret
the history of metaphysics and disclose the long-hidden possibility of a new understanding of being. With Nietzsche, as
the completion of one epoch and the instigation of another,
the task of thinking (about being) is opened up to Heidegger.[9]

      In addition, since Nietzsche discloses the essence of a
tradition to which we are all heirs, this task of thinking
becomes the task of thinking about contemporary man.
Nietzsche's thinking illuminates the nature of the present
world; our thinking, whether for him or against him, moves in
his shadow. By thinking through Nietzsche, we come to comprehend our own thinking, that nihilism is manifest as the history of our own age and is the way and manner in which we are
standing and going today (how we *are*). To ignore Nietzsche is
to ignore ourselves, and our being, whereby we will comprehend
nothing of the 20th century, the centuries to come, and our
place in them (N I 26; N II 86; HW 210; WD 26, 62, 71; WM
424).[10]

      One comes to suspect, as Heidegger does thinking through
Nietzsche, that our thinking remains futile and superficial if
we assume a "defensive vehemence" against nihilism out of
dissatisfaction with the world, or out of moral indignation or
a believer's self-righteous superiority; or if we analyze and
dissect the situation and then propose remedies -- e.g., rein-
stituting values or returning to faith. One suspects that all
of this discloses an uncanny concealment of what is the matter
at stake with nihilism, a treatment of symptoms rather than
the disease, and indeed, to such an extent that those who
believe themselves to be free of nihilism -- those with Christian faith or some metaphysical conviction -- perhaps push
forward the development of nihilism most fundamentally (HW
217-22). Nietzsche, on the other hand, has isolated the
disease, the problem of nihilism, as the revenge of Platonism
against time and existence, separated it from moral considerations (insofar as the last man is happy and content, and what
is needed is contempt for one's happiness), and thus raised
the question of being and time.[11] Hence it is through
Nietzsche and his thinking that Heidegger is able to get at
the problem of nihilism, the *essence* of nihilism, which is
how we *are*, and see that it is not merely a spiritual malaise
of recent times resulting from a collapse of values, but a two

thousand year old destiny lying concealed in the formation of
the Platonic world-structure.[12]

Having thus found Nietzsche, insofar as he illuminates and
exemplifies our thinking today, Heidegger must lose him, "op-
pose" him. Such "opposition", however, cannot consist of a
refutation (which would deny Nietzsche's significance) but
must consist of "a radically different way of taking man's
relation to himself and to beings as a whole; it must consist
of a new beginning that abandons the metaphysical thinking
Nietzsche exemplifies."[13]   Of what does such thinking consist?

Nietzsche has shown us that metaphysical thinking consists
in trying to fill the void with a metaphysical first principle
[Grundstellung] -- a filling that Nietzsche has taught us to
be suspicious of as an attempt by man to secure himself and to
will power. It then appears that the essence of nihilism,
exemplified by metaphysical thinking, consists of taking the
nothing as merely something null and void, non-being, and in
taking nihilism as a deification of such emptiness, to be
offset through vigorous affirmation of some first principle (N
II 53). Metaphysics, then, would be nihilism, as Nietzsche
has taught us, but not for the reason Nietzsche gives (i.e.,
that certain values, the highest values, are no longer effec-
tive, and are in need of replacement), but because the question of the nothing is not asked. "Nihilism would then be,
more originally and more essentially experienced and grasped,
that history of metaphysics which presses toward a metaphysical first position [Grundstellung] in which the nothing *not*
only can*not* be understood in its essence, but no longer *wants*
to be grasped. Nihilism then means: the essential not thinking about the essence of the nothing" (N II 54). The task of
thinking becomes thinking the essence of the nothing.

But in the consummation of metaphysics, at the end of
philosophy, being is nothing -- being is an empty abstraction,
a vapor and a fallacy. "In the place of completed nihilism it
looks as if there were no such thing as *being of* beings, as if
it were nothing with being (in the sense of *nichtigen*). Being
is left out in a strange way. It conceals itself" (WM 415).
The task of thinking is thus similtaneously asking the question of being. But in order to do that, we must come to
consider the oblivion and forgetfulness [Vergessenheit] manifest in metaphysics (i.e., nihilism). We must ask "What is
metaphysics?", a question, but also an essay by Heidegger that
asks the question of the nothing (WM 103ff). However, if we
must once again consider metaphysics, then we are not "overcoming" metaphysics (nihilism) in the way Nietzsche or any
other metaphysical thinker would -- through refutation, over-
turning and casting aside. Instead, we come to abide in the
essence of nihilism (metaphysics), to consider it and the
uncanny way in which it manifests being as an oblivion and
forgetfulness of being. We come to abide in the *essence* of
nihilism, and that means, the presencing [Wesen][14] of being.

We once again ask the question of being (EM 212; HW 264-65; N II 362-63; WM 405, 407, 415, 422).

Such a way of thought that once again asks the question of being, the essence of the nothing, and the essence of metaphysics does not want to overthrow anything, but merely to catch up with something -- the whole essence of man (WD 66). Man hitherto, the last man, undetermined in his essence, would like to remain man hitherto, the *animal rationale*. But this man is unprepared for being, and hence for himself, since the interpretation of man hitherto is a metaphysical interpretation and hence one that has forgotten being and man, insofar as the interpretation of being and man belong together (N II 193). Again, Nietzsche provides the initiative. In *Götzendämmerung* he tells the story of "How the True World Finally Became a Fable" (sec. IV), in which the various phases of Platonism are brought into connection with a certain type of man; the story culminates at noon, "the high point of humanity". What this says is that at the end of Platonism stands a decision, a peak of decision, concerning the transformation of man, whether he will come to an end in the last man, or turn into something else, i.e., into himself (N I 240-41). The decision is especially important now, for as Nietzsche sees it, man is about to assume dominion over the earth, and this portends danger if he remains the last man who takes revenge against the earth (WD 24).

At this high point of humanity Nietzsche declares: *Incipit Zarathustra*. At this high point at which the true and apparent worlds collapse (note that *both* collapse; at this point there is no longer a mere inversion of Platonism which would affirm the apparent, sensible realm while denying the true, supersensible realm, i.e., positivism), Zarathustra begins. He begins here because Zarathustra is the advocate for the one thing that always and first of all addresses man (VA 102) -- his essence. That is why the book *Also Sprach Zarathustra* is "for everyone", as the subtitle says -- "for each man as man insofar as his essence becomes at any given time worthy of thought" (VA 101). As such an advocate, Zarathustra teaches the overman [*Übermensch*], who is not a superdimensional version of man up till now, but

> the man who first leads the essence of man so far over into its truth, and so assumes that truth. Man so far, thus ascertained in his essence, is to be rendered capable of becoming the future master of the earth, i.e., of administering to high purpose the possibilities of power which fall to future man in the essence of the technological transformation of the earth and of human activity (WD 25-26).

The overman is that transition beyond man as he is so far by which man learns to subject himself to himself, to despise what is despicable in his kind as it is so far, to despise his

own happiness, that he might overcome his last essence, the
essence of the last man -- the spirit of revenge. Freedom
from revenge is the essence of the overman (WD 25, 33) whereby
man is underway to his essence, on the way to becoming who he
is. This is why Nietzsche also calls Zarathustra "The Conva-
lescent", i.e., "the man who collects himself to return home,
that is to turn in, into his own determination. The convales-
cent is on the way to himself, so that he may say of himself
who he is" (VA 102).

But to be on the way to himself, on the way to the essence
of man, Zarathustra must *go down*; having risen up into subjectivity, man must go down, back into his essence. He who must
go over -- the overman -- must be one who goes down; "the way
of the overman begins with his going-down [*Untergang*]".   By
that beginning, his way is decided (WD 26), a way that leads
to becoming man again. As Heidegger puts it, the thinking
demanded here, that overcomes metaphysics, is not a climbing
higher, a transcendence of metaphysics, but a "climbing back
down into the nearness of the nearest . . . the ek-sistence of
homo humanus . . . Thinking is on the descent to the poverty
of its provisional essence" (WM 352, 364).

Where does such going-down go? Back to earth. Such
thinking as is now demanded must remain faithful to the earth,
whereby to "sin against the earth" and "to esteem the entrails
of the unknowable higher than the meaning of the earth" is the
most dreadful thing.[15] Zarathustra puts it most eloquently:

> Remain faithful to the earth, my brothers, with the power
> of your virtue. Let your gift-giving love and your knowledge
> serve the meaning of the earth. This I beg and beseech you.
> Do not let them fly away from earthly things and beat their
> wings against eternal walls . . . Lead back to the earth the
> virtue that flew away, as I do -- back to the body, back to
> life, that it may give the earth a meaning, a *human mean-
> ing*.[16]

Such faithfulness to the earth must dwell in time, for
overcoming the spirit of revenge is overcoming revenge against
time. Man must dwell in time, think in time; he may not stand
back and observe the moment of time as a spectator on high.
Since, on high, his vision is disfigured and there is no need
for decision, man must dwell and question within time, even
about the moment of time itself (N I 296f). Zarathustra's
Untergang, then, is such a moment, decisive, and therefore in
time, a moment of transition from that long history of man's
flight from the dimension in which being is disclosed (i.e.,
the history of nihilism, which did not deal with the nothing
[the abyss]) to that region in which the nothing reveals
being, the *Da* of Dasein, that place of lighting and clearing
of beings as a whole. It is a moment, the briefest and most

transient, but at the same time most fulfilled, a moment of decision, of becoming man again (N I 314-15).[17]

And to become man again, dwelling on the earth, means to become mortal once more. In death, man, the still undetermined animal, is determined. With death Dasein stands before itself in its ownmost [eigensten] potentiality-for-being, whereby it is assigned to its ownmost potentiality-for-being; realizing its radical finitude, Dasein receives its own being, comes to itself, such that the future [Zu-kunft] is primordial (SZ 333). Man comes to himself, he is authentic [eigentlich], for das Man, the secure, everyday, tranquillized last man, is shattered, and man is banished from everything familiar. There can be no capture or subjugation (and hence security) with death. The death of man is demanded in the face of the death of God and the logos of subjectivity. This is why the matter of death becomes so important in Sein und Zeit, for Heidegger is following out the implications of the death of God and the disintegration of the Platonic order announced by Nietzsche.[18] Death means the Untergang to which man is called, in which the form of man which decays [verwest] -- i.e., man hitherto, who loses his essence [Wesen] -- is left behind (US 46).

To fulfill the requirement of letting death be, of recognizing our finitude, requires a mode of thought that is alien to representational, valuative, manipulative consciousness which obscures the finitude of Dasein through its will to power. Nietzsche gives us a hint of the bearing of such thinking. When Zarathustra must first of all become who he is, he recoils in "horror" from the task, a horror that gives the whole book a hesitant character that stifles Zarathustra's self-assurance and arrogance (VA 105). Such horror Heidegger calls -- anxiety. It is thinking-within-anxiety in which Dasein is primordially disclosed as being-towards-death, for anxiety takes away from Dasein the possibility of understanding itself in terms of the "world" (the beings around it) and how it has been publicly interpreted. Anxiety takes Dasein away from the tranquillized, self-assured Man and throws it back upon its authentic [eigentlich] potentiality-for-being-in-the-world, its ownmost [eigensten] possibilities, that it may take hold of what is its own [eigen], the uniqueness of its being (SZ 249-51; cf. 333-34). In anxiety, the nothing is revealed; beings as a whole slip away, directing us to the pure possibility of our being-in-the-world. Anxiety leaves us hanging in the nothing of beings as a whole, where there is nothing to hold onto (and hence grab a secure foothold), where there is simply, purely, Da-sein (WM 111-13). Forfeiting the security of ratio, one is resolute, i.e., one stands in openedness [Ent-schlossenheit] (one should think resolution here in terms of re-solution, i.e., the dissolving of the secure, closed das Man) to thinking-within-anxiety, openedness to thinking within the essential ambiguity and ambivalence, the

nothing and nowhere, that is experienced in anxiety.   Learning
how to exist in the nameless, how to sustain one's being held
out into the nothing, becomes the task of human Dasein, whereby representation, valuation and proposition *dissolve* in the
face of human finitude.[19]

Such releasement into human finitude, into the nothing,
compels our coming to the ground question [*Grundfrage*] of
metaphysics: "Why are there beings at all, and not rather
nothing?" (WM 122).   The question does not ask about a ground
in the manner of metaphysics; it does not ask for a *fundamentum inconcussum* whereby we are secured.   Rather, the question
aims at breaking the self-evident character of beings assumed
by the leading question [*Leitfrage*] of metaphysics (i.e., What
is the being?).   Beings then begin to waver between the two
extreme possibilities of being and nothing, whereby beings
become questionable, and questionworthy, of themselves.   We
can no longer belong entirely to such beings and understand
ourselves in terms of them; we ourselves are thrown into
question, our Dasein hanging in the balance (EM 31-32).   Put
another way, the question asks why beings take precedence in
our consideration and lay claim to every "is", and how it is
that that which is not a being, i.e., being, understood as
nothing, remains forgotten, in oblivion.   The ground question
of metaphysics, asking about the *essence* of metaphysics, asks,
and demands the asking of, the question of being (EM 35; WM
382, 420).   The ground question opens up the possibility of a
"ground" for beings which is not a being but an abyss [*Ab-
grund*], the nothing, which is being with regard to its essence
(since being shows itself, presences [*west*], as no-thing).
With that, the question puts an end to metaphysics by demonstrating the futility of seeking to ground Dasein in something, be it beings or itself, and breaks up the self-assurance of Dasein, insofar as the nothing (being) that grounds is
not at Dasein's disposal.[20]

We see here, then, with the ground question of metaphysics, a confluence of a variety of themes in Heidegger's
thought.   Metaphysics (Platonism) is put in question, announced by the death of God.   Being is put in question, as
what is forgotten in metaphysics, yet revealed (as forgotten)
in metaphysics.   Man (the last man, *das Man*) is put into
question, insofar as the nothing revealed in anxiety and
being-towards-death undermines ones ability to control things
by affirming some ground or foundation and directs man to
remember his place, his essence, which is historical(ly).   The
question is decisive, opening up the happening of human Dasein
-- its history -- by opening up unasked possibilities (the
question of being) while reaching back to what has been (metaphysics), and thus sharpening and illuminating the present.
Like Zarathustra's *Untergang*, the ground question is a moment
in time (i.e., historical) that calls for decision, not in the
sense that we draw ideological or ethical *conclusions* after

the fact, but rather in the sense that the basic attitude and bearing of the questioning is itself historical, standing and holding itself in the "timeliness" of Dasein's essence, for the sake of the being (of Dasein) that is revealed in time (EM 48).

What this means -- and this is most important -- is that the anxiety in which we stand with this question is not an experience from which Dasein needs redemption, for it is Dasein's opening onto its ownmost way of being -- i.e., its happening, as history, in time. The task is to persist in such thinking-within-anxiety, to "liberate ourselves from those idols everyone has and to which he is wont to go cringing" (WM 122), for such idols serve as fugitive self-concealments and illusions which attempt to rescue Dasein from the nothing through the "willful" affirmation of some foundation for Dasein. In this spirit, one ought to look at *Entschlossenheit*, resoluteness, in which one is being-toward-the-end and hence anxious, as the effort to resist all interpretations which would "resolutely" handle anxiety and thereby constitute a fleeing from one's *authenticity* and from one becoming who one is. *Entschlossenheit* would then be the effort to shoulder the weight, the guilt [*Schuld*], of one's own being-anxious, i.e., openedness.[21]

It is a lesson Heidegger has undoubtedly learned from Nietzsche, who has made us *suspicious* of every assertion, every representation and every idol (including Nietzsche's) as a manifestation of a will to power and an attempt to secure ourselves. Indeed, Heidegger apparently shows his indebtedness to Nietzsche in this regard most profoundly and most frequently when he constantly notes that things are *fragwürdig* -- questionworthy, as the word is often translated, but also *questionable*, in the critical sense of the word. For example, the meaning of being, like everything else Heidegger questions, is worthy of question because the meaning of being hitherto (constant presence) is questionable.[22]

3. HEIDEGGER AND THEOLOGY?

Given this bearing of anxiety and the ground question of metaphysics, it is a complete misunderstanding of Heidegger and the task he has set before us if we understand the description of Dasein in *Sein und Zeit* as pointing beyond to some greater reality, a ground of beings beyond the thrownness, contingency, and conditionedness of beings as a whole, a creator who is author of man's being. Such an understanding is usually coupled with the criticism that Heidegger needs to go farther than he does in *Sein und Zeit* in order to avoid pessimism and nihilism.[23] But such criticism arises from an unquestioned onto-theo-logical scheme and clings to theological prejudices that imply a philosophical "statement" about a transcendence

somehow "in itself", over and above Dasein, that is to be
expounded. The move "beyond" Dasein to some greater reality
implied in the criticism is one which originates from a radical misunderstanding of being, as we have seen. It is completely different from Heidegger's approach, in which it is
not a question of representing or expounding anything, but a
question of *finding one's resolution in the questioning itself*, attending to being.[24]

The ground question of metaphysics and these misunderstandings of Heidegger's approach bring us to the question
concerning the propriety of any theological use of Heidegger,
i.e., whether Heidegger's sigificance for religion, philosophy
of religion, and religious thinking, properly understood, has
any place in a theological context. That is to say, we now
have to ask whether theologians have attended to, or even can
attend to, the matter at stake in Heidegger's thinking and
remain theologians. For, first and foremost, the matter of
concern for theology would seem to be faith; "faith and what
is disclosed through faith are the theme of theology and that
through which theology is motivated, and that which theology
is supposed to promote" (PT 19-20). Theology is the "science"
of faith, i.e., it gives systematic coherence and conceptual
clarity to what is disclosed through faith. It is not a
science of God nor speculative knowledge of God, nor is it a
philosophy or history of religion dealing with God-man relationships, nor a psychology of religion. All of these rob
theology of its own character as a science geared to its own
matter (PT 21, 25-26).[25]

But what is faith?

> . . . that real being which is man, created in the image of
> God, must above all bring about his reality by holding fast
> to the highest good, i.e., by faith (*fides, qua creditur*).
> Through faith, man is certain of the reality of the highest
> real being, and thus at the same time of his own real con-
> tinuance in eternal bliss. The causality of the highest real
> being allots to man thus created a definite kind of reality
> whose fundamental character is faith.
>
>   In faith rules certainty, that kind of certainty which is
> safe even in the uncertainty of itself, i.e., of what it
> believes in (N II 425).

It is this certainty of salvation and *security* of the individual attained in faith that is the authentic historical-
metaphysical basis for the priority of *certainty* which first
made the acceptance and metaphysical development of the mathematical (i.e., the essence of modern natural science and
metaphysics) possible (FD 100). What this means is that the
self-certainty of the *ego cogito* that rules in modern metaphysics is not a revolt against the doctrine of faith, but a
necessary consequence of it. Metaphysics and Christian faith

are intimately bound up with one another, such that we can
even say that modern culture (including, of course, modern
metaphysics) is Christian even when it "loses" its faith, for
Christian faith has made it necessary that man secure himself,
either through such faith, or by other means (N II 423, 426-
27). Christianity is Platonism for the people (Heidegger
never denies this; see EM 113); metaphysics is onto-*theology*.
Whether security is found in the transcendental or the transcendent (N II 349) is not essential.

What this means is that theology, Christian theology,
embodies the very thinking that Heidegger, following
Nietzsche, finds questionable and is attempting to "overcome".
One cannot get around this criticism by saying that the god
of onto-theo-logy that is "dead" and overcome is merely the
god of the philosophers and not *the* God of faith, for the
dispute is not one of conception, but affirmation. In faith,
and the theology that follows from it, there is an unquestioned *affirmation* and *allegiance* to sacred inscriptions,
doctrines and/or community, and this affirmation, along with
the whole anthropology that follows from it, *secures* man in a
particular place within the cosmos (divine plan) and gives him
the proper means (faith) for attaining security and salvation.
Faith is thereby secure (in its affirmation) even where it is
unsure of its "conception" of God (as in various negative
theologies, or those driven by the "Protestant Principle").
This is especially true today, with almost all theology
beginning from the subject's "experiences" or interiorized
reflection. Take the case of so-called existential theology
and existential faith (and its cognates, e.g., the will to
believe): here existing is faith, whereby man wills himself
as the being who is (e.g., courage to be). Passion and drive
dominate; there is interest, infinite interest (e.g., ultimate
concern) in existence and commitment to what is real. All of
this, however, merely counts as a completion of anthropology
and the *animal rationale* (N II 475ff). Belief and faith
become belief in belief (the will to believe, even a "right"
to believe), which means that there is no longer belief here
(belief cannot be willed) but a *hope* or a *wish*.[26]

Hence faith too stands in the way of the questioning of
being. Heidegger puts it quite plainly:

> Anyone for whom the Bible is divine revelation and truth
> has the answer to the question 'Why are there beings rather
> than nothing?' even before it is asked: beings, so far as
> they are not God himself, have been created through him. One
> who holds to such faith can in a way participate in the
> asking of our question, but he cannot actually question
> without ceasing to be a believer and taking all the conse-
> quences of such a step (EM 8-9).

In other words, what is asked in Heidegger's question is "foolishness" for faith (EM 9), for it asks about matters which are already "known" to faith. If one asks Heidegger's ground question in an authentic manner, and thus opens up the question of the meaning of being and thinks within it, one has to give up the security of faith, and one therefore has to give up theology. Anything else is a subterfuge and misunderstanding of the matter of thinking.

Therefore, though a good deal of theology since the 1920s has made use of Heidegger -- and even that theology which does not use him, or thinks against him, cannot be thought apart from the background of Heideggerian "ontology" -- it is not surprising to find that such theology which has used Heidegger is open to a wide variety of decisive criticisms (from either theologians or Heideggerians) which revolve around the preconceptions such theologians bring to Heidegger's thinking and their failure to ask some basic, fundamental questions about the applicability of Heidegger to theology.[27] As examples of this we might turn to Rudolf Bultmann and Heinrich Ott, who epitomize the two most common theological uses of Heidegger. Bultmann (and others), under the influence of transcendental philosophy and/or Kierkegaardian existentialism, uses *Sein und Zeit* as a formal, transcendental foundation for understanding man, to which he grafts a "concrete" mode of that formal structure -- i.e., Christian existence. Such a procedure might seem justified because of 1) apparent parallels between Christian concepts and Heidegger's *existentialia*,[28] 2) Heidegger's apparent treatment of *existentialia* as parallel to the function of categories in natural science (SZ 59-60), and 3) his talk of seeking the "pre-Christian content" of basic theological concepts apart from any particular instance of theologizing (PT 31), which suggests he is undertaking a formal, philosophical investigation of man. However, the *existentialia* in *Sein und Zeit* are not empty, universal forms like Plato's *ideas* which are above history and separable from any particular content. Instead, the *existentialia* form what Otto Pöggeler has called a "formal-indicative conceptuality", meaning that they are ways of thinking that enable us to once again ask about being and give us the possibility of thinking about being. On the one hand they are "pre-Christian" in the sense that they spring from an experience of and thinking about being that is unencumbered by a petrification of our understanding as occurred with the Platonic and Christian interpretation of the Greek understanding of being. But their content is thereby also post-Christian in that they disclose possibilities of thinking once the albatross of Christian anthropology has been removed. This is all the more apparent when we recognize that, rather than being parallels, some of the *existentialia* (e.g., guilt, conscience) are attempts at rethinking and transforming some Christian concepts according to the matter of thought, and are in that way criticisms of the Christian concepts. This is further borne out by the ways in which this provisional "conceptuality" is disclosed in later writings by Heidegger, ways in which Bultmann and others have recognized to be generally un-Christian and therefore unsuitable for use by the Christian theologian. Ignoring or rejecting the "later" Heidegger (which can be looked upon as the "fulfillment" of the "early" Heidegger), Bultmann and others show an inability to attend to the matter of thought because of an *unquestioning* loyalty to the language and thought of Christianity and the subsequent need to *justify* this language and thought. Basic questions concerning the compatability of the matter of thought and the matter of faith fail to be asked, which has led to the numerous criticisms of the Bultmannian program by theologians and others.[29]

Heinrich Ott, on the other hand, has the same problem manifest in a different way. Insofar as he attempts in *Denken und Sein* to make an appeal to the whole of Heidegger's thought and not simply the "early" Heidegger, Ott ends up being torn between basic theological principles and Heidegger's path of thought. His project is to set up a series of parallels between Heidegger's thinking and the concerns of Christian theology (e.g., response to being/ response to God, primal thinking/thinking of theology, wonder that beings are/wonder at God's creation, *Grundfrage*/Why is there any God . . ?) and thereby draw on Heidegger's insights for parallel use in theology. But a whole host of problems then ensue: 1) the differentiation between theology and philosophy tends to blur, with Christian theology gradually losing its proper place and concern; 2) if God is admitted as a being, which Ott does (p. 142ff), he apparently inspires wonder like other beings, by our thinking his contingency; 3) awe at God's creation does not seem to correspond to Heidegger's awe insofar as the latter does not allow for grounding in a creator; 4) since Heidegger sees theology as a positive science (PT 15), it does not appear that primal thinking and theological thinking are analogous; 5) how can the analogies hold at all, if God is a being, different from being; and finally, 6) God, as a being, if focused on, may stand in the way of the unconcealment of being, which is presumably one reason Heidegger calls his thinking "god-less" (ID 65).[30] Such criticisms have led Ott to back down significantly from his original stance, to a point of vanishing returns.[31]

Despite the fate of both ways in which theology has used Heidegger, theologians such as Alfred Jäger and Joseph O'Leary inexplicably continue to try to appropriate Heidegger for their own purposes.[32] Jäger follows in Ott's footsteps and tries to appropriate Heidegger in developing a variation of dialectical theology. O'Leary has recently sought to call upon Heidegger (and Jacques Derrida) for help in his attempt to separate the "truth of being" from the "truth of revelation" (p. 7ff) and then appropriate "what is most serviceable

in Heidegger's critique of metaphysics" -- namely "the negative, critical side of Heidegger" (pp. 31-32). Both enterprises result in the same sorts of problems met in Bultmann
and Ott. Jäger and O'Leary, like other theologians before
them, do not sufficiently consider that the question of being
raised by Heidegger is so thoroughly radical that it places
all "traditional" enterprises, including theology, at risk,
subverting the certainty of faith by asking how it is that
being (or God) is given to be thought in a certain way.

Of course, Heidegger has repeatedly stressed that theologians have their own task, apart from philosophy (thinking),
and that its project and renewal must come out of its own
origins and according to its own concerns (EM 9; WM 379; PT
14-15, 46). Yet in light of what we have seen regarding
Heidegger's talk of faith and theology, this is an ambiguous
(indeed, almost lame) distinction and proposal. Heidegger's
stress on the distinction between theology and philosophy,
first of all, only seems directed at indicating that philosophy is not a necessary condition for a decision concerning
faith; it does not at all aim at keeping all philosophical
reflection away from man's concern with faith.[33]   Indeed, as
we noted above, the quest for the "pre-Christian" (and thus
post-Christian) content of theological concepts and the development of such concepts in new directions would seem to
indicate a critical stance toward theology. Hence Heidegger's
proposing a genuine and authentic task more often then not
tends to reflect a despair at the possibility of theology
itself. In addition, this despair seems to be something more
than a mere philosophical challenge to faith. Take, for
example, Heidegger's brashness in appropriating the name
"Christian theologian" for himself in a letter to Karl Lowith
in 1921. This claim does not so much reduce Heidegger's task
to that of theology as it expresses a fundamental religious
concern in his thinking (which he could only express at that
time in this traditional way) which he pits against theology.
Theology seems to lose its place at this point (as was mentioned with Ott above) as Heidegger's thinking seems capable
of grappling with the phenomena of existence without theological premises, yet with the hint of a religious concern, as it
searches out the matter to be thought. Theology may indeed by
questionworthy for Heidegger, but only because it is all the
more questionable. Theology may therefore have a lesson to
teach us and some matter at stake in its thought that gives us
pause, but taking that lesson up into a more original thinking
and questioning seems to thoroughly dissolve both faith and
theology.[34]

4. TOWARD A DIFFERENT RELIGIOUS THINKING

Theology and Christianity, then, are very much in doubt in
this time of the world's night, this destitute time in which
the flight of the gods -- Herakles, Dionysus and Christ (note
that the three are given *equal* status) -- leaves us in a time
of the lack of God [*Fehl Gottes*], a time so destitute that it
cannot even discern the lack of God as a lack (HW 269) (e.g.,
there is no lack of theologians in our time). *Fehl Gottes* --
this is Hölderlin's word.[35]   It is a word like Nietzsche's
that speaks in its own way of the destiny of being that shapes
the realm of metaphysics in its self-completion, i.e., in the
oblivion of being (HW 273).
   "Not them, the blessed, who once appeared." With this
first line from Hölderlin's *Germanien* we are set in a determined place (GR 47f) -- the time of the world's night and the
absence of the old gods. With this absence, the ground that
grounds the world fails to appear; we hang in the abyss [*Ab-
-grund*]. Here Hölderlin sounds a message similar to that of
Nietzsche, that the divine claim of the Christian god (among
others) no longer animates our world. "Not them, the blessed,
who once appeared." This also says we may not appeal to these
old gods; we cannot rectify this world-night through the mere
survival of confessions or the Church (GR 80). Willful and
desperate justification of traditional language may provide
comfort to a reactionary few, but this amounts to nothing more
than cursing the darkness, which brings no light, no thought.
Hence Heidegger says quite plainly that

> . . . the people of the country may not attempt to make to
> themselves a god by cunning and thus put aside by force the
> supposed lack. *But neither may they accommodate themselves
> merely by calling on an accustomed god.* True, by this means
> the presence of the absence would be overlooked. But the
> discovery could not be near without the nearness which is
> determined by the absence and hence reserving (EHD 28; my
> emphases).

It is clear from this that Heidegger is in no way on the way
back to faith, to the faith of our fathers.[36]   On the con-
trary, he cites the need to throw the traditional representations open to questioning and thought, though we thereby hang
in an apparently godless abyss, experience it, and endure it
(HW 270).
   But why must we endure this darkness? Heidegger has
already said: "the discovery could not be near in the way in
which it is near . . ." Discovery? Yes, discovery. Descending into the twilight and night we find -- lo and behold! --
we can see: a star. This world-night is not necessarily the
dissolution of all things into a desperate and mindless disarray; Hölderlin, perhaps even moreso than Nietzsche, senses

this.   Though this world-night threatens us with the chaos of
the abyss, it also augers the possibility of change and transformation; it makes ready the going-down by which we enter
into the beginning of our sojourn on this earth (US 52).   Just
as we must go back down into the essence of nihilism and the
oblivion of being so that we might once again ask the question
of the meaning of being, so too we must go back down into this
lack of God, into the abyss, that we might once again ask
after the god and gods (the divine).   For at night, the stars
come out, and the heavens light up.

      Herein we begin to get a glimpse of Hölderlin's contribu-
tion to the thinking of Heidegger over and above his accord
with Nietzsche: he gives to Heidegger, moreso than Nietzsche,
the question whether there could not be a new experience of
the divine along with the transformation of man demanded by
both Hölderlin and Nietzsche.   In Hölderlin, Heidegger finds a
partner in conversation about the homelessness of man and the
lack of God who is outside metaphysics (unlike Nietzsche, who
is thereby tempted to usurp God's place) and free of its
language.   Hölderlin therefore provides both a non-metaphysical model and starting point for once again questioning how
man is to find himself (and find himself [perhaps] under a
divine claim) and a non-metaphysical model for the saying of
such questions.[37]

      Yet the "promise" of a divine claim, of a coming god,
suggested by such questioning and by Hölderlin's words that
this is a time of the gods that have fled and the god that is
coming (EHD 47) (a promise apparently echoed in Heidegger's
proclamation that "Only a god can save us" [Sp 209]) -- this
"promise" is only by virtue of the reserving, sparing night, a
time of godlessness which contains what is undecided (EHD
109).   Hölderlin grounds the inception of another history
"which commences with the fight over the decision about the
advent or flight of the god (GR 1; my emphasis).   There is
therefore no solace here for the theologian who might see in
this attitude signs of hopefulness and expectation.   Nothing
is decided here; we may not rush ahead and refashion a god for
ourselves from the ruins of the old.   Rather, thinking must
abide, as two commentators describe Hölderlin, in "a state of
divinely inspired doubt."[38]   We must remain near the lack of
god, despite the appearance of godlessness, and attend to it,
"for in the face of the god who is absent, we go down" (Sp
209).   The darkness thus revealed bestows new vigilance and
illumination; we grow more in concentration, become more attentive and guarded -- we begin to think again, whereby we
descend into our essence.

      Such thinking is prior to mere questions concerning tradi-
tional religion and confession.   Such thinking is the question
whether and how we will ground our historical Dasein; "it
concerns the true appearance or non-appearance of the god in
the being [Sein] of the people out of its being [Seyn] and for

this. This appearing must be a basic happening" (GR 147). Such a happening have we found in the ground question of metaphysics, that decisive point at which we go down into our essence and once again ask the meaning of being. Only out of this question, of who and how we *are*, opened up and compelled by the death of God, might we once again even begin to ponder a divine claim upon us.

Such thinking places historical Dasein in need and decision, for such thinking is suspicious, doubtful, born of a collision of knowing and not-knowing, light and darkness; it makes Dasein questionworthy, for it is not clear what is happening (GR 100-101). The traditionally pious way of unobstructed vision, of cleanliness and purity, implied in otherworldly ideas and ideals or the antiseptic procedures of science, knows what is happening, "since they see to it that nothing can happen to them in general" (GR 100). It is a way ruled out for Heidegger by Nietzsche and Hölderlin; theirs (and his) is a twilight vision ruled over by an enigmatic, chaotic god such as Dionysus (Hölderlin, Nietzsche) or a tricky messenger who grants favor -- or leads astray, one cannot be sure (Hermes -- hermeneutics -- Heidegger). There is much danger in such a vision; not surprisingly, too much danger for theologians: even a mystic is to be preferred to Heidegger.[39] But such danger teaches us to be *care*-full, and *thought*-full, whereby we may yet see a star, and ourselves.

We can see here, then, that whatever religious dimension we might discover in Heidegger, and whatever direction it leads us in, it will not emerge along the track of theology, but rather from a turning away from theology. This is clearest, it seems, when we look to his considerations of Nietzsche and Hölderlin, who tell of the darkness they see spreading over the Western world in similar religious terms (death or lack of God) and thereby press for a radical transformation of our language and thought. Attempts to defend or justify a religious tradition, which is the task of theology, do not satisfy the questions they raise and which Heidegger hears. Thus even if theology is questionworthy in the new beginning that he seeks, as Heidegger seems to think, it is because it is nevertheless at the same time deeply questionable, for the old gods are gone.

> I said to my soul, be still, and let the dark come upon you
> Which shall be the darkness of God. As in a theatre,
> The lights are extinguished, for the scene to be changed.
> With a hollow rumble of wings, with a movement of darkness
>   on darkness
> And we know that the hills and the trees, the distant panorama,
> And the bold imposing facade are all being rolled away -- [40]

NOTES

1. David Farrell Krell, "Nietzsche and the Task of Thinking," p. 1n, relates that "One is hard pressed to find an essay or lecture by Heidegger in which Nietzsche is not explicitly called into play; it would scarcely be an exaggeration to say that Nietzsche's impact on Heidegger's thinking is visible on every page of his published writings." Hildegaard Feick's *Index zu "Sein und Zeit"*, 2nd revised ed. (Tübingen: Niemeyer, 1968), p. 118, shows that Hölderlin holds a similar fascination for Heidegger, occupying him in eight essays (six of which are gathered in EHD) and warranting citation in at least a dozen other essays. And all of this does not take into account Heidegger's unpublished work, just now being published.

2. Erich Heller and Anthony Thoreby, "Idealism and Religious Vision in the Poetry of Hölderlin," *Quarterly Review of Literature* X (1959), pp. 25, 33.   For observations on Hölderlin's style, see Michael Hamburger's remarks in Friedrich Hölderlin, *Poems and Fragments*, trans. Michael Hamburger (Ann Arbor: University of Michigan Press, 1967), pp. xiii, 15.

3. Note that it does not matter when the meditations on Nietzsche and Hölderlin were conducted or came to fruition. What is important is coming to understand the claim put on Heidegger's thinking (the oblivion of being, which covers the whole of his thinking from *Sein und Zeit* onward) and how Heidegger clarifies his thinking about that claim by interpreting this thinker and this poet.

4. Otto Pöggeler, *Der Denkweg Martin Heideggers* (Pfullingen: Neske, 1963), p. 261.

5. Nietzsche, *Also Sprach Zarathustra*, Preface, 5. (Note that all references to all of Nietzsche's work will be by section and paragraph number, as is customary).

6. The   last man bears   comparison with Heidegger's inauthentic man in *Sein und Zeit*; likewise the overman and Heidegger's authentic man bear comparison.   See Michael Zimmerman, "A Comparison of Nietzsche's Overman and Heidegger's Authentic Self," *Southern Journal of Philosophy* 14 (1976), pp. 213-31.

7. Krell, "Nietzsche and the Task of Thinking," pp. 68, 114, 130, 319. Cf. Krell, "Nietzsche in Heidegger's *Kehre*," pp. 200ff.   For Nietzsche on truth, see *The Will to Power*, # 493, 507, 602.

8. Krell, "Nietzsche and the Task of Thinking," pp. 183-84.

9. *Ibid.*, pp. 101, 317. Cf. Eckhard Heftrich, "Nietzsche im Denken Heideggers" in *Durchblicke*, pp. 343-44, 348. This latter essay is probably the most important analysis of how the required "destruction of ancient ontology" declared in SZ evolves into an eschatology of being and the required meditation on Nietzsche.
It should be clear at this point that in naming Nietzsche the *eschaton* of being he names the basic experience of *Sein und Zeit*, i.e., the oblivion of being. Nietzsche's thinking can hence be said to "haunt the entire region of that experience which gives *Being and Time* for thought"; Krell, "Nietzsche in Heidegger's *Kehre*," p. 202.

10. Lawrence Lampert, "Heidegger's Nietzsche Interpretation," *Man and World* 7 (1974), pp. 354, 363; Krell, "Nietzsche and the Task of Thinking," p. 110.

11. Michael Gelven, "From Nietzsche to Heidegger: A Critical Review of Heidegger's Works on Nietzsche," *Philosophy Today* 25 (1981), pp. 70-73. Cf. Nietzsche, *Zarathustra*, Preface, 3: "What is the greatest experience you can have? It is the hour of the great contempt. The hour in which your happiness, too, arouses your disgust, and even your reason and virtue.

12. Krell, "Nietzsche and the Task of Thinking," pp. 23, 35, 118; Lampert, pp. 357-58. Cf. Nietzsche, *Will to Power*, # 19, 28.

13. Lampert, p. 368. Cf. WD 23: "It belongs to what is thought-provoking that it [Nietzsche's thinking] has still not been found. It belongs to what is thought-provoking that we are still not in the least prepared truly to lose what is found, rather than merely pass it over and by-pass it."

14. *Wesen* normally means "essence". However, for Heidegger, the essence of something, i.e., the way it is, is always how something shows itself, i.e., emerges into presence, comes-to-presence (e.g., in this case, being shows itself, comes-to-presence, as nothing, as no thing). Hence, throughout this work, we will be translating *Wesen* as "essence" and "presencing" and occasionally "coming-to-presence" (though the latter more often translates *Anwesen*).

15. Nietzsche, *Zarathustra*, Preface, 3.

16. *Ibid.*, I, 22:2 (my emphasis); see also Preface, 1, and I, 3.

17. Krell, "Nietzsche and the Task," p. 166.

18. *Ibid.*, pp. 16, 25, 320-21.

19. *Ibid.*, pp. 208-209. Cf. Nietzsche, *Beyond Good and Evil*, 203, for Nietzsche's thoughts on the anxiety one suffers when one knows of the danger that man degenerates and what may yet be made of man.

20. James M. Robinson, "The German Discussion of the Later Heidegger," in *The Later Heidegger and Theology*, ed. James M. Robinson and John B. Cobb, Jr. (New York: Harper & Row, 1963), p. 12.

21. Krell, "Nietzsche and the Task," p. 294.

22. Noteworthy in this regard is Heidegger's discussion of authentic historiography (in which, incidentally, he explicitly cites Nietzsche) (SZ 523-24), which illustrates the questionworthy/questionable tension in Heidegger's thinking in the *monumental* and *critical* modes that are essential to authentic historiography.

23. Examples of this way of thinking are: Williams, *Martin Heidegger's Philosophy of Religion*, p. 109 ("the description in *Sein und Zeit* of Dasein as being-towards-death definitely points beyond Dasein to some greater reality"); John Macquarrie, *An Existentialist Theology* (1955; rpt. New York: Harper & Row, 1965), pp. 71, 74-75; Helmut Danner, *Das Göttliche und der Gott bei Heidegger* (Meisenheim: Anton Hain, 1971), p. 175, who claims that Heidegger seeks "god" but "only" comes as far as to "assert" (sic) the "lack of god" and thereby does not "attain" the God of the Old and New Testaments. Karl Rahner and other Thomists also think along these lines, insofar as they seem to feel that Heidegger does not pursue the question of being as far as they can, to the question of God; see Robert Masson, "Rahner and Heidegger: Being, Hearing, God," *The Thomist*, 37 (1973), p. 487.

24. See Annemarie Gethmann-Siefert, *Das Verhältnis von Philosophie und Theologie*, p. 263, and Masson, pp. 487-88. See also John Caputo, "Being,

Ground and Play in Heidegger," *Man and World* 3 (1970), p. 42; Hans-Georg Gadamer, "Sein Geist, Gott" in *Heidegger: Freiburger Universitätsvorträge zu seinem Gedenken*, 2nd ed. (Freiburg/München: Karl Alber, 1979), pp. 50-51; James L. Perotti, *Heidegger on the Divine* (Athens: Ohio University Press, 1974), p. 18; Otto Pöggeler, "Being as Appropriation," trans. Rudiger H. Grimm, in *Heidegger and Modern Philosophy*, ed. Michael Murray (New Haven: Yale University Press, 1978), p.106.

25. When Heidegger later says (in 1964) that theology is not a science (PT 46), this is not so much a contradiction of his 1927 essay as it is an elaboration; in the later essay, Heidegger would appear to be stressing that theology has little in common with the natural sciences and their exact language and that, indeed, there is danger in their being so conceived. See Gethmann-Siefert, pp. 134-35.

There is undoubtedly some question to be raised here concerning Heidegger's account, insofar as he says that theology is not a science of God nor speculative knowledge of God, yet it is a reasonable and coherent account of what is disclosed through faith, of which God (as creator, for example) must be counted a part.

26. Alasdair MacIntyre, "The Fate of Theism" in MacIntyre and Paul Ricoeur, *The Religious Significance of Atheism* (New York: Columbia University Press, 1969), pp. 21-23. See also N II 378-79, where Heidegger talks about theological transcendence in subjectivity, and Jean Beaufret, "Heidegger et la théologie" in *Heidegger et la Question de Dieu*, eds. Richard Kearney and Joseph O'Leary (Paris: Bernard Grasset, 1980), pp. 20-21, who notes that this line of thought (which we have directed at "liberal" theologians) makes it clear that Heidegger is not secularized Kierkegaard, suggesting that Karl Barth is thus also subject to the same criticism.

27. Gethmann-Siefert, pp. 140-262, gives the most exhaustive treatment of the theological use of Heidegger, and the most pointed criticisms of that use (pp. 262ff). See Danner, pp. 147-49, 154, for other criticisms. Williams, pp. 11-16, gives the most extensive summary in English of the theological use of Heidegger.

28. For such comparisons, see Pöggeler, *Denkweg*, pp. 36-46; Sheehan, "Introduction to Phenomenology"; Hans-Georg Gadamer, "Heidegger's Later Philosophy" in Gadamer, *Philosophical Hermeneutics*, trans. and ed. David E. Linge (Berkeley: University of California Press, 1976), p. 214; Hans Jonas, "Heidegger and Theology," *Review of Metaphysics* 18 (December 1964), p. 212; Macquarrie, *Existential Theology*, p. 53, and *Principles of Christian Theology*, 2nd ed. (New York: Charles Scribners' Sons, 1966), pp. 59-83, 99-100, and *passim*. Walter Biemel, in *Martin Heidegger: An Illustrated Study*, trans. J. L. Mehta (New York: Harvest, 1970), p. 15, vehemently denounces the effort to draw a dependency between *Sein und Zeit* and the theology of the 1920s, and Danner, p. 161, points out the insignificance of such comparisons.

29. For discussions and examples of the Bultmannian use of Heidegger, see Bultmann, "Die Geschichtlichkeit des Daseins und der Glaube. Antwort an G. Kuhlmann" in *Heidegger und die Theologie*, ed. G. Noller (München: Chr. Kaiser, 1967), pp. 72-94 (as well as other works by Bultmann); Gadamer, "Heidegger and Marburg Theology" in *Philosophical Hermeneutics*, pp. 206-207; Gethmann-Siefert, pp. 140ff; Jonas, pp. 231-33; Macquarrie, *Exis-*

tential Theology, pp. 34, 73-74 and entirety, and *Principles*, pp. 59-120 and *passim*; Williams, pp. 18-19. See also the articles in Robinson and Cobb, which largely argue along Bultmannian lines. For criticisms of Bultmann, see Gadamer, p. 207; Heinrich Ott, "Die Bedeutung von Martin Heideggers Denken," p. 30; William J. Richardson, "Heidegger and God — and Professor Jonas," *Thought* 40 (1965), pp. 15, 37; Paul Ricoeur, "Preface to Bultmann" in Ricoeur, *The Conflict of Interpretations*, ed. Don Ihde (Evanston: Northwestern University Press, 1974), pp. 399-400. For a discussion of the formal-indicative nature of the *existentialia*, see Pöggeler, "Being as Appropriation," pp. 110-12.

30. For these criticisms, in order: 1) Danner, pp. 167f; 2) Robinson, p. 42, and Jonas, p. 221; 3) Robinson, p. 42; 4) Jonas, pp. 226-27 (note that Heidegger's apparent admission of this analogy between primal and theological thinking, reported by Robinson, p. 29, was apparently more hypothetical and for argument's sake than a statement of his position on the matter; see Jonas, p. 222n.10); 5) Jonas, p. 222; 6) Jonas, p. 221, and William J. Richardson, in response to Ott's "Hermeneutics and Personal Structure" in *On Heidegger and Language*, ed. Joseph J. Kockelmans (Evanston: Northwestern University Press, 1972), p. 190.

31. This retreat is documented by the series of articles and statements Ott has made since *Denken und Sein* (1957): "What is Systematic Theology" in Robinson and Cobb, pp. 77-111, "Bedeutung," pp. 27-38, "Hermeneutic and Personal Structure," p. 193, and finally a statement in Richard Wisser, ed. *Martin Heidegger in Conversation*, trans. B. Srinivasu Murthy (New Dehli: Arnold-Heinemann, 1977), p. 29. This last statement is very cautious, only advancing that Heidegger's prudence and patience in thinking are a good example for theology.

32. Jäger, *Gott. Nochmals Martin Heidegger* (Tübingen: Mohr, 1978); O'Leary, *Questioning Back: The Overcoming of Metaphysics in Christian Tradition* (Minneappolis: Winston/Seabury, 1985).

33. Gethmann-Siefert, pp. 131-32. Cf. Gadamer, "The Religious Dimension in Heidegger" in *Transcendence and the Sacred*, ed. Alan Olson and Leroy Rouner (Notre Dame: University of Notre Dame Press, 1981), p. 202, in which Gadamer sees in Heidegger's call to theology a "task of thinking".

34. Cf. Heinz-Horst Schrey, "Die Bedeutung der Philosophie Martin Heideggers für die Theologie" in *Martin Heideggers Einfluss auf der Wissenschaften aus Anlass seines 60. Geburtstag* (Bern: Franke, 1949), pp. 9-10; Otto Pöggeler, "Heideggers Begegnung mit Holderlin," *Man and World* 10 (1977), p. 23; Gadamer, "Heidegger's Later Philosophy," p. 198, and "The Religious Dimension in Heidegger," pp. 193, 195-96.

35. And an ambiguous word it is, too. It comes from the last line of "The Poet's Vocation" (*Dichterberuf*), which reads: *so lange, bis Gottes Fehl hilft* ("God's being missed in the end will help [the poet]" [?]). *Fehl* is highly ambiguous. *Fehlen* can mean absence, lack or want, non-appearance, non-attendance (as in school). *Fehl* can mean fault, blemish or flaw, and the verb *fehlen* can have meanings of to do wrong, err, sin or blunder, in addition to what is listed above for *Fehlen*. Both "lack" and "non-attendance" seem best. But then the genitive is equally ambiguous, especially if lack is used. Hamburger notes (p. 659): "The last line has puzzled many commentators. Hölderlin's disgust with the exploitation and

debasement of religion, science and art is such that the allusion to God's absence has been construed as irony. Yet Hölderlin is quite serious in stating that the dominant trends in our civilization will never be reversed until there is a general recognition of God's absence in our lives. Only this awareness of God's absence can bring about a general *metanoia* -- and release the poet and prophet from his irreligious solitude."

36. Contra Charles H. Malik, "A Christian Reflection on Martin Heidegger," *The Thomist* 41 (1977), p. 60.

37. Hence Hölderlin is not a "replacement Bible" to which Heidegger refers, nor does Heidegger's thinking become "mythological" in conversation with Hölderlin, anymore than it becomes theological in conversation with Christianity or nihilistic in conversation with Nietzsche and metaphysics; see Pöggeler, "Heidegger's Begegnung," pp. 28, 38, 48, and "Metaphysics and the Topology of Being in Heidegger," *Man and World* 8 (1975), p. 17.   See also Gadamer, "Sein, Geist, Gott," pp. 55-56, 62, and Mehta, p. 474n.42.

38. Heller and Thoreby, "Idealism and Religious Vision," p. 34.

39. Jonas, pp. 225-28, laments the ambiguous realm into which Heidegger thrusts us, and John D. Caputo, *The Mystical Element in Heidegger's Thought* (Athens: Ohio University Press, 1976), pp. 246-47, 249, much prefers the plenum of being, goodness, and intelligibility that is Meister Eckhart's lovable God to Heidegger's inscrutable being and *Ereignis*.

40. T.S. Eliot, "Four Quartets," p. 126.

CHAPTER 3

RELIGION AS TRUE: DISCLOSURE OF A WORLD

> *At the still point of the turning world.*
> T.S. Eliot

1. THE PROBLEM -- WHAT IS TRUTH?

Following Heidegger along the way in which the question of the
meaning of being is raised anew with the dissolution of any
sort of transcendent-transcendental world, thinking is immediately confronted with questions concerning truth and the cor-
ollary subjects of world and meaning. Traditionally, the
locus of truth has been found in assertions (judgments), and
the essence of truth (i.e., how truth manifests itself) in the
agreement of the assertion with its "object", i.e., the "true"
world, however construed (*ideas*, sense-data, the divine plan
of God, the plan of reason, etc.). Meaningful and true knowledge was therefore obtained through a correct orientation to
that "true" world. Now, however, at the end of philosophy and
onto-theo-logy, that "true" world dissolves before the suspicion that assertion is exactly that -- assertion, of the will
to power and permanence that decides what is really in being
and hence what is justified as the correct orientation toward
the world. Truth as adequation becomes an exercise in justification of one's own stance *vis á vis* the world, a world that
has become nothing more than what can be justified for securing the permanence of the will to power. Truth, for all
intents and purposes, can be an illusion and an error, as long
as it enhances one's power and efforts to secure permanence.
But now where there is no telling truth from illusion and
error, truth is indeed questionable.

The problem is of course no less acute for religious
thinking, and is perhaps most amply illustrated in the current
dilemma over the plurality of religions and the diversity of
"truth-claims" they present to us. Exclusivist approaches (we
have *the* Truth) are all too obviously suspect as exercises in
securing permanence and power. Yet, on the other hand, to
make every religion "partly true", i.e., part of, or a facet
of, the whole Truth that transcends us, seems wholly unsatis-
factory, for it mimics Nietzsche's proclamation that truth is
a kind of error (any "truth" that is "partly" true is "partly"
false, i.e., error). We come to question what we can say,
think, or do, if anything, within the realm of religious
thinking in the midst of a plurality of truth-claims.

Clearly a new approach, one that is neither theological
nor nihilistic, is called for if we are to recapture any sense
of meaning in thinking and religious thinking in particular.

Heidegger's efforts to grapple with the meaning of being and
therefore the problems of truth, world, and meaning seem
ideally suited to illuminating the problems and pitfalls in
this area, at the very least. In addition, if Heidegger's
thinking proves helpful in grappling with the problem of
religious plurality, we will get a first glimpse of what
significance he has for religious thinking. Toward these
ends, we will be concerned in this chapter with two things:
1) a rather lengthy interpretation of Heidegger's considerations of the problems of truth, world, and meaning, and where
such thinking takes him, and then 2) an application of
Heidegger's reflections to the plurality of religions, both in
criticism of some of the more prominent ways in which this
problem has already been addressed, and towards developing a
satisfactory way of dealing with the plurality of religions
on our own.

2. TOWARD *EREIGNIS* -- MEANING, WORLD, TRUTH

As we have already noted, previous ontologies have dealt with
the "world" in terms of beings as a whole and the sum of what
is, whether that is represented as the whole of creation
(beings present-at-hand created by God) or a secularly represented universe of nature and history. The epitome of such
an approach in modern metaphysics would be Descartes' treatment of the world as *res extensa*, which Heidegger finds to be
dependent upon the idea of substantiality and hence being as
constant presence (SZ 119ff), the unquestioned assumptions of
the whole of metaphysics. Such a metaphysical approach results in the development of true and apparent worlds, world-
views, and a variety of epistemological conundrums as to how
the subject (man) is to relate to, or even know that there is,
an object (the world) "out there". To avoid such a questionable approach, Heidegger begins his considerations by taking
up a piece of equipment as an example of a being within-the-
world and asking how this being shows itself to us and therefore *is*. Heidegger finds that such equipment *is* more than a
mere object [*Gegenstand*], present-at-hand [*vorhanden*], standing over against a subject. As ready-to-hand [*zuhanden*]
(Heidegger's term for the being of equipment, its being ready
to be used), we find that equipment is used *in order to* do
something; it has some function(s). Its use is geared towards
something *toward which* the work is done; its use has some
"goal" which, though it may initially be some other being
within-the-world (e.g., a house), is ultimately Dasein, the
being that we are, and *for the sake of* which the work is done
(e.g., a house is for the sake of Dasein). Finally, a piece
of equipment never *is* in isolation, but is always found amidst
other equipment and other beings within-the-world *with which*
and *in which* it is used (SZ 92ff). These assignments and

references [*Verweisung*] (the "in order to", the "towards
which", etc.) show that the ready-to-hand is *that* which is em-
ployed *for* [*mit . . . bei*] some end, and hence that the being
of the ready-to-hand does not lie in some sort of constant
presence, but in destination [*Bewandtnis*][1] (GP 413-15; SZ
112). In using a piece of equipment, or comporting ourselves
in any other way towards beings within-the-world, we refer
ourselves, and are referred, to a context of assignments and
destinations; we signify [*be-deuten*], i.e., point out, interpret and explain, a context of relations in our comportment
toward beings. Heidegger calls the relational totality of
signifying "significance" [*Bedeutsamkeit*], and it is that,
already disclosed in our comportment toward beings, which is
the world (GP 410; SZ 116-17).
        World is then for Heidegger that in terms of which beings
are what they are; they are significant only by virtue of
world. World is thus not a being within-the-world, but what
determines and makes possible the manifestation of beings
within-the-world (though not as abstractions or categories of
beings in general). Only insofar as "there is" [*es . . .
>>gibt<<*] world can beings show themselves and thus be encoun-
tered and discovered by Dasein. World is the "how" of beings
which defines them in their totality and is ultimately the
possibility of every limit and measure (SZ 97, 111; WM 143).
        Now since beings are first accessible only by virtue of
the the world, world is "that by means of and in terms of
which Dasein is given to signify [*sich zu bedeuten gibt*] what
beings it *can* behave toward and how it can behave toward them"
(WM 157). World is thus what permits and allows us to encounter beings within-the-world. But what permits and allows us
something gives us possibilities and therefore enables [*ermög-
licht*] us to be (US 199). As enabling us to be, world is
constitutive of our being. World marks out the projects of
Dasein, that is, its being and its potentiality-for-being.
Put another way, since world has the basic character of 'for
the sake of' Dasein (the ultimate destination), world belongs
to the selfhood of Dasein (self thought as a way of being,
not substantially) and is essentially related to Dasein. In
signifying in terms of world, "Dasein calls forth [*zeitigt*]
itself as a self, i.e., as a being to which it is left *to be*"
(WM 157). Dasein understands the world in its comportment
toward beings, meaning that it discloses the 'for the sake of
which' [*Worumwillen*] and significance whereby beings are and
it may be. Such understanding has the structure of projection
[*Entwurf*] whereby Dasein throws [*wirft*] possibilities ahead of
itself, projects a world, and understands itself (always) in
terms of such projection and possibility. World then is a
characteristic of Dasein and relative to Dasein, although it
encompasses all beings in its totality (GP 421-22; SZ 87, 190,
193; WM 143).

Yet as a characteristic of Dasein (which makes it essential to Dasein's being) world is then also that to which
Dasein finds itself [befindet sich] already submitted as well;
world is "wherein" Dasein as a being already was. Through its
disposition [Befindlichkeit], its mood [Stimmung], whereby it
is attuned [gestimmt] to the world as that in which it already
moves and dwells, Dasein has already got itself delivered over
into definite possibilities that it is and has to be as Dasein.   Such thrownness [Geworfenheit] is a determination [Be-
stimmung] of Dasein equiprimordial with the projection of
possibilities in understanding. Projection then is never an
explicit grasping of being and possibilities of being that are
free-floating and indifferent, but thrown projection, whereby
world is disclosed and Dasein constituted and determined in
its being and is 'there' [da].   Thrownness and understanding
are equiprimordial determinations of Dasein whereby, in being
(hear this verbally), world is disclosed. World is "there" in
the disclosedness of being that is Dasein (SZ 179-80, 183,
191; WM 32, 158).

In all of this it must be kept clearly in mind that the
world is not some network of forms which a worldless subject
has fabricated (or has had fabricated for it) and then throws
over some kind of material "out there". World is not some
sort of possession which Dasein has; it is therefore not a
world-view, nor a web of beliefs or hypotheses or rules as we
have in structuralism or Wittgensteinian conventionalisms
wherein meaning and significance can be calculated out of a
finite set of relationships like mathematical functions. Such
representations or categorical interpretations as these are
already too late, already "presupposing" a world, for they are
ways of comporting ourselves towards beings which are manifest
only by virtue of the world. Instead of these rigid networks
of relationships with which the world is usually identified,
we must think of world as "worlding" [weltet], as Heidegger
puts it. With this figura etymologica ("the world worlds")
Heidegger emphasizes the dynamic way in which the world is
shown and shows itself (indicated by the throwing and the
counter-throw [Ent-wurf], the signify-ing and disclos-ing) and
a way that cannot be explained by grounds and causes. Grounds
and causes are suitable for beings within-the-world but do not
reach the ever nonobjective worlding world to which we are
subject in our dealings with beings (HW 30; SZ 78n, 86, 118).

Now one way of being towards beings available to Dasein is
asserting and assertion, the traditional locus of truth. We
should therefore expect to see, in the disclosing which Dasein
is, some connection between world and truth.

Taking a look at assertions, Heidegger finds that they
have three significations: 1) pointing out, letting a being
be seen from itself, which is the primary signification, 2)
predication, which asserts a predicate of a subject and thus
gives it a definite character, and 3) communication [Mitteil-

ung], which shares with [*teilt . . . mit*] the other what we
have pointed out with a definite character (SZ 205-206).
Heidegger thus defines assertion as "a pointing out which
gives something a definite character and communicates" (SZ
208). This threefold character mirrors the threefold fore-
structure of interpretation, which is the way in which understanding becomes itself, working out projected possibilities.
Interpretation in every case is grounded in a fore-having
[*Vorhabe*], i.e., it unfolds in being towards a totality of
destinations already understood ("had"); in pointing out,
assertion clearly operates within such a totality (in order to
be able to point out). Interpretation is also grounded in a
fore-sight [*Vorsicht*], which is the 'first cut', as it were,
out of the forehaving, the unveiling of something from a point
of view with the intention of providing a definite way of
interpretation; predication does exactly that. Finally, interpretation involves a foreconception [*Vorgriff*], the decision for a definite way of conceiving, because it involves
what can be held in common and shared (SZ 197ff).

The thrust of this analysis is to point out that assertion
is a mode of understanding and interpretation, and indeed, a
derivative mode in that it covers up its interpretative character, i.e., its operating within a totality of destinations
and significance as disclosed in circumspective concern (SZ
209-10). What this indicates is that something is going on in
the assertion more primordial than the agreement of a proposition with some object "out there" in the external world.
Indeed, that asserting is primarily a pointing out indicates
that something must have been uncovered beforehand such that
it may be pointed to by the assertion. This is clear from any
demonstration that attempts to confirm an assertion, for con-
firmation of an assertion involves a being showing itself in
the way it has been pointed out by the assertion.[2] Assertion,
then, as a way of being towards the thing itself that is,
uncovers the being towards which it is. Thus Heidegger concludes that

> to say that an assertion *is true* signifies that it uncovers
> the being as it is in itself. Such an assertion points out,
> 'lets' the being 'be seen' (*apophansis*) in its unconcealed-
> ness. The *being-true* (*truth*) of the assertion must be under-
> stood as *being-uncovering* [*entdeckend-sein*] (SZ 289).

What this means then, however, is that the primordial
meaning of truth is not agreement but that of uncovering
beings, taking them out of their hiddenness and letting them
be seen in their unhiddenness. Such an interpretation of
truth, though apparently highly arbitrary, finds support in
the oldest parts of our tradition (e.g., Heraclitus,
Aristotle) in which *alētheia*, commonly translated as "truth"
but etymologically indicating uncovering, is found to concern

beings in the "how" of their uncoveredness. Surprisingly
enough, Heidegger's "defining" truth as unconcealedness is a
reappropriation of the tradition, not as an attempt to revive
Greek philosophy, obviously, but as an attempt to remind us of
what, unthought even by the Greeks, underlies our familiar
conception of truth as correctness and agreement (SZ 290-91;
HW 38; cf. GP 295ff).[3]

We have seen now that asserting, wherein truth is traditionally found, is a derivative mode of interpretation and
hence founded on understanding, which is constitutive of the
disclosedness of Dasein. In other words, with and through the
disclosedness of Dasein, the uncovering that is truth is
possible. Dasein's disclosedness, then, is the existential-
ontological foundation, i.e., the primordial phenomenon, of
truth. Insofar as Dasein is its disclosedness, it is "in the
truth", whereby "all truth is relative to the being of Dasein"
(SZ 292, 300; cf. GP 313). Heidegger concludes that "'there
is' [>es gibt<] truth only insofar as Dasein is and as long as
Dasein is (SZ 299).

Truth then is linked to Dasein -- unconcealment (alētheia)
is tied to disclosedness. This however does not at all mean
that all truth is subjective. Though truth now is certainly
not something existing beforehand, "outside" and "above" us
"among the stars" that later descends among beings and toward
which we comport ourselves (HW 49; SZ 301), truth is not
thereby a presupposition we make at our discretion. Rather,
'truth' is what makes it possible for us to be able to presup-
pose anything at all, and is hence a "presupposition" that has
already been made; we, in being, have already been set down
before the truth (SZ 301-302). This is clear when we recall
that in uncovering, Dasein is brought before beings themselves
as they show themselves, as they stand in unconcealment (SZ
300); there can then be no question here of relativizing truth
to the whim of Dasein. We understand a being, uncovering it,
only insofar as we have already been thrown into the unconcealment of beings.

We note now, however, that how beings are uncovered belongs to the disclosedness of world; to understanding, as
uncovering, belongs understanding (something like) a world --
to thrownness, a prior submission to world. Truth and world
belong together to the disclosedness of Dasein. As one com-
mentator on Heidegger puts it:

> Truth is the way of being open to the world which is consti-
> tutive of the possibility of inquiry at all. It is the
> openness (dis-closedness) of the whole in-order-to-for-the-
> sake-of-which structure within which particular beings (in-
> cluding ourselves) are freed to be encountered for the first
> time.[4]

We may better see the interconnection of truth and world and the matter at stake if we turn our attention to what William Richardson considers to be the unifying theme of "early" Heidegger: transcendence "to" world *as* freedom and *as* truth.[5] Heidegger says that the world is that "toward which" Dasein *transcends*, meaning that Dasein first attains to the being that it is (disclosedness) by *surpassing* beings "to" world and letting the world happen. In this way Dasein may encounter beings and itself; it is *free* to discover the world it has been submitted to and understand its potentialities given by the world (WM 138-39, 158; cf. GP 424-26). Put another way, we could say that we are able to encounter beings, finding them significant and meaningful, only if we are free to ask about them, which ultimately means going *beyond* beings (surpassing, transcending) to ask *how* they are in this way (the "how" meaning the world) and not in another.[6]

Such surpassing and *letting* the world *be* involves freedom. Freedom here has nothing to do with the causality of willing but concerns the dynamics of the unconcealment which discloses possibilities granted by the world. Freedom alone lets the world govern and is thereby that which makes bonds and obligations in the first place. Freedom is letting-be, i.e., engagement in the disclosure of beings, and thus the essence (presencing) of truth, for correctness (truth in the traditional sense) is only *possible* on the basis of the opening up carried out by freedom. Through freedom, Dasein is ex-posed [*aus-setzend*] to the world, set out into the world, that he may be free to encounter beings and comport himself toward them in any number of ways. Freedom, by possessing man (man never possesses freedom, just as he never 'has' world or truth in the sense of having them at his disposal), attunes man to his world such that he finds himself and his possibilities, one of which is asserting. Hence there can be truth in the traditional sense of conformity of statement to object only if Dasein has freely entered into an open region for something opened up by freedom (WM 164-65, 185-86, 188-90, 192).

Freedom thus governs the open [*Freie*] in the sense of what is cleared and lit up [*Gelichten*], i.e., the revealed; it involves a clearing [*Lichtung*] (heard verbally) within which beings may stand in the light [*Licht*] of their being and show themselves. The open, the clearing, is the realm of unconcealment, governed by disclosure, and is called *alētheia* (HW 40; VA 32-33,258; WM 185-86, 201). In this region beings come to shine in their being. This region then is not only a clearing of beings but, first and foremost (so that beings may show themselves), a clearing of being. So we find Heidegger also saying: "*das Wesen der Wahrheit ist die Wahrheit des Wesens*" -- what makes truth (as adequation) possible (essence -- *Wesen*) is the unconcealment (truth -- *alētheia*) of presencing (*Wesen* thought verbally -- being) (WM 201). Since beings come to shine in this clearing, it is only by *standing out* into this clearing, comporting itself toward beings and hence exposed to how beings are and may be, and how it is and may be, that *Da-sein* is the 'there' [*da*] of being -- the clearing of being, the "place" of the clearing of being -- whereby being is taken into 'care' and "guarded". This is why the essence of Dasein is called existence (from *ek-stasis*, "standing out".) by Heidegger. "*Das 'Wesen' des Daseins liegt in seiner Existenz*" (SZ 56-57) says: The presencing of being, 'there' (in the clearing, unconcealment), lies in the standing-out (*ek-stasis*) (of man into that clearing, whereby he comes to be in his proper essence [being]) (WM 189-90, 325-27, 329-30, 350, 373).

We find then that the topics of world (being), truth (as adequation) and man converge on a single matter, the openness or clearing in which being is cleared and beings may thereby show themselves and be encountered. Only through a standing-open comportment which is, in some sense, the clearing (in that it discloses, though it does not first create this clearing but enters into, takes over, and dwells in it),[7] is there any dealing with beings, including truth as conformity to the object.   This project domain "upon which" being is understood (intelligible, meaningful) and beings are significant in that they are understood in their being, is the meaning of being, the original issue of Heidegger's thought. This "meaning", this "place" in which being and beings are cleared, is clearly not a matter of reference (something denoted by the word "being") but a process or event in which and from out of which there is meaning.   It is what makes truth possible and is therefore 'truth' in a more primordial sense -- *alētheia*, the truth of being.   It is not something free-floating and "outside" of beings -- an empty generality or abstract universality -- but what is *essential* to whatever shows itself (SZ 47, 429-30; WM 184 and note, 185 and note, 200-201, 337).[8]

Now insofar as truth in this primordial sense is characterized as unconcealment and clearing and thereby bound up with light metaphors, it may seem as if there is very little that is radically new in Heidegger with regard to truth. However, as Heidegger himself notes: "Only someone who is thinking superficially or, indeed, not thinking at all can content himself with the observation that Heidegger conceives truth as unconcealment" (Preface, xii). This is because over against both the philosophical tradition in which being is in principle intelligible (e.g., Aristotle, Hegel) and the religious tradition in which Truth is (ultimately) sheer transparency and pure light, Heidegger stresses a character of hiddenness and concealment inseparably bound up with the unconcealment characterizing truth as *alētheia*.   Concealing [*Verbergen*] is constitutive of revealing [*Entbergen*] and unconcealment [*Unverborgenheit*]; *lēthē* lies at the heart of *alētheia*.   Concealing is furthermore not a lack or privation in the sense of something that could or eventually would be

uncovered; it is not like a shadow which can be eliminated if
we changed the light source. In order for there to be revealing, disclosure, and unconcealment, there must be concealing
and closure. Concealing, then, shelters [bergen] the possibility of revealing [Ent-bergen] and preserves it, and is
therefore essential to revealing as what makes it possible (VA
271; WM 193-94; ZD 78).

This revealing-concealing character of the unconcealment
of being and beings is manifest in a number of ways throughout
Heidegger's thinking. For example, in the analysis of Dasein
in *Sein und Zeit*, Dasein is found to be constituted by *thrown*
projection. In having been already thrown into the world,
Dasein, and the beings it discloses, are characterized by a
pure and simple "that-it-is" [Daβ] that refuses any further
explication; at some point there can be no further manipula-
tion on our part. Dasein (and beings) simply *is* (are), and is
what it has to be. Dasein then is fixed in place, which does
not mean made rigid and secure but that it is outlined,
bounded, and circumscribed. Such limitation is not a harmful
restriction or deficiency, a cessation or a failure. This
"refusal", this boundary, must be thought in the Greek sense
of boundary (*peras*), i.e., that from which and wherein something begins and arises as that which it is (e.g., Dasein
comes to be, "begins", in thrownness and its "that-it-is",
from which Dasein understands its being). Thrownness as a
limit is that whereby Dasein and beings begin to be, begin to
stand out and come to stand in the open of the clearing.
Beings are given form (*morphē*), completed and fulfilled [*voll-
endet*], by their refusal. The pure that-it-is of Dasein and
the refusal of beings are the boundaries that set both free
into unconcealment (EM 64; HW 40, 71; SG 125; SZ 179-81;VA
17).

In already having been thrown into the world, Dasein has
also already submitted to and been taken up into an everyday
understanding and interpretation of beings within the world.
Such immersion [*Verfallenheit*][9] in the world, constituted by
common talk [*Gerede*], curiosity, and ambiguity, disguises and
closes off what has been uncovered and disclosed. Dasein
falls into understanding what every*one* knows, projecting possibilities every*one* has, thereby foregoing any primordial
appropriation and understanding of the world that is its *own*.
Dasein thereby falls away from itself, losing itself and
becoming absorbed in the publicness of *das Man* (the ambiguous
"they" or "one"). For example, in the common talk of being-
immersed, one understands the words spoken -- what is said in
the talk -- but one passes over what the talk is about, i.e.,
Dasein, the open region, the unconcealment of being. One
simply passes the word (the public interpretation of the
world) along and promotes an undifferentiated kind of understanding that has been *uprooted* from the matter at stake
(since passing along removes the saying from its original

place) and which everyone and anyone can have. Such a public
interpretation is tempting, for it knows all (it has passed
the word along from everywhere) and hence covers up the need
for a genuine reappropriation and understanding of the possibilities of Dasein. (A good example of this is the fugitive
way in which das Man deals with death, making it impersonal
["everyone dies"] and thereby concealing that it is Dasein's
ownmost potentiality-for-being; see SZ 336-38). In short,
Dasein, the unconcealment of being (what is talked about, the
disclosing), is forgotten. Yet this immersion and its concealing is nothing negative, but essential to Dasein. All
genuine understanding, interpreting, and communicating are
performed in, out of, and against this being-immersed; all
existing (standing-out into the unconcealment of being) is as
it is out of and back into everydayness. Immersion preserves
an understanding of the world (possibilities of Dasein) and is
thus disclosive, but in a disguised and hidden manner, in a
mode of semblance (SZ 58-59, 168-69, 222-26, 233, 293-94; WM
332).[10]

It is because the state of being of Dasein is thrown
projection that Heidegger can also say that Dasein is equipri-
mordially "in the truth" and "in the untruth" and thereby name
the concealing that is necessary for unconcealing in another
way (SZ 294-95; WM 193). However, as becomes clear from the
discussion above, this concealing, this un-truth, is of an
uncanny, twofold nature. On the one hand, concealing is a
refusal, a boundary, and thus the beginning of the clearing
and unconcealment; it reveals an indefiniteness and mystery
[Geheimnis] in beings and being that makes everything ordinary
extraordinary, as they never allow themselves to be completely
at our disposal and completely disclosed. We therefore have
to learn to be at home with this mysterious and indefinite
character of beings and being, that beings may come to shine
in the clearing. But concealment is also manifest as a dis-
sembling, pretension, and semblance, as attested to by the
character of being-immersed. Because being consists in offering an appearance [Schein] and view, the possibility of an
appearance which covers up and conceals what beings are in the
truth (i.e., the possibility of semblance [Anschein]) is necessarily and constantly there as well. One is thus constantly beset by the possibility that the concealment allowed
for and accomodated so that beings and being may be disclosed
is a mere illusion and thus a fleeing before the matter at
stake. Disclosing then becomes a matter of taking concealment
seriously both in its deceptive and bestowing power. Concealment compels restraint and prudence, in refusing complete
disclosure and thus total control by us, and suspicion, in
that we are never sure whether such concealment is illusion
that carries us away and displaces us (EM 111-13; HW 40-42).

This uncanny character of concealment is perhaps nowhere
better evoked than in Heidegger's concern with the nothing

[*das Nichts*]. From the nothing, all beings come to be as
beings; the nothing makes the openness of beings possible for
human existence. The repelling gesture of the nothing, which
Heidegger calls nihilating [*nichtigen*], directs us to beings
and discloses them, opening them up in their full yet hitherto
concealed strangeness -- that they *are* rather than nothing (WM
114-15). Yet the nothing, as making possible, belongs then to
being and its presencing; nothing is the way in which being
presences [*west*], revealing beings while withdrawing, holding
back, and keeping to itself. Such withdrawal, however, fos-
ters the oblivion and forgetfulness of being that is the
history of metaphysics (nihilism). The nothing, belonging to
the being of beings and the clearing of being as the *lēthē*
lying at the heart of *alētheia*, both bestows and disguises (WM
114 & note, 115 & note, 306, 359-60).
     To explain this, we might take a look at science, which
Heidegger says needs to call upon the nothing for help in
expressing its positive and exclusive behavior toward beings
(WM 106). What does this mean? On the one hand, it points to
the totality of significations, the total context of behavior,
in which science is rooted and can be what it is, revealing
beings in a particular way according to the comportment of
science. Science itself is always going to rely on a concealed context, an unexamined and unexplained world (which is
"nothing" compared to beings) whereby beings are first revealed, that it may behave toward beings in the way that it
does. Recent philosophies of science have tended to bear out
the extent to which an unexamined "background" plays a part in
science.[11] On the other hand, since everything else is nothing to science except the way beings show themselves to science (e.g., as objects), science tends, for the most part, to
remain oblivious to other ways in which beings may show themselves to us (e.g., a rat *is* a tool for a cancer researcher;
it can*not* also *be* a pet). But then, finally, beings oftentimes *refuse* to conform to the way science sees them (e.g.,
subatomic particles refuse to act according to Newtonian laws,
which were adequate at a macrophysical level). This refusal
(which cannot be accounted for by the existing theory and is
therefore nothing to that theory) forces the scientist to
rethink the way things are, revealing new possibilities of
being.[12]
     There is one final way in which Heidegger deals with the
concealing of disclosure, and it first arises in the context
of his consideration of the artwork: the strife between world
and earth. In the artwork, its "material" does not get used
up but is brought forth for the first time. The massiveness
of stone, the darkness and glow of color, the singing and
clanging of tone, the hardness, luster and glimmer of metal --
all these are brought forth for the first time in the work.
But what is brought forth is precisely the earth in its concealedness and self-concealing; the earth presences (shows

itself) by denying any sort of penetration or explanation
(e.g., color does not glow when analyzed in terms of wave-
lengths; it simply disappears). The work, in opening up a
world (i.e., disclosing), sets forth the earth as concealing
and sets itself back into the earth in order to disclose the
world it discloses. The clearing of paths, of possibilities
and decisions, opens up at the same time something not mastered, i.e., something concealed, confusing: the earth, the
ground on which any projecting of world rests. The phenomenon
of the earth shows us that such truth as is disclosed in the
artwork is not a simple manifestation of meaning, but a truth
that is sheltering and concealing, and is therefore an unfath-
omableness and depth of meaning brought about by the artwork
standing in itself and holding within itself a fundamental
opposition to our will to control.[13]   Earth belongs essentially to world, or, as Heidegger later puts it in the context of
the fourfold [Geviert] that makes up the world, earth and sky
belong together in the worlding of the world (HW 35, 42, 50-
51, 63).[14]
      We must be clear on the relationship here between reveal-
ing and concealing, world and earth, and their unity: it is
no dialectic, no reconciliation of contradictories in an encompassing unity. As Heidegger puts it,

        the relation between world and earth does not wither away
        into the empty unity of opposites unconcerned with one an-
        other. The world, in resting upon the earth, strives to
        surmount it. As self-opening it cannot endure anything
        closed. The earth, however, as sheltering and concealing,
        tends always to draw the world into itself and keep it there
        (HW 35).

The opposition, then, is a striving that raises each up into
what it is; the world is opening in surmounting the earth, and
the earth is closing in jutting out into the world. Neither
can dispense with the other if they are to be what they are.
At the same time, the striving carries each opponent "beyond"
itself such that each, in being what it is, gives itself, of
itself, to a "unity" and repose (HW 35-36). This is no synthesis, but an instigation and maintenence of the striving of
world and earth. Thus the work of art (art's working) consists in uniting the opposition of world and earth into a
unit. The intimacy [Innigkeit] of the striving constitutes the
truth, the unconcealment, the open region.
      We might get a better sense of this striving if we consid-
er Heidegger's meditations on an early Greek word for being:
physis. Heidegger does not translate physis with the word
"being" or "Nature" [Natur], as is customary, but as Aufgehend
-- upsurgence, emergence, arising. Physis

says emergence from out of itself (e.g., the blossoming
[*Aufgehende*] of a rose), self-opening unfolding, the appearance in such unfolding and holding itself out into it and
remaining; in short, the emerging-whiling away.   This emergence and in-itself-standing-out-of-itself must not be taken
as a process among others that we observe among beings.
Physis is being itself, by virtue of which beings become and
remain observable (EM 16-17).

Physis, then, is the never-setting, the always enduring arising whereby beings come to shine in their being.   But
Heraclitus, in Fragment 123 (*physis kryptesthai philei*, usually translated as: 'Nature [or the essence of things] likes to
hide'), names arising [*Aufgehen*] -- *physis* -- and concealing
[*Verbergen*] -- *kryptesthai* -- in closest proximity, indeed, in
such a way that they are not separated from each other but
mutually inclined toward each other (insofar as *philein* and
philia name a reciprocal favoring).   Thus Heidegger, after a
lengthy examination, translates this fragment as: "'Rising
(out of self-concealing) bestows favor upon self-concealing'
[*Das Aufgehen (aus dem Sichverbergen) dem Sichverbergen
schenkt's die Gunst*]" (VA 271; cf. EM 122).   What is decisive
here in this thinking of *physis* is that "self-revealing [*Sich-
entbergen*] not only never dispenses with concealing [*verbergen*], but needs it, in order to presence [*west*] in the way
that it presences, as dis-closing [*Ent-bergen*]" (VA 271-72).
The *kryptesthai* of *physis* is not to be overcome or stripped
from *physis*; rather, the task in thinking *physis* "is the much
more difficult task of allowing to *physis*, in all the purity
of its presencing, the *kryptesthai* that belongs to it" (WM
301).
        An illustration might be in order here.   A plant, e.g., an
oak tree, rooting itself in the earth and reaching up to the
sky, is a picture of a dynamic abiding that draws on both the
earth (concealing) and sky (revealing) for its nourishment and
is what it is by *becoming* what it is.   Hence Heidegger "defines" *physis* as "the on the way [*unterwegs*] of a self-placing
thing towards itself as what is to be pro-duced [*Her-zustel-
lendem*]", and this such that "the placing is itself wholly of
a kind with the self-placing thing and what is to be produced."   *Physis* then is "a mode of coming-forth into presencing [*Anwesung*] in which the 'from which', the 'to which' and
the 'how' remain the same," such that it is a "going-forth
[*Aufgang*] towards a going-forth [*Aufgehende*] and thus remains
a going-*back*-into-itself, towards *itself* as always going-
forth" (WM 292-93).   To return to our example, *how* an oak tree
is (a "rooted reaching up", so to speak), is the same as that
to which it attains (an oak tree, in growing, further roots
itself that it may reach higher) and *from which* it goes forth
(the oak tree already is a rooted reaching up).

This description of the double direction of *physis*, and
thus the revealing-concealing openness that is the issue for
Heidegger, indicates a unity that has nothing to do with any
notions of improvement or of surmounting inadequacies to reach
a goal of overall understanding and knowledge as in traditional philosophy (e.g., the oak tree does not uproot itself to
reach higher, but reaches back even deeper into the earth).
This description also indicates that the dynamic unity of
physis is not to be thought dialectically or circularly, á la
Hegel's "good infinity". For as Heidegger puts it,

> the merely spatial image of a circle is fundamentally inad-
> equate because this going-forth which goes back into itself
> precisely lets *something* go forth from which and to which the
> going-forth is on the way (WM 293).

Nothing is *aufgehoben* here; there is simply an abiding in the
unity of striving.[15]
        By now, if we have been attentive to the language being
used (clearing, meaning, revealing, concealing, disclosing,
arising), it should be clear that the essence and presencing
of truth is not static, a rigid stage with a permanently
raised curtain, so to speak, on which the play of beings
occurs. Rather, truth is a struggle, a "primal strife [*Ur-
streit*]", as Heidegger puts it, "in which the open center
[*Mitte*] is one within which beings stand and from which it
sets itself back into itself" (HW 42). Strife lets beings
come to stand, for cleavages, intervals, distances and joints
are opened up by its separating within which beings may
emerge, just as a field furrowed and cleared [*auf- und unreis-
sen*] opens up the field to seed and growth. Beings then have
their "unity", their rest and repose, in the strife. Such
strife is a gathering, for this rift [*Riβ*], which is the
intimacy with which the opponents in the strife belong to each
other, is a basic design [*Grundriβ*] and outline sketch [*Auf-
riβ*] which sketches out the basic features of the clearing of
beings and draws them together into a unit. A being comes to
be, and is preserved in its being, by having the conflict open
up in it, such that it is brought into the rift, and thereby
is (EM 65-66; HW 50-51; US 252).
        Such strife is accomplished and "won" by a work. The
work, thought in the Greek sense of the word (*ergon*) (i.e.,
bringing forth what is present into unconcealment), sets up a
world and sets forth the earth; earth is worked, set free to
be itself, whereby it is formed, and a world shines forth (HW
51-52). For example, a painting of a pair of peasant shoes, a
working of pigments on canvas, opens up the peasant's world
-- the roads and fields he must trod, the length of time he
must work, etc. -- by revealing the material (the "earthi-
ness") of the shoes (HW 19). Likewise a temple, a working of
stone, as another example, gives things their look and men

their outlook before the divine one -- who is present as
concealed within the temple -- all the while standing firm on
the earth and revealing it as man's abode (HW 27-29).   Other
examples could be added: the work of the word in thinking and
poetry, the work of the *polis*, the political state, the work
of worship and sacrifice (EM 200; HW 49).   All such workings
project a world, e-rect [er-<u>richten</u>] it, opening up the *right*,
the guiding measure, which opens up and closes off paths
wherein beings may be (HW 30).

     If truth is accomplished by work, if it comes-to-pass in
works and is thereby essentially dynamic, then it is not an
attribute of beings or propositions but a *happening* [*Gescheh-
nis*], i.e., the prevailing movement of the clearing *and* concealing in their union, the movement of the clearing of self-
concealing (HW 25, 41, 71-72).   As such movement and happening, truth is necessarily bound up with history [*Geschichte*],
thought here in the sense of "an acting and being acted upon
through the *present* which is determined from out of the future
and which takes over what has been [*Gewesene*]" (EM 47-48).
Such an understanding of history, we can see, is entirely in
keeping with the description of Dasein as thrown projection
and the general description of the revealing-concealing, back-
and-forth movement of the unconcealing of being (*alētheia*,
the clearing).   Yet it is not history as we commonly understand it and which is the object of study in historical science [*Historie*; "historiography"].   Normally we think of history as some sort of flow of events that happen to men or
which is created by men.   Such a view, Heidegger points out,
represents history as a series of "nows" or *present*ations;
history is understood as what is past or "gone by" [*Ver-
gangene*] and thereby some*thing* belonging irretrievably to an
earlier time or *now present* left over from the past. Historical science thereby aims at reckoning up history as what is
fixed and stable (constantly *present*), i.e., what is past and
now fixed, unchanging.   What is past is presented as the "al-
ways-has-been-once-already" [*Immer-schon-einmal-Dagewesene*],
meaning that what is unique, solitary, and therefore great
(i.e., authentic history), is levelled off into (*re*-presented
as) something that can be compared with something else.   The
great is measured against the ordinary and average and thereby
becomes controllable.   Historical science is then even able to
predict what is to come from the images of the past it determines by the present (EM 47; HW 82, 326; SZ 500-501; WD 104).

     History for Heidegger, on the other hand, concerns not man
but the truth of being into which man stands out; time is the
first name of the truth of being, and history *is* only when the
essence of truth (i.e., unconcealment) comes-to-pass, takes
place, and is decided (EHD 76; G 56-57; WM 377).   Put in terms
of Heidegger's analysis in *Sein und Zeit*, Dasein is said to
stretch itself along "between" birth (thrownness) and death
(projection) such that its being is this stretching along, and

birth, death and the "between" *are* as a unit. In other words,
Dasein, in disclosing and interpreting, "happens", and is
therefore historical in the very basis of its being (and not
"accidentally", as a matter of a worldless subject standing in
history to be buffeted by events in the world) (SZ 495-98,
513). In its standing-open comportment toward beings (i.e.,
anticipatory resoluteness or openedness), Dasein lets itself
be encountered undisguisedly by that which it seizes upon in
such comportment, i.e., it lets beings be *present*, thereby
disclosing its possibilities and thus *coming towards* itself
[*zukommen -- Zu-kunft* -- future] as its ownmost potentiality-
for-being, and this by *coming back* understandingly to its
ownmost *having been* [*Gewesen*], by taking over its thrownness
and what it has to be (SZ 430-31; cf. GP 374-77).

   Put in a way perhaps less esoteric, we must realize that
Dasein has grown up both into and in a traditional way of
interpreting itself in terms of which it understands itself
proximally and, within a certain range, constantly, such that
possibilities are disclosed and regulated. Dasein's "past",
its heritage, then, is something which already goes ahead of
it (SZ 27). Tradition [*Überlieferung*] presences by handing
down [*überliefern*] ways of thinking (e.g., concepts and ideas,
all of which "have a history") to which we are delivered over.
But such being delivered over does not surrender us to what is
past and irrevocable. Instead, that which has been [*Gewesen*],
as a gathering of essential being [*Ge-wesen*],[16] shelters and
conceals within it a happening that is resting and bound in
the thinking which has been and lies here in every proposition
and each everyday opinion. Tradition then is a delivering
[*liefern*] in the sense of *liberare*, a setting free into those
essential possibilities that are sheltered and concealed within it, whereby we are delivered over to ourselves and fit into
tradition. In resoluteness, openedness, then, we are opened
up to the inner dynamic, the happening, bound up and concealed
in what has been, set free for a conversation with what has
been and the possibilities for being that have been disclosed.
We stand in the moment [*Augenblick*] (the authentic present; SZ
447), letting the past and the future collide, and thereby
unfold and endure the clash of what is relinquished and what
is given, acting into the future while simultaneously taking
over and recalling ("repeating" -- *wiederholen* -- holding
again) what has been (FD 42-43, 47; N I 311; SG 83, 171; SZ
27, 507; US 57; WD 71; WP 14-15).

   Talk of tradition handing itself down, i.e., imparting and
communicating, and of a conversation with what has been opening up in resoluteness, suggests that language might be the
"element" to consider for a better understanding of the interplay of being, truth, and time that Heidegger is trying to
unfold for us. Traditionally, language has been considered as
human expression which presents and represents the real and
the unreal, such that words and language are thought of as

wrappings we use in order to package things for our commerce
(EM 16; US 14-15). However, Heidegger notes that, more primordially, language brings beings as beings into the open for
the first time. This is clear when we note that to speak of a
being means to understand it in advance as a being and thus
understand its being (how it is). Words, in naming beings,
first nominate beings to their being, bringing them out into
the open for the first time and letting them lie before us in
the light of their being. Put another way, language be-things
[be-dingt], i.e., conditions, things as things; conditions,
not as an existing ground that gives reasons and grounds (not
an efficient cause), but as an *allowing* the thing to presence
(show itself) as a thing by projecting its being. Being
presences as language itself, whereby language is called the
house of being; it is the lighting-concealing place or province in which being is cleared and through which we go to
reach beings (EM 87-88, 180-81; HW 61, 310; TK 40; US 118,
164, 232-33; VA 223; WM 313, 326, 333).
     For this reason, Heidegger calls the essence of language
Saying [*Sage*], from the Old Norse *sagan*, *saga*: to show
[*zeigen*], to let what is present appear, and let what is
absent fade and thereby presence in its own way. Pervaded by
ways of saying [*Sagen*] and what is said [*Gesagte*] and therefore what is to be said [*zu-Sagende*] (and thus withheld from
saying), language speaks by saying (i.e., showing) beings in
their being, whereby we may then speak. Each word is a hint
[*Wink*], a way-marker, beckoning [*winken*] in one direction and
away from another, towards regions of thought in which we
should or should not make our way. Each word serves as memory
at work for us, an inexhaustible wellspring of what was once
spoken and is still to be spoken, whence language speaks.
Language thus reaches into the past, the present, and the
future and gathers them together in a clearing-concealing-
freeing offer [*lichtend-verbergend-freigebend Darreichen*] of
world, whereby we are. Through this offer we are put in
dialogue with our forebears and those who come after us in
that we are directed upon the linguistic meaning that has been
handed down to us and which we pass on into the future through
our "use". Language, then, is a fluid, dynamic, creative,
historical "action", a way-making movement [*Be-wëgung*] that
disposes and determines us in one way or another in our essential possibilities according to the interpretation of the
words (the understanding of being) that comes to prevail by
the mysterious play of language (EHD 37-38; GR 67; N I 169-70;
US 123, 145, 214, 253-54, 257, 264; WD 89).[17]
     The "element" of language gives us a further sense of how
being and time co-jointly pervade our lives and our comportment toward beings, yet we still need to clarify the interplay
and belonging-together of these two, being and time. We might
learn more along these lines if we consider the revealing-
concealing play of unconcealment in terms of presencing, or

coming-to-presence [*Anwesen*], and absencing [*Abwesen*].   Here
it seems best to quote Heidegger at length:

> What is presently present in unconcealment lingers [*weilt*] in
> unconcealment as in an open region. Whatever lingers [*Weil-
> ende*] (whatever whiles [*Weilige*]) in the region proceeds to
> it from concealment and arrives in unconcealment. But what
> is present *is* arriving whilingly [*ankünftig weilend*] insofar
> as it is already departing from unconcealment toward conceal-
> ment. What is presently present lingers awhile. *It endures
> in approach and withdrawal. Lingering is the transition from
> coming to going.* What is present is what in each case ling-
> ers [*Je-weilige*]. Lingering in transition, it lingers still
> in approach and lingers already in departure. What is for
> the time being present [*Das jeweilig Anwesende*], what pre-
> sently is, presences [*west*] out of absence. This must be
> said of whatever is truly present . . . (HW 350; my emphases)

We find in this dense and difficult passage a summary of
the connections between the revealing-concealing interplay of
disclosure (*alētheia*, the clearing), the coming-to-pass and
taking place [*sich ereignen*] of this interplay, and time as
this coming-to-pass, this "happening". Beings, which are
present, in being disclosed, are rising up out of the absence
(concealment) of what has been (as what is to come) and a
departing back into the absence (concealment) of what is to
come (i.e., the future [*Zu-kunft*]). Presencing, coming-to-
presence [*Anwesen*], i.e., being, belongs not only to the
present but to what has been and is to come as well. Being
then is *ontologically different* from beings, which are what
are *present*. Being is thus not constant presence and therefore not a being to be thought as the most in being or beings
in general (onto-theo-logy). Instead, it is an interplay of
presencing and absencing, a pre-ab-sencing, as it were, withdrawing in its arrival. Beings then too must be thought in a
different way. "Placing something into appearance always lets
something (a being) come to presence in such a way that *in* the
coming to presence an absencing comes to presence" (WM 297).
This simply follows from the supposition that a being comes to
shine in its being, which is both presencing and absencing. A
being is unified, steady, in repose (in being), joined [*ge-
fugt*], "between" the twofold absencing in which it lingers,
not as a slice between two absences, but by letting itself
belong to the absencing -- i.e., withdrawing and differing
from what has been (which is absent) and withholding and
deferring what is to come (which is also absent). A being is
thereby fitting, proper, and in order [*Fug*], i.e., it is what
it is, gathered into its order by surmounting dis-order [*Un-
Fug*] (HW 347, 354-55; ZD 13-14; cf. EM 169).[18]
Being is not a being, yet there is/it gives [*es gibt*]
being in the realm of the clearing. This clearing is the

throw of projection whereby nearness to being is granted; its movement is a sending [*Schicken*] of being, a dispensation [*Schickung*] of presencing [*Anwesen*] which furnishes man with the open and thereby first sets man free for (i.e., sends him) his proper [*schicklichen*] essential possibilities at any time. Such presencing is extended and offered [*gereichte*] in the past, present, and future in such a way that in each offering there is a withholding and distancing of each: the present is withheld from what is coming, that it may be (presence) as what is coming, and what has been is denied its advent as present, that it may be (presence) as what has been.   What has been, present, and future offer themselves to one another and thereby belong to one another (but not "at the same time"), lighting up an openness in which presencing plays.   Time, then, is a clearing of self-concealing, a reaching out that clears and sends presencing (being).   Such sending is the destiny [*Ge-schick*] of being, the gathered sending of being. Such destiny is nothing fatalistic, but the coming-to-pass and taking place [*sich ereignen*] of the clearing of being.   Such is the history of being, which is not like the history of a city, but is determined solely by the way in which being happens, the way in which it is sent (e.g., as *idea*, *ousia*, *substantia*, will, etc.) in the mutual reaching-out of what has been, future, and present (EHD 14;   G 57;   Preface, x; SG 158; VA 32, 251-52; WM 336-37; ZD 7-8, 14-16; cf. SZ 507-509).

Of course, time is not something either, though there is/it gives [*es gibt*] time in the unconcealment of being. Being, sending itself and revealing itself, withdraws and conceals itself.   Being keeps to itself, holds back (*epochē* in Greek) in its sending such that the destiny of being is epochs of being, a holding back in favor of the gift that is given (i.e., being as revealed).   In the dispensation, being is not completely handed over, but is spared, still to be sought, though "won".   In presencing, being denies what has been, and withholds what is to come.   Thus in the unconcealment and sending of being there is/it gives time (EHD 14; HW 338; SG 122; ZD 9; cf. ZD 14-16).

There is/it gives being; there is/it gives time.   The two, being *and* time, belong together, belonging to the giving -- giving as destiny, and giving as the reaching out that clears. Each is thereby its own [*Eigenes*] -- being, as presencing, and time, as the realm of the open -- in the sending and extending granted by the giving.   What gives both in their belonging together, whereby each is its own, Heidegger calls: *das Er-eignis* (ZD 20).

Ereignis -- not the subject of *Es gibt* and thereby some third "thing" beside being and time, an isolated "It" that then gives being and time, but a "neutral tantum", so to speak, the neutral "and" in being and time.   *Ereignis* belies explanation and interpretation -- like the Dao in Taoism or *śūnyatā* in Buddhism -- for it does not stand for anything yet

points and indicates. *Ereignis* -- not a genus or encompassing
general concept under which being (and its sendings) and time
are subsumed; rather, a pervading and penetrating of everything everywhere in its gathering reach such that it is the
"absolutely concrete", so to speak. But this is wrong too,
for we cannot even say that it *is* (and likewise that it is
not), for it is the giving of being and time that is to be
thought in the manner of the giving that belongs to it and
grants each its own [*Eigen*]. In the end, all we can say is:
Ereignis ereignet, whereby "object" and "activity" dissolve
into one another; time and being *ereignet* (take place, come-
to-pass and are appropriated) in *Ereignis* (ZD 18-19, 21-24,
46-47;   cf. VA 272-73; ZD 41).

     To understand our difficulties here, we might use a pic-
ture Heidegger provides us, that of a clearing in the forest
in which we stand (ZD 71-72).[19]   The clearing is neither those
things in the clearing (beings) nor is it the light that
shines down into the clearing whereby beings come to shine
(being). How do we point out the clearing, particularly as we
stand in it and are illuminated as being within it?   In much
the same sense, *Ereignis* does not tolerate discussion [*Erört-
erung*], which situates [*beortet*] and sights things, for it is
the locality [*Ortschaft*] of all locales [*Orten*], bringing all
present and absent beings each into their *own*, from where they
show themselves in what they are, and where they abide according to their kind (US 37, 258).   As a "bringing to sight that
brings into its own [*eigende Eräugnis*]," whereby there is an
inflashing [*Einblitz*] of being itself (TK 44), *Ereignis* withdraws in favor of its gift (being and beings) and is thus an
Enteignis belonging to *Ereignis* in which it preserves what is
its own (WD 5; ZD 8, 23).

     Mindful of the problems in speaking, we might now venture
forth, as a summation of this section of our chapter, and as
an approximation to *Ereignis*, to say --
     Ereignis: essence [*Wesen*] as the way that something holds
sway, is administered, develops and decays, i.e., presencing;
enduring [*währen*], but not as permanent enduring [*Fortwähr-
ende*], enduring permanently as an absolute, but in the sense
of *fortgewähren* (a word from Goethe) -- to grant permanently,
hearing *währen* and *gewähren* (granting) in one unarticulated
accord. Being endures, and is thereby pre-served and con-
served [*be-wahrt und ver-wahrt*], only as what is granted.
Thus *Ereignis*: what safe-guards, keeps safe [*Wahrende*], the
preserve [*Wahr*] in the sense of that gathering that clears and
shelters -- truth [*Wahrheit*] as the preservation [*Wahrnis*] of
being granted permanently, and hence something of an "origin"
[*Ur-sprung*] or "beginning" [*Her-kunft*] from which beings
spring forth in their being and *come here* (EHD 171; HW 348; VA
38-39; WD 97, 143).
     Ereignis: Saying [*Sage*], as showing; Saying is the mode
in which *Ereignis* speaks. Language is the "house" of being,

i.e., what keeps and preserves coming-to-presence, by *letting* beings shine in their being (because language as Saying is the mode of *Ereignis*).   Hence *Ereignis* might be called an "event of meaning", a constantly granting presencing of meaning that happens *within* language, a wellspring and origin of meaning that gives us to signifying beings in their being.   Likewise, *Ereignis*:   not a cause which effects, an antecedent to some consequent, not a making or founding by which it could be derived.   Instead, *Ereignis*:   yielding [*er-gibt*], the giving-yield [*Er-gebnis*], to be experienced as the abiding gift [*das Gewährende*] in the showing of Saying.   Thus *Ereignis*:   not God, nor a cosmic ground (WM 331)[20] but an abyss [*Ab-grund*] that grants and sends being without why, and simply plays, as long as it plays.   It remains "only play, the highest and deepest -- *Ereignis ereignet*" (ID 28; TK 42-43; SG 187-88; US 258, 262-63, 266-67).

Ereignis: permanently granting, thus the Same [*das Selbe*] that concerns all thinkers, but not the identical [*das Gleiche*].   The identical always moves toward the absence of difference; it is the reduction to a common denominator, the stale emptiness of that which persists without relation, i.e., persists *indifferently*.   In the Same, however, the difference appears all the more pressingly; we can only say 'the Same' if we think difference [*Untershied*].   The Same -- the belonging together of that which differs, a gathering by way of the difference, holding together in keeping apart in the most extreme disparity, a perdurance or carrying out [*Austrag*] of difference which gathers what is distinct into an original being-at-one [*Einigkeit*], rather than a dispersion into the dull unity of mere uniformity (ID 35; SG 152; VA 193).

Ereignis: difference [*Unterschied*, *Differenz*], of being and beings, world and thing (as well as being and thinking, being and man).   Difference is not to be thought as a relation which we have added to the two (being and beings), a distinc-tion of the intellect added after the fact that mediates and connects the two.   Indeed, rather than difference it is per-haps better thought dynamically -- as a differing -- in keep-ing with the disruption, dislocation, and distancing in the giving of being and time.   Thus it is already there, before our understanding, making possible all naming and experiencing and grasping of beings as beings, and thus already encountered everywhere in the matter of thinking so unquestioningly that we do not even notice the encounter (e.g., in metaphysics). The two do not subsist alongside one another but penetrate each other, whereby they traverse a middle in which they are at one and therefore intimate.   But this middle, this intima-cy, is not a fusion, but only holds sway when the two that are intimate are divided [*schiedet*] and remain separate (cf. the distancing of past, present, and future).   The "between" then is an intimate scission [*Unter-Schied*] that holds apart the middle whereby the two are at one with each other; it is a carrying out that carries through [*durchtragenden Austrag*], a rift that gathers.   It is "as if Being and beings shared a common center that remains interior to both, a common measure that serves as a primal unity by reason of which each adheres to the other and out of which both 'issue forth'"[21] (ID 8, 53-57; N II 208-209; US 24-27).

We comport ourselves towards beings and keep ourselves above all in relation to being.   We therefore stand in the difference, i.e., in *Ereignis*.   *Ereignis* brings man into his own [*Eigen*] as the being who catches sight of [*er-äugen*] being standing in authentic time.   Man is admitted into *Ereignis*, appropriated [*geeignet*], assimilated.   This is why we cannot place *Ereignis* in front of us and re-present it either as object or all-encompassing.   "It" is the most inconspicuous of inconspicuous phenomena, the simplest of simplicities, the nearest of the near and the farthest of the far, in which we dwell (ID 24-25; N II 207-208; US 259; ZD 23-24).

Ereignis: the matter [*Sache*] of thought, not as something we establish, but what is decisively at stake in all our thinking, the state of affairs [*Sachverhalt*] which holds [*hält*] such matters as being *and* time together.   It is the "controversy" [*Streitfälle*] that alone concerns thinking, a strife [*Streit*] that is not a feud but, according to the promptings of the word, an affliction [*Bedrängnis*], what is pressing [*Bedrängende*], a need [*Not*] and therefore a necessity [*Notwendigkeit*] of thinking.   It is the "undefinable defining something" that guides a dialogue, the conversation that we are.   Such conversation and dialogue is a discussion [*Er-örterung*] through which we are situated [*beortet*] in that place [*Ort*], that locality of all places, in which being is granted (ID 31; US 37, 100, 112; WM ix, 363, 440; ZD 4, 20). This conversation is first and foremost the "soul's dialogue with itself", as Plato put it, i.e., thinking.

We see then that Heidegger's thinking, which we have followed here in its matter from his considerations of truth and world to *Ereignis*, has been a topological thinking, a thinking of the *topos*, the plac-ing of being, truth and world. Such thinking asks how being is situated and thereby directs us to the unthought, the unsaid, in our situated thinking and saying, not as a fault but as the "how" that grants us our thinking and saying by situating it.   Heidegger's thinking thereby encourages us to be attentive, in both our saying and that of others, to how we are incorporated in the silent coming-to-pass and taking place [*sich ereignet*] of truth.[22]

3. TRUTH AND THE PLURALITY OF RELIGIONS

To better understand the significance and meaning of Heidegger's considerations of truth, we now bring his thinking to bear on the problem of truth as it arises in the context of

the plurality of religions.   The apparent problem with a
plurality of religions is this: on the one hand, different
religions, different cultures, make sense of their being in
different ways; they constitute a very diverse collection of
particular and irreducible contexts of behavior, meaning, and
truth.   On the other hand, truth is traditionally considered
to be something which is somehow valid in itself, beyond time
and therefore eternal, rooted in the unchanging depths of the
universe, so to speak.   Anything less than this truth in
itself -- eternal truth -- seems trivial.   Indeed, anything
less than eternal truth seems to suggest relativism, which in
turn leads to sheer caprice, anarchy and nihilism, for nothing
is fixed and stable any longer.   The question then is this:
How do we reconcile the radical diversity of religious traditions and cultures, and their unique contexts of meaning and
truth, with the apparent need and necessity of having some
eternal and lasting truth and meaning?

The usual response to this dilemma (and it takes many
forms) is to try to develop a scheme in which religious traditions are seen as somehow reflecting, or participating in, or
building toward, some Absolute or Ultimate Reality.   The classic example of this kind of approach is a kind of "transcendental esotericism" in which the diversity of religious truths
are seen as intimations of and emanations from the one, supersensible Truth that grounds these diverse truths, such that
there is a transcendental unity of all religions or an atemporal, primordial "tradition" with which we have lost contact
in our historical lives.   By such a scheme all religions are
the temporal manifestations of an Absolute Reality relatively
glimpsed through the fractured crystal of time.   To that
extent, at least, these religions are "partly true".   But
this, of course, is not good enough.   The temporal, limited,
exoteric aspect of religion must be transcended to attain a
speculative and intellectually unlimited understanding at the
esoteric level of religion (which forms the "core" of each
religion), whereby truth is seen in all its glory and lumines-
cence.[23]

This sort of classic monism as expressed by transcendental
esotericism is not a particularly popular choice for dealing
with the plurality of religious truth in the West, for the
approach tends to discriminate against revealed religion
(i.e., Western religion) in favor of contemplative religion,
and is all too apparently presumptive and assertive of an *a
priori* common core to religions that appears to abstract us
from historical realities.   Hence in the West another procedure arises for attacking the problem of religious diversity.
Here the *a priori*, theological assumption of a common core of
religions is suspended, "bracketed out", whereby one attends
simply to a description of the facts as they present themselves (i.e., of the things themselves).   The goal here is to
flush out the basic categories, the structural and formal

differences and comparisons, by which we may then make a judgment concerning a common core of religious experience, or on
the basis of which we may then account for a dialogue between
different religions.[24]

   In order to avoid vacuity and superficiality, such a
procedure seems obliged (if it is not already doing so by
virtue of its categories) to eventually make some reference to
a transcendent or transcendental reality (even if it is only a
"speculative hypothesis"). Such is the case with John Hick,
who points out the *possibility* that the different encounters
with the transcendent within the different religious traditions are all encounters with the one infinite reality. Hick
does not really argue for this standpoint so much as profess a
certain *faith* that all the major religious traditions have a
common referent, a faith based on his dubious perception that
all the main religious traditions refer to an ultimate divine
reality that is infinite and as such transcends the grasp of
the human mind. The result is a vision of religious plurality
not much unlike that of transcendental esotericism insofar as
the different religions are seen a providing many different
accounts of the divine reality which "may be true", though
imperfectly, as temporal human analogies. This view allows
Hick to look to a convergence of religions, presumably on the
supposition that we are now finally interacting with one
another in "one world", but more than likely based on his
view of religions as ways through time to eternity, and hence
ultimately expendable before the face of God.[25]

   Hick relies for a good deal of his insight into the nature
of religions on the work of Wilfred Cantwell Smith, who has
perhaps the most thoroughly researched and far-reaching view
of anyone on the nature of religious plurality. Though osten-
sibly an historian of religion, Cantwell Smith's main concern
is not with history -- which he sees as the various percep-
tions, expressions, and beliefs accumulated in a tradition and
which can be observed by the historian -- but with the religious *person*, and thus ultimately with that person's *faith*.
Faith, which is greater than a people's history, involves the
person in his inner religious experience or involvement with
the transcendent, his ability to say "Yes!" to truth, to the
abiding and the ideal. This transcendent truth is considered
by him to be ultimately one (though the forms of faith "decor-
ate or bespatter our world diversely"), whereby we have our
unity. Ultimately, Cantwell Smith also looks to a convergence, a world *theology*, constituted by a "corporate critical
self-consciousness" in which everyone, observers and observed,
synthesize their subjective and objective knowledge in one
conceptual apprehension of a given observable.[26]

   What is noteworthy about all these approaches to the
problem of truth as it arises in the context of the plurality
of religions -- from transcendental esotericism to Cantwell
Smith's "fideistic personalism" -- is that they do not offer a

solution to the problem, for they do not address the matter at hand, i.e., religions in their *particularity*, their *different* contexts of meaning and truth. Ultimately, and that means essentially, they reduce them all to a *common* denominator, the one transcendent (or transcendental) truth or meaning that is ultimate and absolutely valid for all. It does not matter that some of these approaches give the appearance of being "historical" while others do not; even those "historical" approaches look to overcoming time and history in a teleological convergence or phenomenological categories. By such thinking as lies behind these approaches to religious plurality, experiences and concepts are *uprooted* and *abstracted* from their temporal and contextual roots and represented as something comparable and therefore able to fit into broader, all-inclusive categories of thought and experience (e.g., faith, God, mysticism). Possibilities are thereby *levelled down* to possibilities that every*one* else has as well. Everything essential is already known, hence nothing is strange and uncanny. Assured of the transcendent, we are no longer threatened by other religions but are *tranquil*, for in our awareness, which has risen up to such a height that we can see the global history of mankind "the way that God has seen it all along," we are able "to feel at home in the world -- the whole world."[27] Through one's *faith* and/or *certainty* (in/of the convergence of religions, or the transcendent unity of religions), one is *disburdened* of having to answer for one's being, for in that one's religion refers to the same (identical) transcendent reality as all others, one is *secure* in the knowledge that one's religion is good enough, no matter where one was born. One thereby also keeps other religions at a *distance*, where they cannot threaten one, because one already knows what they are all about. Other religions are a *curiosity*, a change of pace which one can take or leave on a whim.

Such "thinking" as this, that has uprooted concepts and experience and passed them along, levelling them down to what is common, what everyone has, that is tranquil because it is certain and secure and thereby disburdened of thinking, that keeps its distance and is thus rather indifferent, venturing forth only out of curiosity -- such "thinking" as is found in the various approaches to religious plurality -- is the nihilistic thinking of the last man, *das Man*, the inauthentic man. It is nihilistic because being -- our comporting ourselves toward beings -- comes to nothing; it does not *matter* how we comport ourselves because there is *no difference* one way or the other. We are thereby indifferent to our *own* being, and inauthentic. It is nihilistic thinking because such thinking does not want to know of the nothing that is past and future; it *forgets* about its *own* history and situatedness and insists on the present, clinging to it and trying to control things, but only throwing everything out of joint and into disorder and chaos. (Such is, e.g., Cantwell Smith's emphasis on faith interpreted in a very Protestant, 20th century existential, experiential, subjective way, yet applied to everyone else.) The eternal that it insists upon in an effort to gain control is merely a suspended transiency, the void of a durationless now (HW 320), and "durationless" means: not having duration, not enduring, and therefore *not essential*.   Such thinking also does not want to know of the nothing in the sense that it does not want to know *why* it is as it is and thereby open itself up to the unspoken context of what has been and is to come in which it stands and is thereby situated (sited/sighted) (i.e., given possibilities to think).   Such questioning would only give nihilistic thinking pause, unsettle it, and keep it from running around to all other places (and away from itself) in a curious, turbulent effort to gain control.

In short, such "thinking" as exhibited by the approaches to religious plurality we have had up till now is nihilistic because it *closes off* what is essentially open (i.e., truth) with an absolute truth, or by avoiding truth altogether by dealing in the phenomenology of religious experience and the categories of religious experience (and not, notably, religious thinking).   Rather than taking up the plurality of religions as a bounty of possibilities that challenge our thinking and the way we are, such approaches as we have had engage in apologetics and justification of familiar categories to which all religions are reduced.   The whole enterprise reeks of the desperation of Western religious thinking trying to save itself from the well-aimed criticisms of science and philosophy by retreating to the security of numbers (other religions) and personal experience (religious experience), but thereby abdicating thought, and being.

A genuine engagement with the problem of truth as it arises in the plurality of religious truths, and a "solution" to the problem, seems much more likely along the lines of Heidegger's thinking, which pays heed to the situatedness of our being and the open contexts of truth and world in which being presences.   Such thinking does not wish to empathize and reach some sort of complacent agreement with another as, e.g., Cantwell Smith does, for that would be to deny one's own situatedness and foster the illusion that one is somehow outside of time and history and able to step back in at any time (somewhat in the manner of the traditional Western God). From such a vantage point "outside" time, one ends up noting the "limitations" of a religion or a religious thinker, minimizing the greatness of that religion or thinker by making their utterance a mere opinion that was not quite well enough informed about things we know to be true, and therefore at best only relatively true.   One then needs to "save" such thinking by linking it with some transcendent or transcendental purpose, elevating [*aufheben*] it to a greater goal (e.g., esoteric religion, or world theology) which *we* now of course know.   There is in such a stance the implicit polemics of the

petty and vengeful inauthentic man who knows better than
others (even if he calls them great) (cf. EM 123; VA 121, 261;
WD 72, 113).

Such thinking as Heidegger effects, on the other hand,
recognizes the thinking of a thinker not as a mere deposit of
opinion which he has expressed, but a thinking of being. As a
thinking of being, a saying of what is, such thinking is seen
as loyal to its "limitations" (though not necessarily "con-
scious" of them), i.e., the unsaid and unthought contexts of
meaning that are disclosed in his thinking and from which his
thinking originates. By setting thinking that has been back
into the open realm in which it moved (i.e., the free space of
what is unsaid and unthought in which is sheltered the original dynamic of the truth he speaks), we enter into the force
and greatness of that thinking and encounter the thinker and
what he has to say to us. The unsaid and unthought, then, are
the gift which the past thinker bestows upon us, i.e., what
has been spared of being and might now be granted to saying
and thinking. Our thinking becomes then not a step forward
onto some higher plane, but a *step back* into that opening
realm from which thinking has its origins and is still already
happening in our thinking (ID 38-39; KM 182; N I 158; N II 43,
484-85; SG 123- 24; WD 71-72, 113; WM 440).

Such a step back into the origin [*Anfang*], the incipience
that is the "truth" of the saying, tries to repeat (again
hold) [*wieder-holen*], the essential openness of the saying (or
other work) that has been handed down to us. Repetition does
not merely trot out what is past, but fetches and gathers what
is concealed in the old and is always coming toward us as what
has been granted, i.e., the dispensation and destiny of being.
Repetition is going back into the possibilities still open,
still unfolding, in what has been, rather than tying us down
to something finished (EM 199-200; N II 481; SZ 509-10; US
131). Applied to religious forms, such a step back that
repeats avoids an "idolatry" of those forms by trying to lay
bare the originary meanings beyond what is said, thought, or
produced, giving voice to the dynamic origin out of which the
historical forms have crystallized, whereby we hear the "message", the possibilities of being inherent in what has been
said.[28]

Such thinking that finds the force of past thinking in
what has been unthought and unsaid, and is thus *re*-petitioning
(petitioning again) such thinking for possibilities, is clearly not empathy with or mimicry of what has been; justification
and apologetics are not in order here. Rather, such thinking
is essentially confrontation or conflict [*Aus-einander-setz-
ung*] in which one differs from what has been. There is then a
certain "violence" to the interpretation, a "destruction" of
merely historical assertions that have been passed along and
cover up what is to be thought -- the matter at stake, the
opening region out of which past thinking originates. Such

destruction and violence, as we have said, is not a refutation
or polemic but an attempt to excavate what stands to be decided, a reflection [Besinnung] on what is decisive in the
thinking of past thinkers and which is still granted to us to
be thought. Such violence and destruction opens up the thinking that has been, recognizes its meaning [Sinn], and thereby
opens us up to what has been granted to us -- the destiny of
being and what is our own (EM 185; KM 183; N I 13; N II 97-98;
WD 103; WP 33-34; ZD 9).

Put another way, set apart from what has been thought in
thinking what has been, our thinking past thinkers becomes a
dialogue with the work and saying that has been. A dialogue,
which is a speaking to one another, is to tell of "something"
together, and is thereby "to show to one another what that
which is claimed in the speaking says in the speaking, and
what it, of itself, brings to light" (US 253). We understand
what has been (e.g., a text), not better than its author, or
others, but differently, and out of this difference belong to
the same matter, corresponding with, through, and to the
essential origin that is an ever-granting of being. Our
corresponding and dialogue with past thinkers opens up "between" us the essential realm out of which each in their own
way is; the discussion [Erörterung] gives rise to the places
[Orten] in which we site/sight ourselves. Our dialogue, possible only by virtue of our difference, binds us to the matter
of thought (our place), whereby we devote ourselves to the
same matter, though each in his own way (EM 104; HW 213-14,
233; N I 45-46; US 37; VA 239; WD 110; WP 30-33).

In the same vein, our dialogue with other religions is not
going to be a set of parallel monologues which merely publi-
cize the premises of each religion, nor is it a "dialogical
dialogue" which pursues dialogue for its own sake in an indeterminate conversation between religions.[29] Our "dialogue" is
going to be a "talking" to each other from out of each other's
differences, not to mediate them or justify them, but to hold
them open that "truth" may open up in such speaking and saying
and new possibilities of thinking emerge. Here we see the
full significance of Heidegger's realization that truth is not
a quality that things (e.g., other cultures and religions)
have, but "something" that comes-to-pass and takes place.
Truth takes place in and through the conversation "within" a
tradition or in and through the conversation "between" cultures. It might take place in the dialogue between two thinkers at the same time and place, or it might take place in the
"soul's" dialogue with itself, i.e., thinking, which is already a dialogue with those who have come before and those yet
to come.[30] We -- mankind -- are a conversation (as Hölderlin
indicates and Heidegger affirms [EHD 38-39; GR 69-70]), and
this conversation joins opponents together in their differing,
drawing us together as it sets us apart. Through the conversation and dialogue that is thinking and interpretation [Aus-

legung], we lay out [*legt . . . aus*] our *own* possibilities and
site/sight ourselves by entering into the opening region that
grants being.

What is essential here is to consider thinking as a way or
path. Thinking (interpreting, "conversing") is itself a way,
and only takes place on the way, clearing the way. On the way
is where we "find" the truth, opening ourselves up to the
emerging prospects and directions of the path of thought, and
taking steps (being on the way) in those directions, confused
and indeterminate as they are and must be. Thinking is not
taking up a position on the way and then talking about the
differences and incompatabilities of earlier and later
stretches. Such "stopping" takes one outside the way, outside
the movement of thinking and its imbeddedness in time, whereby
one sees everything askew and "all is the same" indifferently,
because one is outside the moment. For Heidegger, "all is the
same" in the moment, that is, in their decisiveness and *difference* (cf. N I 311ff; WD 164).

Extending the metaphor, we might say that each tradition,
religious or otherwise, is a path, akin to the *Holzwege* of
Heidegger's beloved Black Forest: "Each proceeding separately, but in the same forest. Often it seems, one is the same
as the other. Yet it only seems so" (HW, preface). It only
seems so, for though they are all paths (the same), they are
not identical (the same as each other), for they wind and
twist in different directions at different times and places.
Even when they crisscross and meet for a time, they are not
identical, for even those who walk the same way are given what
is their own each in their own way, though drawn on by the
same surroundings (cf. AED 88-89). It is this way that we must
think the plurality of religions, as paths going their own way
and not merging, even where they meet.

The dialogue with other religions, in fact, may be the
most risky and dangerous conversation of all, though it thereby may be the most rewarding. Most dangerous, because the
conversation is most often in one language or another, and we
thereby risk overlooking the hints and messages granted to us
by a word in another language by thoughtlessly translating
(i.e., interpreting) it with a word in our language which we
have not thought through in its history and hints. Indeed,
Heidegger explicitly points to this danger and how, especially
when conducted in a Western language, it promotes the tendency
to Europeanize all thinking and being, even though, dwelling
in different languages, we presumably dwell in different
"houses" of being. Thus Heidegger even goes so far as to
seriously question the extent to which dialogue is possible
(US 88ff). Yet such a dialogue may be the most rewarding, for
not only are we rewarded with hearing all the hints available
to us and are perhaps able to open ourselves up to other great
origins, we also benefit from the most radical kind of siting/
sighting: an encounter with another culture most forcefully

throws us back upon ourselves and our tradition in our attempts to understand the other culture, for we are forced to
examine our own thinking and saying for new possibilities to
interpret them.   Such an encounter, besides making us more
sober in our thinking, also opens up whatever possibilities
there may be for a genuine "planetary" thinking that is capable of meeting the challenges placed before us.

In the end, we see that there is no problem with the
plurality of religious truths, for such a problem only begins
with an emphasis on truth claims and an overemphasis on the
subject and his "faith" posture, instead of an emphasis on
thinking.   The problem ends when we recognize that truth
comes-to-pass in conjunction with a situated, contextual
thinking that takes place in the world, within the event of
meaning and worlding of the world that grants it ever-emerging
possibilities of thinking.   The "truth" that emerges has its
own kind of endurance, an endurance of granting being and the
possibilities of being.

> At the still point of the turning world. Neither flesh nor
>   fleshless;
> Neither from nor towards; at the still point, there the dance
>   is,
> But neither arrest nor movement. And do not call it fixity,
> Where past and future are gathered. Neither movement from
>   nor towards,
> Neither ascent nor decline. Except for the point, the still
>   point,
> There would be no dance, and there is only the dance.[31]

NOTES

1. As J. L. Mehta points out (in *Martin Heidegger: The Way and the Vision*, p. 149n.11), "destination" is a much better translation of the word *Bewandtnis* than "involvement" (as translated by Macquarrie and Robinson), since what Heidegger is talking about is the end, object, point, of the use of the piece of equipment -- its *raison d'être*.

2. Heidegger gives the example of a picture hanging askew on a wall, and someone, with their back to the wall, making the true assertion that the picture is askew, then turning around to perceive the picture and demonstrating the truth of the assertion. The person looks to the being itself to demonstrate the truth of the assertion, and it is the being which confirms the assertion by showing itself in the same way as the assertion uncovers it (SZ 288-89).

3. Heidegger later withdraws the connection between the question of *alētheia* and the question of truth as "inadequate" and "misleading" (ZD 77-78), largely, it seems, because of criticism of his thesis in "Plato's Doctrine of Truth" (WM 203-38) that Plato initiated a change in the Greek understanding of truth from unconcealment to agreement. This reneging is curious, insofar as using the connection is helpful in raising questions about what exactly is happening when we talk about truth and insofar as Heidegger was surely not making an argument and trying to "prove" anything (except perhaps in the Plato essay) on the basis of etymology. One might therefore venture to guess that this late concession on Heidegger's part may have been an attempt to keep alive the question of unconcealment without getting bogged down in philological technicalities.

4. Joseph Rouse, "Kuhn, Heidegger and Scientific Realism," *Man and World* 14 (1981), p. 288.

5. Richardson, *Through Phenomenology to Thought*, p. 193.

6. Note the difficulty of this language, in that transcending "to" and "toward" world could suggest a metaphysical scheme in which the world is above and beyond Dasein as the "true" world; Heidegger even says that the world is transcendental. Yet since he does not mean this in a metaphysical sense, he eventually drops the whole vocabulary of transcendence and the transcendental in order to emphasize his distance from the tradition. For an interesting attempt at reinterpreting "transcendence" in Heideggerian terms, see Robert P. Orr, *The Meaning of Transcendence: A Heideggerian Reflection* (Chico, California: Scholars Press, 1981).

7. We touch here on the complex relationship "between" being and man that will be taken up in greater detail in Chapter 5. On the one hand, Dasein, as being-in-the-world, "is cleared [*gelichtet*][a] in itself, not through any other being, but in such a way that it *is* itself the clearing[b]." To dispel any subjectivism here, note a, added in the *Gesamtausgabe* version of SZ, says "Alētheia -- openness -- clearing, light, lighting up", and note b indicates that though Dasein is itself the clearing, it "however does not produce" it (SZ 177). Hence we also find Heidegger saying that "if the essence of the unconcealedness of beings belongs in any way to being itself (cf. SZ ◊44), then being, by way of its presencing [*Wesen*], lets the place of openness (the clearing of the there [*da*]) happen, and introduces it as *such* [a place] wherein each being emerges in its own way" (HW 49 & note). One could then say that unconcealment is

itself presencing -- the Same, but not identical (HW 370). Being and man belong together in the clearing which, however, is not a third thing.

8. One of the most confusing aspects of Heidegger's thought, and one upon which we must try to be clear in following his arguments as presented here, is the multiple use of the word *Sein* (be-ing, heard verbally) and the various names he gives to his matter of thought. On the one hand, *Sein* means "the being of beings", the presencing of what is present, and thus the light in which beings stand so that they may appear; being here is what Heidegger sometimes calls "beingness" when he talks about meta-physics, i.e., the "condition" for beings being what they are. On the other hand, *Sein* means what makes something like the being of beings (i.e., what makes something like the presencing of what is present) pos-sible, and it is this that has always been the matter of thought for Heidegger. It is this matter which is called forth in various ways: the meaning of being, the truth of being, the unconcealment of being, the essence of being, being itself, *Seyn*, being, that which regions [*Gegnet*] (in *Gelassenheit*), the ontological difference, *Differenz*, *Ereignis*. This dual sense of *Sein* is not a confusion on Heidegger's part, for tradition-ally being is what makes possible, what is essential, and *Sein* in the sense of the clearing or unconcealment of being "is" what makes being (presencing) possible (i.e., "is" the essence of being). In addition, Heidegger cannot easily direct us to the matter of thinking without changing our thinking about being in the sense of beingness, further entangling the question of being and the question of the meaning of being. Gradually, of course, Heidegger leaves the term *Sein* to the realm of metaphysics (as the being of beings) and talks of *Ereignis*.

For discussion of this problem, see US 109-10, and the following ar-ticles: Otto Pöggeler, "Metaphysics and Topology of Being in Heidegger," pp. 3-27, and Thomas Sheehan, "Introduction: Heidegger, the Project and the Fulfillment" in *Heidegger: The Man and the Thinker*, pp. vii-xx, espe-cially vii-xii. See also: Joseph J. Kockelmans, "Ontological Difference, Hermeneutics and Language" in *On Heidegger and Language*, p. 211, and Kenneth Steiner, "Appropriation, Belonging-together and Being-in-the-world," *Journal of British Society for Phenomenology* 10 (May 1979), p. 130.

9. This translation is suggested by Theodore Kisiel and Murray Greene in their translation of Werner Marx's *Heidegger and the Tradition* (Evan-ston: Northwestern University Press, 1971), p. 191n. Macquarrie and Robinson translate *Verfallenheit* as "fallenness", keeping the connection with the verb *verfallen*, which must usually be translated as "falling". However, this could suggest a "fall" from a "purer" and "higher" primal status, given our metaphysical and religious tradition, all of which has nothing to do with *Verfallenheit* as Heidegger is using it (SZ 233).

10. This is of course why metaphysics, as the history of being in which being itself is forgotten and remains in oblivion, is not something simply to be rejected, for it harbors within it possibilities yet to be revealed, as a disguised and hidden disclosure of the unconcealment of being.

11. Cf. Paul Feyerabend, *Against Method*, and Thomas S. Kuhn, *The Structure of Scientific Revolutions*. Both Kuhn and Feyerabend provide us with a variety of historical evidence that science depends on a variety of

amethodical, "irrational" elements in its discovery and maintanence of various theories, elements that are ignored, forgotten, or concealed by the method of science. Unfortunately, their philosophical insight has not been a match for their historical insight, causing some difficulties. For a masterful attempt at showing how Kuhn's philosophy of science may be "rescued" with the help of Heidegger's insights, see Rouse, pp. 269-90.

12. Cf. Michael Gelven, "Heidegger and Tragedy" in *Martin Heidegger and the Question of Literature*, ed. William V. Spanos (1976; rpt. Bloomington: Indiana University Press, 1979), p. 221; Rouse, pp. 286-87. See N I 460 for how this applies to philosophy as well.

13. Gadamer, "Heidegger's Later Philosophy," pp. 222-23.

14. There is a certain change in Heidegger's use of the term "world" from his early to his later works that parallels the multiple use he makes of the term *Sein*, a use which is also no more arbitrary than his multiple use of the word *Sein*. In early works, world, as the "how" of beings, seems to be confined to openness, opposed to the closure of earth and concealment. But already in his essay on artwork, Heidegger is saying that the earth juts out into the world, presencing as concealing in the world, thereby suggesting that world encompasses both revealing and concealing. Thus in other writings from about this time (e.g., early Hölderlin essays), the revealing-concealing character of unconcealment is evoked by naming the earth and the sky [*Erde und Himmel*], and the whole context of earth, sky, divinities and mortals, the opening region of unconcealment, is called world. Regarding the fourfold [*Geviert*], see Chapter 4, below.

15. Cf. Marx, p. 143. The inadequacy of the circular image is undoubtedly one reason Heidegger eventually dropped all reference to the famed "hermeneutical circle"; see US 151. Note that Gadamer, who emphasizes the idea of the hermeneutical circle in his own thinking, is one who tries, despite the evidence, to see a great deal of Hegel in Heidegger, much, I think, to the misunderstanding of the "polarities" in Heidegger's thought. See Gadamer, "Hegel and Heidegger" in *Hegel's Dialectic*, trans. P. Christopher Smith (New Haven: Yale University Press, 1976), pp. 100-116.

16. It is important to note that the "ge-" prefix signifies a "gathering" in German, and is meant by Heidegger in his choice of words.

17. Barrett, *Illusion of Technique*, pp. 193-194; Ronald Bruzina, "Heidegger on the Metaphor and Philosophy" in *Heidegger and Modern Philosophy*, p. 196; John McCumber, "Language and Appropriation: The Nature of Heideggerian Dialogue," *The Personalist* 60 (1974), pp. 378, 392. The latter two essays are excellent for an understanding of Heidegger on language.

Though we cannot go into it here, we should note that Heidegger develops his understanding of language alongside his consideration of the early Greek words *logos*, as a primal gathering, and *legein*, as letting-lie-together-before, and their interrelatedness with the other key words of early Greek thinking, *physis* and *alētheia*. See especially the last three essays in VA (207-82) and HW 321-74. See also Chapter 5, below.

18. Cf. Albert Hofstadter, "Enownment" in *Martin Heidegger and the Question of Literature*, p. 21, and Vincent Vycinas, *Earth and Gods: An Introduction to the Philosophy of Martin Heidegger* (The Hague: Martinus Nijhoff, 1961), p. 125.

19. Too static. A better picture might be that of a man walking
through a dense forest, making his way by clearing away bushes and
branches so that he may go through, after which they fall back into place,
concealing his trail. In making his way, light filters through every now
and then in the clearing he makes, lighting his way. And he makes his way
by being attentive to what is granted to him and denied him; he does not
go through trees or very heavy undergrowth, for instance, but goes another
way. Such a picture, it seems, captures more fully the lighting-concealing clearing action in rest to which Heidegger is pointing with the word
Ereignis.

20. The Heideggerian text ("The Letter on Humanism") talks of being
itself, but this names *Ereignis*; see ZD 46.

Cf. Williams, *Martin Heidegger's Philosophy of Religion*, in which
Williams reads *Ereignis* as God in Heidegger's "philosophy", since It gives
being and time. This insistence on reading *Es gibt Sein* in a subject-
predicate mode reminds one of a saying from Nietzsche: "I am afraid we are
not rid of God because we still have faith in grammar" (*Götzendämmerung*,
III, 5).

If the negative character of the exposition of *Ereignis* still tempts
one to think of *Ereignis* as God along the lines of a negative theology, it
might be helpful to consider what Jacques Derrida has to say about his
negative exposition of *différance* (which is not unlike Heidegger's *Ereignis*):

> Thus, the detours, phrases, and syntax that I shall of-
> ten have to resort to will resemble -- will sometimes be
> practically indistinguishable from -- those of negative
> theology. Already we note *that* différance *is not*, does not
> exist, and is not any sort of being-present (*on*) And we
> will have to point out everything *that* it *is not*, and con-
> sequently, that it has neither existence nor essence. It
> belongs to no category of being, present or absent. And
> yet what is thus denoted as différance is not theological,
> not even in the most negative order of negative theology.
> . . . if we deny the predicate of existence to God, it is
> in order to recognize him as a superior, inconceivable, and
> ineffable mode of being. Here there is no question of such
> a move . . . Not only is différance irreducible to every
> ontological or theological -- onto-theological -- reap-
> propriation, but it opens up the very space in which onto-
> theology -- philosophy -- produces its system and history.
> It thus encompasses and irrevocably surpasses onto-theo-
> logy or philosophy.

"Différance" in *Speech and Phenomena and Other Essays on Husserl's Theory
of Signs*, trans. David B. Allison (Evanston: Northwestern University
Press, 1973), pp. 134-35.

21. Kockelmans, "Ontological Difference, Hermeneutics and Language," p.
215.

This is clearly one of the more difficult ways of approaching *Ereignis*,
because to talk of being and beings in our onto-theo-logial language could
suggest two "things" in and for themselves before they are brought togeth-

er by the difference. Heidegger continually tries to break-up such notions by talking about being and beings in terms of coming-to-presence and
what is present, or, in *Identity and Difference*, in terms of overwhelming
[*Überkommnis*] and arrival [*Ankunft*]. Cf. note 20, above.
   Heidegger's talk of the ontological difference is also one of the more
controversial formulations for those who do not think he has gone far
enough in his radical rethinking of Western thought, and still retains
some "nostalgia" for metaphysics and its emphasis on presence; see, for
example, Derrida, "Différance," pp. 155ff, and Charles Fu, "The Trans-
onto-theo-logial Foundations of Language in Heidegger and Taoism," *Journal
of Chinese Philosophy* 5 (1978), pp. 301ff, the latter criticizing
Heidegger from the standpoint of Taoism. Whether these criticisms read
Heidegger more metaphysically than he wanted to be read, i.e., take
Heidegger's apparently metaphysical language metaphysically, will be taken
up in Chapter 6.
   22. Henri Birault, "Thinking and Poetizing in Heidegger" in *On Heidegger and Language*, pp. 167-68; Otto Pöggeler, "Heidegger's Topology of
Being" in *On Heidegger and Language*, pp. 123-27, and "Metaphysics and
Topology of Being in Heidegger," pp. 23, 26; Mehta, p. 44.
   23. Examples of such an approach are: Frithjof Schuon, *The Transcendent Unity of Religions*, trans. Peter Townsend (New York: Harper & Row,
1975), and Huston Smith, *Forgotten Truth* (New York: Harper & Row, 1976).
The term "transcendental esotericism" is Carl Raschke's; see his article
"Religious Pluralism and Truth: From Theology to a Hermeneutical Dialogy,"
Journal of the American Academy of Religion 50 (1982), p. 38.
   24. A classic example is Mircea Eliade, *Patterns of Comparative Religion*, trans. Rosemary Sheed (1958; rpt. New York: New American Library,
1963). Another taking this approach is Ninian Smart; see "Truth and
Religions" in *Truth and Dialogue in World Religions*, ed. John Hick (Philadelphia: Westminster Press, 1974), p. 55.
   25. *God and the Universe of Faiths* (New York: Macmillan, 1973), pp.
139-40, 146-47. Cf. *Philosophy of Religion*, 2nd, revised ed. (Englewood
Cliffs, NJ: Prentice-Hall, 1973), pp. 125-29.
   26. *Faith and Belief* (Princeton: Princeton University Press, 1979),
pp. 163, 170-71; *The Meaning and End of Religion* (New York: Macmillan,
1963), pp. 152-53, 156-57; *Towards a World Theology* (New York: Macmillan,
1981), pp. 26-27, 59, 66. For an excellent summary and criticism of
Smith, see Raschke, pp. 37-38.
   27. *Towards a World Theology*, pp. 18, 21.
   28. Cf. Raschke, pp. 40-41.
   29. Raschke, pp. 39-40.
   30. Here we must seriously doubt Raschke's criticism of Heidegger's
"dialogue" (in *Alchemy of the Word* [Missoula, Montana: Scholars Press,
1979], pp. 85ff) as vapid and lacking the "concrete" tension of reciprocal
speakers as found in Buber's I-Thou relationship. The suggestion that
dialogue between two present interlocutors is more "concrete" than thinking shows a metaphysical bias in favor of the present. We would have to
say instead that thinking is primary, for in order for a dialogue between
two present people to be successful the two would have to be thinking and
thereby open to the possibilities of their own and the other's saying.
   31. T.S. Eliot, "Four Quartets," p. 119.

CHAPTER 4

RELIGION AS FINDING MAN'S PLACE:
GODS AND THE FOURFOLD

In order to arrive at what you are not
You must go through the way in which you are not.
T.S. Eliot

1. THE PROBLEM -- THINKING THE DIVINE

Having brought truth and meaning down to earth such that it takes place and comes-to-pass in conjunction with a situated thinking -- whereupon that thinking is granted ever-emerging possibilities to be thought -- we can now more easily pursue the make-up of a "religious" world and a "religious" thinking. Specifically, we now turn our attention to one of the more controversial and misunderstood aspects of a most controversial and misunderstood thinking, a matter that gives even devotees of Heidegger's thinking some discomfort: Heidegger's speaking of the gods, and of the holy. Such talk is easily confusing. First of all, Heidegger's talk is not at all "uniform" with regard to this matter, insofar as he talks of gods, divinities, angels, the god, aether, and the holy. In addition, since such talk arises first of all in the context of his elucidations of Hölderlin's poetry, it might be considered unimportant, a bit of poetic license with no bearing on "theology" and "religion". Furthermore, to the Judeo-Christian mind, such talk smacks of paganism; and, to those who hoped for better things from a thinker who is trying to overcome metaphysics and its onto-theo-logical thinking, it suggests a relapse by Heidegger into some sort of "quasi-onto-theo-logical" thinking that vacillates between metaphysics and "transmetaphysics".[1] Many things to many people, Heidegger's speaking of the gods and the holy is most certainly in need of clarification.

Such clarification is also all the more necessary for this study in that by coming to Heidegger's talk of the gods and the holy we have come upon the most obviously "religious" dimension in his thinking so far. Clarifying his talk of the gods and the holy, then, will help us see more clearly the "religious" dimension of the thinking of Heidegger, and therefore the extent to which his thinking is significant for future religious thinking. Toward all these ends, then, the present chapter is divided into three sections: 1) a clarification of the thrust of Heidegger's talk about the holy and the gods, 2) an explanation of what this means for human thinking and dwelling, and finally, 3) an examination of what significance this has for our understanding of religion, and

specifically, how it bears upon what has already been said of
th death of God.

2. GODS, THE GOD, AND THE HOLY

In approaching this topic of the gods and the holy, we might
first turn our attention to Heidegger's elucidations of
Hölderlin's poetry -- specifically, his meditations on Hölderlin's hymn *Wie wenn am Feiertage*. In that hymn, the word and
theme reverberating throughout is *Natur*, nature, which has
nothing to do with the "natural world" and "nature" as we
understand it scientifically today. Nature is what educates
and brings up [*er-ziehet*] the poet, educating him to a "won-
derful omnipresence" [>>wunderbar allgegenwartig<<], for it is
coming-to-presence [*anwesend*] in all reality, presencing in
all things of heaven and earth, and in all human endeavor.
Pervading everything with its presencing, yet withdrawing and
never letting itself be encountered as a being or a collection
of beings, nature is the clearing before everything and in
which everything gathers and rests, the "fixed law" whereby
everything can first be present.   It is the dark abyss,
"chaos", the gaping open which prepares all things and thereby
lets all things be what they are.   It is spirit [*Geist*], not
in the sense of German idealism, but as inspiration [*Begeist-
erung*], the omnipresencing, all-creative arising and awakening
that inspires [*begeistert*] thinking and poetry.   "Older than
the ages", but not thereby timeless or eternal, it is time
itself, the oldest time, before the ages by which man reckons.
Yet it is younger than everything subsequent too, for it is
the original, the incipient [*Anfängliche*] -- what is coming,
emerging, arising, and remaining as such.   Nature is the word
for being itself, *Ereignis*, the worlding of the world -- what
the early Greeks named in such words as *physis* (which is often
translated as "nature"), *logos* and *kosmos* -- the ever-enduring
arising which abides in itself and preserves all coming-to-
presence, gathering everything together in the appropriateness
of its essence (EHD 52-63; EM 16-17; US 259; VA 275; WM 240).[2]
      Older than the ages, before everything real and working
[*allem Wirklichen und Wirken*], nature then is also before the
gods -- "higher [*über*] than the gods of Occident and Orient",
as Holderlin's poem puts it. As what is constantly of old and
of the future [*das stets Einstige*],[3] and before the gods, it
remains intact as the incipient, and is therefore the whole
[*Heil*].   It is the original hale and whole, the integralness
of the whole of beings which grants each thing the welfare
[*Heil*] of its abiding.   Nature, then, is the holy [*Heilige*] --
"holy chaos", as Hölderlin puts it -- the opening and abysmal
difference that stands "between" gods and men, from which they
arise and in which they meet one another (EHD 59, 62-63, 147-
48).

The holy, then, is not a property borrowed from an established god, from one who is divine, but is the gleaming
strife, the fire and *polemos* (as the early Greek thinkers saw
it) which manifests some as gods, others as men, illuminating
[*beleuchtet*] and enlightening [*er-leuchtet*] each from it and
to it, that they, cleared [*gelichtet*] in their essence, may
fulfill its lighting and clearing [*Lichtung*], each in their
own way. The holy is the open and clearing itself which
arranges [*vermittelt*] the relations between everything real,
the mediateness [*Mittelbarkeit*] which is in the midst [*Mitte*]
of everything as the immediate [*Unmittelbare*], enclosing within itself all fullness and every structure. Before the holy,
nothing more primordial can be thought. It is the intimacy
[*Innigkeit*] which precedes everything and retains everything,
that lies at the heart of things, the incipient remaining of
which is the "eternity" of the "eternal" (which is no empty
duration). Thus it is called the "eternal heart" by
Hölderlin. Simple, immediate, withdrawing from our grasp and
therefore inaccessible, it is the serene [*Heitere*], making
everything clear, granting the essential space in which everything belongs according to its essence and may therefore come
to stand in the still light and brightness [*Helle*] of its
essence, serenified [*aufheitert*]. It is the clarity (*clari-
tas*) in which everything rests, the highness (*serenitas*) in
whose gentle yet firm embrace things abide, the joyous and
joyfulness (*hilaritas*) in whose play everything hovers. Healing [*heilt*], it lets and keeps everything in tranquillity and
wholeness (EHD 16, 18, 53, 59-75; VA 277-79).
It is from such considerations as these that we can better
understand Heidegger's treatment of the holy and the gods
elsewhere, as in this now famous passage:

> Only from the truth of being can the essence of the holy be
> thought. Only from the essence of the holy is the essence of
> divinity [*Gottheit*] to be thought. Only in light of the
> essence of divinity can it be thought or said what the word
> 'god' is to signify (WM 351).

This is not a hierarchy, a chain of being, but an indication
of the priority and primordiality of being itself, the clearing of being as holy, out of which the god, as divine it its
own way, comes forth and stands in the light of being. The
gods, insofar as they *are*, and however they are (present or
absent), stand "under" "being", i.e., they come to presence
out of the splendor of the worlding of the world, the clearing
and opening region, the constellation, of being. Being -- the
holy -- in which and from out of which the god and gods "of
Occident and Orient" may first become present (HW 30-31; TK
45-46; WM 240, 351-52; cf. WM 159).[4]
In and from out of the clearing of being, the gods are
themselves enchanting. Unlike men, who may become immersed in

things such that everything is familiar and ordinary (concealed), the gods themselves cannot remain concealed, for
their exceptional character in relation to the clearing is
nothing other than the clearing itself. Gods and goddesses
therefore awaken the enchantment and rapture of the serene
best of all, for they themselves are serenifiers and carriers
of the light and brightness of the holy (the clearing of
being) and thus enable the highest shining of the holy. Gods
gather together and reflect a world and its happening, and are
thus important -- not as existent beings, but -- as extraordinary occurrences of meaning, as beckoning [*winkenden*] messengers of the godhead [*Gottheit*], as heralds of the holy in its
embrace of man and things (EHD 20, 54, 68; VA 150, 177,
278).[5]

    The epitome of the gods, in which they have their essence
and which they disclose (godhead, divinity, "godness" -- *Gottheit*), is the god,[6] who dwells in the "highest" (i.e., the
holy) and therefore often assumes its name (e.g., the high
one, aether). He is the joyous one, giving to man the joy of
the joyful serene, the "father" of all that gives joy (i.e.,
of all the gods). His essence is serenification; thus does he
love to illuminate, opening up things to the joy of their
presence and illuminating the heart [*Gemüt*] of man for the
courage [*Mut*] to be open to the holy. Taking upon himself
that which is "over" him (the holy), he gathers it into the
sharpness of a single, unique blow (the "holy ray") and brings
it to man, throwing the lightning bolt that ignites the glow
of light from the holy that is contained within the soul of
man. His lightning abruptly lays before us in an instant
everything present in the light of its presencing; it steers,
bringing all things forward to their essential place. The
highest god, the highest "being", is therefore called destiny
[*Geschick*], for he fulfills the dispensations of fate [*Schick-
ungen des Geschickes*] in the aim of his bolts. He is the
unique event of meaning, the unconcealment of being *par excel-
lence*, whereby he even at times takes the name of that unconcealment (for the Greeks, *logos*, "the laying that gathers")
for himself (EHD 18f; HW 272; VA 222ff).[7]

    The nearness of the god and gods to the *logos* -- the
unconcealment of being, the holy -- such that the god may even
at times appropriate its name, indicates a certain ambiguity
and danger in the essence (presencing) of the god and gods.
The danger lies in the fact that the highest *being* does not
properly name the holy. The god -- as immortal, "timeless",
unchanging, constant presence -- threatens the holy with the
loss of its essence, for the holy is not some *thing* but a
revealing and concealing that makes the holy ever-emerging,
incipient, dynamic. The perfection of a god is misleading,
blinding us to the essence of being, even as it discloses
being, resulting in a concern with theo-logy (with the highest
being) and a forgetfulness of (or "obliviousness" to; *Verges-*

senheit) (the whole of) being. (One is reminded here of the
divine blindness [atē] that often strikes the hero of Greek
tragedy, who gets carried away in his or her piety and suffers
for it.) The essence of man is not grounded in the conception
of the god, but in the embrace of the holy.   Mortals must
recall that the god and gods are but beckoning messengers, and
hence *are* only insofar as they *hint* [*winken*]. The language of
the gods is hinting; it is not to be taken as definite assertions to be abided by, but directions to be considered and
thought about.   What is important is being directed to the
wholesomeness of the holy, the unconcealment of being. Or,
put another way, the manifestation of the god and gods directs
man to the *polemos*, the fiery irruption of being itself which
"happens" in the difference between gods and men, the veiled
destiny of truth and being (the holy) in which man dwells (EM
148; EHD 65, 69, 73-74; GR 32; HW 39; VA 224).

The god and gods therefore provide a measure [*Maβ*] for
human dwelling. Man spans [*durchmiβt*] the dimension of his
dwelling, the dimension which measures out and metes out
[*zumessen*] what and how he may be, by sighting/siting himself
against the divinity, measuring [*miβt*] himself by the upward
glance from earth to sky. The pathless places [*Stellen*] of
the earth cannot provide the site [*Ort*] for man's dwelling;
there is no measure on the earth. Rather, looking up to the
sky, which belongs in the dimension of man's dwelling just as
much as the earth, man takes measure [*ver-miβt*] of "his"
dimension, his site. "Only insofar as man takes the measure
of his dwelling in this way is he able to be commensurate
[*gemäβ*] with his essence" (VA 195; WD 117-18).   But this
measure is strange, for the sky is the measure only in that it
manifests the god as unknown. The manifestness of the sky
consists in a disclosing that lets us see what conceals itself, but lets us see it not by seeking to wrest what is
concealed out of its concealedness, but only by guarding the
concealed in its self-concealment. Whether in the darkness of
the thundercloud and storm, wherein the voices of destiny
resound in lightning and thunder, or, more veilingly, in the
darkness of the brightest brightness of its lovely blueness
and the radiance of its height, the darkness of its all-
sheltering breadth and unfathomable depth, the sky discloses
the god as unknown. Into everything that shimmers and blooms
in the sky and thus under the sky, on the earth, into all that
is intimate to man but alien [*Fremde*] to the god(s), the
unknown one sends himself and thus remains a stranger [*ein
Fremdes*] to man (EHD 165f, 169f, 173, 189f; VA 197ff).   In
this way, in the appearance of the god as unknown, there
shines the holy, being itself, the mysterious dimension which
is alien to everything in that it is no thing, yet pervades
everything by granting being, opening up and spanning [*durchmiβt*] the various regions of being, measuring out and appor-
tioning [*er-miβt*] each to its own and thereby meting out

[*vermisst*] the measure of their essence, even while withdrawing, concealing, and therefore preserving itself in its essence (US 25-26, 44-45).[8]
     Measuring himself [*sich messen*] by the god, man misses
himself [*sich missen*] if he sets out to measure by measuring
up to the god and "imitating" the god, giving himself up
solely to the god as made in his image. The reason is that
such measuring takes God as a final repose and resting place,
a constantly present "yardstick", which leads either to the
presumptive security of imitation (e.g., *ego cogito*) or the
security of degradation (e.g., the certainty of faith, given
up completely to the god as supreme value and the earth as
worthless). Taking measure in the god as unknown, on the
other hand, knows no security. Such an abysmal measure directs one to taking measure in being itself, the holy abyss
which is no measure (as usually conceived) but demands thinking. Man is thus thrown back upon himself and his dwelling on
the earth (where there is no measure). The advent of the god,
then, as unknown, calls upon man to become more radically man,
as needed, for he too, in his own way, belongs to the holy.[9]

3. BUILDING AND DWELLING -- MORTALS AMIDST THE FOURFOLD

To better understand this measured-measureless dwelling of man
that spans the dimension of being in the sight of the god, we
should look to the "authentic man" in Heidegger's later writings -- in this context, the "poet" -- and his saying. On the
one hand, the poet stands "bare-headed" "beneath God's thun-
derstorms", i.e., stands open, exposed and without shelter,
before the unique event of meaning in which the advent of the
gods lies, and is therefore bound to the signs [*Winke*] of the
gods. Yet, on the other hand, the poet must think about and
re-call [*denken . . . an*] that which first of all concerns the
"sons of the earth", if they are to dwell in their place.
Hence the poet is also bound to the "voice of the people", to
an interpretation and elucidation of the traditional language
and saying (which sometimes grows weary and dumb, as opposed
to the signs [language] of the gods) in which a people recalls
that it belongs to being (the whole, the holy). Hence the
poet stands as one cast out into the "between", between gods
and men, thinking from out of this between that is above both
and hallows both differently, glimpsing the opening in which
the gods first come as guests and men can build an abode. The
poet, then, speaks from "holy compulsion", i.e., from out of
the holy, the clearing of being. The poet attests to the
holy, and thus first lets the belonging-together of god and
man appear (EHD 45-46, 64, 69, 123, 148, 187; GR 30f, 165ff).
     Since the holy reaches "from high Aether down to the low
abyss", the poet, in attesting to the holy, names gods, and
names all things insofar as they are. Compelled [*genötigt*] by

the holy to a naming of the gods, the poet is taken into use
[braucht] in order to let the advent of the gods appear. The
gods then need the word of the poet for their appearance. But
this word, which nominates the god and gods to their being,
does not name them as something asserted [Gemeinte] and in-
spectable, but names them in their hinting, as which they are.
Poetic saying is a further hinting [winken] of the signs
[Winke] of the gods, a "silent" naming in accordance with the
character of responding and corresponding that simply lets the
presence [Gegenwart] of the god be said, greeting him and
letting him enter originally into the nobility of his essence.
The poet wants nothing for himself, and hence wills nothing.
Instead, his saying becomes "a quiet, exuberant bow, a jubi-
lant homage, a eulogy, a praise: laudare," laudes, song.
Poetry is song, the celebration of the advent of the gods, the
singing of which is an art, for it guards the god and gods as
reserved and spared [Gesparte] -- i.e., as unknown, remaining
far and coming -- yet grounds a nearness to the gods in thus
unfolding this distance between gods and men. In this way,
through song, a silent naming, the immediate (the holy) is
left in its immediacy, yet its transmission and mediation is
undertaken, in order to show that stillest of all events
[Ereignisses]: the coming to light of the clearing presencing
in all -- the light embrace of the holy (EHD 25, 41, 58, 71,
96, 170, 187ff; GR 32; PT 47; US 182, 229).

   At the same time, called on and compelled to a naming of
the gods, the poet brings human Dasein into a firm relation to
the clearing and gives it a basis. His intercepting the signs
of the gods is therefore not only a receiving but also a
giving which boldly presents in the word what he has glimpsed
-- what is full, the whole, the holy -- and so tells in advance of the not yet fulfilled, of the possibilities open to
man. Thus is the poet a "prophet", not, of course, in the
sense of a seer or fortune teller, but as one who speaks for
(pro-phetes in Greek) the holy,[10] showing the opening of the
between out of which it is first decided who man is and where
he is settling his existence [Dasein]. Dwelling on the earth,
yet mindful of the sky, the poet takes measure of the breadth
of human existence, measuring out and spanning the dimension
in which man dwells and in which human dwelling has the warrant [Gewähr] by which it endures [währt]. Dwelling near the
origin and thus the remaining [Bleiben], watching over
[wahren] it and what is proper [Schickliche] to man's essence,
the poet founds the history [Geschichte] of a people -- i.e.,
the gathered sending of fate [Schicksals], destiny [Ge-schick]
-- and thereby lays out (interprets) and securely establishes
("consecrates") the ground or earth [Boden] on which man may
build his existence (EHD 41,46-47,105-106,114,148; VA 195ff).

   However, we should not be misled by this talk of founding,
ground, and security. Though the "harmless" song of the poet
mediates the horror and tremor of the arising incipience

[aufgehenden Anfänglichen] of the holy for the "sons of the
earth" -- such that the latter are visited with a "lack of
danger" -- this has nothing to do with the supposed safety of
a final resting place. Of course, the poetic word (and perhaps even more so, the word of the thinker) might be taken as
such a final resting place, for its "mildness" mediates the
holy for man and thereby threatens to convert the holy from
its arising incipience and make it infirm and rigid.   However,
properly construed, the "security" of the poetic word is a
warrant [Gewähr] to be, a granting [Gewähren] of being, a
"housing" of being wherein man is called to dwell.   And indeed, he is called to dwell poetically, for if poetizing first
lets dwelling be dwelling, the original dwelling of the "sons
of the earth" is the founding dwelling that is poetizing.
"Dwelling poetically" is obviously not some façon, some self-
decoration of life, but the basic character of human Dasein --
an exposedness to being itself (the holy), suspension in the
superiority of being [Ausgesetzheit in die Übermacht des
Seyns].   Such openedness is attained between heaven and earth,
mortal and divinity, maintaining, within the domain of the
word, a tension between our concern for heaven and the divine
and our rootedness on the earth.   Such tension thereby confers
a dimensionality to our being and a locus to our dwelling,
which is given as gift in the coming of the god.   Thus is
man's authentic being a "poetic" dwelling (EHD 42, 71-73, 148-
49; GR 30-31, 36; VA 189).[11]
     Put another way, the building [bauen] that is poetizing
and poetry is dwelling [wohnen], a correlation which shows
itself if we let language speak, as Heidegger is inclined to
do: the Old English and High German word for building, buan,
means to dwell, to remain [bleiben], to stay in a place [sich
aufhalten].   In addition, the rootedness of the German bin --
as in ich bin (I am), du bist (you are), and the imperative
bis -- in buan and bauen gives further testimony to the interplay of how we are, dwelling and building.   Finally, bauen
also means, at the same time, to cherish and protect, preserve
and care for [hegen und pflegen], specifically to till [bauen]
the soil and cultivate [bauen] the vine.   Hence, listening to
language, we find that building is dwelling, which is the
manner in which we are, and unfolds as both a cultivation (of
growing things) as well as an erecting (of structures).   Building is "habitual" [Gewohnte -- what we inhabit], what we do
because we are, dwelling (VA 146ff; cf. SZ 73).
     This characterization of building and dwelling is in keep-
ing with the characterizations of human Dasein which we have
already found in Heidegger: the remaining and staying in
place give voice to our standing out in the clearing of being,
the cultivation, cherishing, and protecting give voice to our
care, our letting beings be in their essence (being).   But
what now is a thing in its being, i.e., what is a thing as
thing, that we let it presence (a letting which Heidegger

sometimes calls sparing)? A jug, for example: how is it as
the thing that it is, as jug?   Clearly it is not an object
[Gegenstand], something standing before us, nor is it some
unknown x to which properties are attached, nor is it even the
material of which the jug consists, for we are interested, as
Heidegger stresses, in how the jug is as jug, as a holding
vessel, and not as material, object, substance, or whatever
else.   The jug is a holding vessel, and what holds, Heidegger
notes, is the emptiness which has been formed by the sides and
bottom of the jug.   Thus the emptiness that holds is that in
which the thingness of the jug lies, is that in which the jug
presences [west] as jug.   Now this holding takes what is
poured in, and keeps it, and this twofold holding has its
unity in the outpouring, since a jug holds in order to be able
to pour out and give what it holds (i.e., it is "designed" to
pour out something which it holds).   Thus Heidegger concludes
that the jug-character of the jug, the way in which the jug is
jug, presences in the gift of the outpouring (VA 165ff).

But Heidegger's analysis does not end there, for he goes
on to say that the gift of pouring out manifests sky and
earth, mortals and divinities.   The wine or water that are
poured out from the jug attest to the sky and the earth.   In
the wine presence the nourishment of the earth and the sun of
the sky that yield the fruit of the vine; in the water presences the rock that serves as the source of the spring and
which receives the rain and dew of the sky.   Furthermore, the
gift of the outpouring is a drink for man, and, in the celebration of the festival, a consecrated libation poured out for
the immortal gods.   In the gift of the outpouring that is
drink, in which the jug is as jug, each of these four -- earth
and sky, divinity and mortal -- linger [weilt] in their own
way.   And so it is with other things, e.g., a bridge: it
gathers the earth as landscape around the river or stream,
letting each bank be as such (set off against one another,
whereby they are banks), and is set up with due consideration
for the weather (winds, flooding) that may batter it; it
grants men a way to go to and fro and thus gathers the various
precincts of man, and it does so before the divinities, as
shown by the thanksgiving attested to in the figure of the
saint of the bridge. (If this seems quaint, note the modern
day parallel, which Heidegger does not mention, of the dedica-
tion of a structure by the powers that be, i.e., city, state,
national, and international figures, who give their blessing
by cutting a ribbon or shovelling dirt and then commemorating
the event with a plaque or cornerstone.) In the jug as jug,
or the bridge as bridge -- the thing as thing -- these four,
this fourfold [Geviert] of earth, sky, mortals and divinities,
while [weilt] together all at once in a simple onefoldness
[Einfalt] (VA 152f, 170f).

This simple onefoldness in which the interplay of the four
gathers is described by Heidegger as a kind of mirroring:

Each of the four mirrors in its own way the essence, presencing [Wesen], of the others. Each therewith reflects itself
in its own way into its own [Eigenes], within the simple
onefoldness of the four. This mirroring does not portray a
likeness. The mirroring, lightening and clearing [lichtend]
each of the four, appropriates [ereignet] their own essence
and presencing into simple belonging to one another. Mirroring in this appropriating-lightening-clearing [ereignend-
lichtend] way, each of the four plays to each of the others.
The appropriative mirroring sets each of the four free into
the simple onefoldness of their essential being toward one
another (VA 178).

With this image of mirroring, Heidegger gives his consum-
mate "description" of the movement and rest, revealing and
concealing, that is the worlding of the world, the "happening"
of truth, the arising incipience of the holy -- Ereignis.
Caught up in a "round dance of appropriating [der Reigens des
Ereignens]" which lightens and clears the four into their own
through a play of mirroring, these four belong in one by a
primal oneness, in a groundless playing, such that no one of
the four produces the other three, nor the four the oneness,
nor the oneness the four. In the midst [Mitte] of the simple
onefoldness, none is in and for itself, cut off and standing
on one side for themselves. Rather, each being face to face
with one another [Gegen-einander-über], each is expropriated
[enteignet] out of such onesidedness and appropriated [vereig-
net] into the in-finite relation that holds the world regions
together thoroughly in their midst. The middle [Mitte] makes
way [be-wëgen] for the mirror-play, whereby each is open for
the other, open in its self-concealing (mirroring requires
opacity -- concealing -- for revealing) and is thereby freed
to belong to the other in-finitely, i.e., by virtue of being
in its own (bounds, limitations, "finitude") from within the
intimacy of the middle. For, keeping to one another [halten
sich aneinander] in-finitely, the four are what they are from
out of the in-finite relation, such that they are whole and
the holy itself. In other words, to name one is to name the
other three, and thus the whole. The middle, the in-finite
relation, is being as being, the obliteration of being (as
substance) in favor of the jointure [Fuge] of the four which
lets the four reach one another and holds them in the nearness
of their distance and difference, "mediating" [mittelt], de-
creeing [fügen], and disposing [verfügen] the four, destining
them, into their own. The mirroring is the intimacy of the
four, the marriage [Hochzeit] which celebrates the coming of
the whole of the in-finite relation (the birth of a world),
and thus commemorates and remembers the beginning [Anfang] in
which the four are betrothed [zutraut], extended, entrusted,
and abandoned to one another in a singular event of meaning,

such that each is itself. The mirroring is the still, gathered ringing [*Gering*] which joins [*ringt*] the four while it
plays, a *Zeit-Spiel-Raum* which throws open times and places in
which each may presence, a nighness [*Nähnis*] which spares its
appearance for the presencing of the four, and thus remains
unapproachable and farthest from us whenever we talk "about"
it (EHD 163,170, 172ff, 179; US 211, 214-15; VA 149, 178-79;
WM 411; ZD 58).

It is out of this ringing mirror-play of the four that the
thinging [*dingen*] of the thing takes place, i.e., the thing *is*
and shows itself as thing. Thing (*thing*) is the ancient word
for gathering; things gather to themselves earth and sky,
mortals and divinities, letting the fourfold of the four stay
[*verweilen*] with them. This staying, of course, no longer is
the mere persisting of something present-at-hand (as the essence of thing traditionally is thought) but is an appropriation which brings the four into the light of their mutual
belonging. Thus the thinging of a thing is a gathering-
appropriating staying [*versammelnd-ereignend Verweilen*] of the
fourfold, the unfolding of the world in which things while.
Thinging, things gesture [*gebärden*], gestate, carry out and
bear [*tragen . . . aus*], world, the gathered onefold of the
fourfold of the world (US 22; VA 153-54, 172, 176, 179).

All of this, of course, bears on our dwelling (being) in
the world. For if to dwell means to spare things as things,
to let them come into their essence (and not try to control
them), then dwelling involves sparing the fourfold, letting
the fourfold presence in things. Such a sparing gives to us a
way to dwell, and a place to dwell. The way to dwell is *as
mortal*. With this name, Heidegger recalls to our thinking
that only in being-towards-death, being capable of death as
death, is man able to stand out in the clearing of being,
enter into the mirror-play of the four and thus attain to his
essence, to what is his own. Death is the shrine of the
nothing, harboring within itself the presencing of being; it
is the gathered sheltering, the highest keeping [*Ge-birge*], of
being, and hence a beginning for man. Georg Trakl, a favorite
poet of Heidegger, calls the dead one a madman, for in his
madness [*Wahnsinn*] he remains without (*waha*, Old High German
root of *wahn*) the sense [*Sinn*] of others, of another mind
[*Sinnes*] than *das Man*. The dead one is without the direction
(*sinnan* originally means journey, striving, taking a road) of
the others, on the way in another direction, pondering [*sinnt
. . . nach*] a greater stillness -- the meaning of being that
reaches from earth to sky, mortals to divinities. Mortals die
death in life, and so, let into the in-finite relation of the
clearing of being, become *im*-mortal [*un-sterblich*] in death.
This is not meant in any "substantial" sense (e.g., regarding
the immortality of the soul, or literally living forever); it
simply means that in mortality, in-(being)mortal, man belongs
to the meaning of being that is (for)ever-granting being to us

(EHD 165; KM 206; SZ 349, 436-37 and *passim*; US 23, 53, 55; VA 150-51, 177, 256; WM 374).[12]

Corresponding to this way of dwelling is a place to dwell for man. In death, i.e., as mortal, man is on the way in another direction, called to go down [*Untergang*] -- back to the earth, and thus back down into the abyss of being. In death, mortals seek the earth, that they may build and dwell upon it. Instead of rising up above the earth and taking revenge against it by re-presenting it in a way in which they want, mortals spare the fourfold by "saving" the earth, i.e., letting it show itself and thus setting it free into its own presencing [*Wesen*]. Such is already implied in man's relation to things. For things be-thing, condition [*be-dingen*], man, calling him into the play of the four by visiting him with a world. It is things which reveal being to man. They are a location [*Ort*], allowing a site [*eine Statte verstattet*], making room [*räumt . . . ein*] for the fourfold. Things thereby determine the places [*Plätze*] and ways by which a space [*Raum*] for our dwelling is provided, since the cleared space for settlement and lodging that is space is let into bounds, granted and joined by things as locations gathering the four. Mortals *are* by persisting through and pervading spaces -- and are thus "out there" in the world -- only by virtue of their stay [*Aufenthalt*] with things. Never abandoning such a stay, always coming back to himself from things, man dwells on the earth, letting things *as* things be in their presencing, such that the fourfold -- ~~being~~ -- is accomplished (US 22, 41; VA 36, 149-52, 154-55, 157-59).

All of this is certainly quite strange. Indeed, Trakl tells us that "something strange is the soul on the earth [*es ist die Seele ein Fremdes auf Erden*]." Here, as in the first chorus from the *Antigone* of Sophocles (lines 332ff), Heidegger sees man called the strangest, the uncanniest [*Unheimlichste*]. He is such in a twofold sense: on the one hand, he cultivates and guards the familiar -- the things of the earth -- but in that loses himself in the ordinariness of the everyday, strangely forgetting the clearing of being to which his essence belongs and which brings even the self-evident to light. But, on the other hand, man cultivates and guards the familiar in order to "break out" of it and let being break in; man's "darkness", his capacity for failure, for falling, for losing himself amidst beings and thus forgetting himself, is, strangely enough, a "dark light" wherein the truth of being may shine. On the earth, man, the strange one, goes forth, ventures forth (as the Old High German root of *Fremd* -- *fram* -- suggests); he ventures forth toward being, in search of that where he may remain, on the way into his own. Going down, back to the earth, mortals go down into something strange -- into the abyss -- a "home" which does not let him be at home [*einheimisch*]. Such a "home" casts him out of the "homely" [*Heimlichen*], the native [*Heimischen*] and secure

(wherein man is one-sidedly for himself as e.g., *ego cogito*,
or the self-justified knight of faith) and sets him apart from
others (*das Man*), making him a stranger to them. Such exile
from home first discloses the home, for in the happening of
uncanniness and homelessness [*Unheimlichkeit*], beings are
opened up -- the happening of unconcealment takes place.
Homelessness becomes the summons that calls them home into the
strangest of all -- *Ereignis*, the holy -- wherein they *are* (EM
158-60, 172, 175-76, 178; EHD 129; US 41, 49-51, 54-55; VA
162; cf. KM 210-11; VA 264-65, 280-81).
     With this, man responds to the summons of homelessness by
going home; dwelling becomes a homecoming, a return to the
nearness of the origin, the source, from which all things are.
But we are where we are, dwelling near the origin, in such a
way that we are at the same time not there; the nearness that
holds sway through dwelling lets the near be near and yet, at
the same time, be what is sought, and therefore not near.
Homecoming consists of becoming at home in the still withheld
essence of home. Thus man is indeed strange, always on the
threshold, always going out in search of the site where he
remains as wanderer. Only in this going, going back into the
origin, which remains, is there the remaining and lingering of
dwelling near the origin. Man finds his way, his balance, his
path and saying, only in the repetition of homecoming, i.e.,
in a constant wandering and travelling. His nearness to the
origin is then indeed a mystery, both joyful and sad: joyful
in its homecoming, sad in its renunciation, of not having the
home, once and for all, in his grasp, but reserving and preserving it in its withdrawal. Man's dwelling must thereby be
patient, submitting to the "rift of pain" that lets the far be
near and the near be far,[13] and enduring the constant wandering in which man resides (AED 75; EHD 23ff, 92, 109, 117, 146,
150, 164; US 62, 73-74, 199, 235-37; VA 176).
     Thus the need of dwelling, of constantly responding to the
summons of homelessness by learning to dwell, by trying to
bring dwelling to the fullness of its nature, searching ever
anew for the essence of dwelling. This man accomplishes by
attesting to his belongingness to the earth in various ways,
building out of dwelling and thinking for the sake of dwelling, bringing forth things that admit and install the fourfold. Whether working in the fields, nursing and nurturing
the things that grow, or working to construct things that do
not grow, or fashioning works of art from materials and pigments, or naming things in the work of the poet or the thinker, dwelling thereby discloses a world, sparing (i.e., looking
after and taking care of [*hüten*]) things and the fourfold. It
saves the earth (i.e., does not assault or attack the concealing that is part of the whole), receives the sky (i.e., allows
things their openness), awaits the divinities (who signal the
unique grant of things) and thus initiates mortals into their
possibilities, their dwelling. Man is therefore "saved" --

saving and salvation meaning being brought home into one's
essence and therefore set free and kept safe (EM 166; EHD 36;
HW 21-22; TK 41; VA 36, 150-52, 159-60, 162).

And in this, the place that man now inhabits -- the earth
-- comes anew. The earth shelters and bears the holy, and
becomes whole, holy, itself, as the gathering of the fourfold
by the thing shows. It is this familiar abode that is the
opening region [*Offene*] for the presencing of the unfamiliar
one -- the god -- and the upsurgence of healing [*Heilens*]
brought about by the advent and address of the unfamiliar one,
that directs man into his stiller essence. Indeed, both the
earth, which houses and grants [*einräumt*] a people its historical place wherein they can be "at home" in their essence, and
its seasons (i.e., time, temporality), which gives to man that
whiling [*Weile*] which has been measured out for his historical
sojourn in his essence, are "angels", heralds, of the serene
in their own right, revealing the clarity in which the essence
of man and things are safely [*heil*] preserved. The earth, as
well as the aether, is a godhead [*Gottheit*]; the place of man
has its own fullness of being and dignity alongside the splendor of the divinities. We ourselves, in our own way, are
divine, precisely in that we dwell in time and on the earth.
"It is the mortals/Who reach sooner into the abyss. So the
turn is/With these," says Hölderlin in *Mnemosyne*, and in that
we find the divinity of man -- that the gods need man to let
them appear, and that it is given to man to take the whole of
the fourfold, the holy, under his care, and let it shine forth
(EHD 16-17, 60, 161; US 79; WM 354-56, 359).[14]

4. RETHINKING THE DIVINE

The introduction of divinities into the matter of thinking
provides us with a traditional religious subject with which we
can see even more clearly just how far we are from traditional
theological thinking in following Heidegger, and thus to what
extent this "religious" dimension in Heidegger's thinking
gives us an entirely different understanding of religion and
religious thinking than that to which we are accustomed. For
instance, by bringing the god and gods into the play of the
world, and specifically, into the gathering of the fourfold
that is the thing, Heidegger (in keeping with what we have
learned so far) radically questions the tendency on the part
of thinking to deal with the god and gods as such, i.e., in
terms of a transcendent-transcendental, otherworldly scheme.
With its emphasis on the god and gods presencing within the
familiar abode of man, as unfamiliar, the Heideggerian scheme
suggests that the matter of the god and gods is less that of
dogma and doctrine and more that of our being on the way,
going out into the world, giving thought to what has been
given, and thereby perhaps catching sight of the divine. This

is not meant sentimentally, as a matter of "experience" versus reflection. Despite a certain similarity, the Heideggerian scheme does not suggest a theology of consciousness or an inductive possibility (as Peter Berger calls it) of religious affirmation in which human experience is the key to a theologizing that senses signs and intimations of the infinite in natural and common events, such that the empirical universe is a symbol of the infinite.[15] Such an inductive possibility retains a true world/apparent world dichotomy and is too subjective in its conception of the core of religion in comparison to the thinking proposed here. Things in a Heideggerian scheme are not ciphers of the divine which man experiences. Instead, things are initiators and signifiers *within* (and not simply through) which the divine is shown, making the religious thinking proposed here a much more "active" and "creative" movement wherein the divine is *brought forth* and *shown* by the active and enterprising participant in the world's manifold life. This would also fit well with the increasing awareness in religious studies of the importance of such matters as art, architecture, and maybe even landscape[16] in religious traditions, for their importance tends to confirm what Heidegger has been telling us: that the extent to which the divinity shows up for man lies in his dwelling in the world, i.e., staying with things and sparing them, building and creating places in which to dwell by word and deed.

Of course, by moving away from an emphasis on the god or gods as such, we are then able to deal with an important part of religious traditions without resorting to a transcendent-transcendental scheme that either makes various religious traditions mere variations on a universal theme, or leads to a premature dismissal of religion on the basis of our discomfort with such a transcendent-transcendental scheme.[17] By not understanding the god or gods as objects of belief, nor arguments and explanations for particular happenings and events, but as hints of the divine and holy, the fullness of their meaning and concreteness can be "justified" for us whether we believe in them as gods or not. For the matter at stake, as was suggested in our chapter on truth, is not the god or gods as such, but the event of meaning that takes place in the advent and withdrawal of the divinities, the dimension for taking measure of that place in which we are. Thinking about the signs of the gods, thinking about the signs that *are* the gods, whereby we attend to and respond to the message of being (the holy) that concerns us all, we are able to understand and converse with our own religious tradition and other religious traditions without converting and "believing" in those gods (i.e., asserting them as [a] foundation[s] of the world).

These insights are diluted if we allow ourselves, as others have,[18] to focus on Heidegger's talk of "the god" and "the divine god" and interpret this as God-talk that is easily squared with our Western philosophical and religious tradi-

tions. To a great extent, the Heideggerian account stresses a
plurality in our experience of the divine ("gods") that should
not be taken lightly and systematically reduced to the symbol-
ic representation of an all-encompassing Supreme Being.   The
plurality of divinity is in keeping with the tensions, ambiguity, and differing that are constitutive of our "place" in
the world by the Heideggerian account. Taking stock of this
might enable us to better understand those traditions in which
plurality is an integral part of the appearance (and non-
appearance) of the divine (e.g., Hinduism, Buddhism, Greek
"religion").   It might also raise some disturbing questions
for our own, traditionally monotheistic, religious background.
For example, to what extent, phenomenologically speaking, do
different religious thinkers "within" the "same" religious
tradition "think" or "experience" the "same" God, and how does
the answer bear upon our understanding of religious traditions? A full-blown Heideggerian account might tend to stress
a greater diversity "within" a religious tradition and therefore seriously question the simple, neat unity that is often
assumed to be constitutive of a tradition.

It seems important to note at this point that the submission of the god or gods to the *Zeit-Spiel-Raum* that is the
mirror-play of the four is in no way a reduction of the divine
ones to things in the world; the god and gods remain strange
and alien to the things familiar to man, however such alien-
ness is understood. It is therefore erroneous and misleading
to simply brand this thinking "pagan" and "idolatrous".   In
submitting the god and gods to the play of the four gathering
in things, however, Heidegger does provide us with the possibility of a religious thinking that does not take revenge
against the earth by taking its meaning somewhere beyond. We
now become aware that what is important is not, e.g., the
absolute transcendence (even to the point of "absurdity") of
God as such, but the *difference between* man and God evoked by
such radical transcendence and which provides the measure for
human dwelling. The matter at stake is not God as such, but
the whole which is to be understood, what is opened up (sky)
and closed off (earth) and thus granted to man to be in the
advent of God as "absurd".   That matter of Christian doctrine
is the Same as the matter in, say, Pure Land Buddhism, in
which the divinity (Amida Buddha) is different from man in
another way, setting up a *different* measure for human dwelling
and therefore granting different possibilites. It is then
only by heeding this matter -- the event of meaning that lays
out *how* it stands with gods and men and is the Same in Christianity and Pure Land -- that we will see the very *different*
possibilities each of these religions grants us and therefore
the decisive and important nature of the two. If, as often
happens, we were simply to pay attention to the divinities as
such (e.g., note that both Christianity and Pure Land comport
themselves toward a transcendent Other who grants otherworldly

salvation), the whole matter at stake -- of how and in what ways human dwelling is to be made whole and holy -- is overlooked and forgotten.

The submission of the god and gods to the play of the fourfold also allows for a reconsideration of time and eternity with respect to the gods. Walter F. Otto has pointed out that in ancient and "primitive" societies, the three "phases" of time were the sources for the manifestations of the god and gods.[19] We can see this in other traditions as well: 1) the future manifests the promise of the god or gods (as in the [2nd] coming of the Messiah); 2) the past manifests the eternity, or the age and previous existence, of the god or gods (e.g., the covenant in Judaism, the many lives of the Buddha in Mahāyāna Buddhism, even the appeal to the Buddha's example and a transmission of that example in supposedly "timeless" Zen Buddhism); 3) the present manifests the nearness of the god or gods (as in the varieties of religious "experience", or the performance of a ritual such as the Catholic Mass). All of this points to how the gods are meaningful and significant: by a manifestation of the divine *in* and *through* time. And this, of course, immediately raises questions about the extent to which we can talk, as some do, about a distinction between "historical" and "atemporal" religions.

The Heideggerian account is significant in other ways as well. Given the unique relation between the god and gods and the holy, it allows for understanding traditional doctrines that associate the god or gods with the holy, for with the advent of the gods within the world, "completing" the site, there too is the holy. Yet this same unique relation also lets us see how the god or gods can become of overriding concern, to the extent that they become arguments and objects of belief instead of hints of the holy. This gives religious language that peculiar double-edgedness that all language has according to the Heideggerian account (e.g., is the sentence "It is the will of Allah" an assertion, an argument, an explanation, or is it a realization of the overriding and unpredictable sway of the holy?). In addition, since the gods in this way can "get in the way" and lead to a forgetfulness of the matter at stake (being, the holy), the Heideggerian account also allows us to see how it is that the gods are of lesser importance, or not the central issue, in some religions (e.g., Confucianism, some schools of Hinduism, though the latter retain the notion of *Brahman*) or how the gods may even be absent in some traditions (e.g., "philosophical" Taoism, some schools of Buddhism, such as Zen, even Judaism in exile in which God abandons Israel to its enemies). This is of course simply the consequence of the fact that with the Heideggerian scheme we have gone beyond theism and atheism in our characterization of religion. The matter at stake in religion is not whether a god or gods is asserted or denied, believed in or rejected, but what is disclosed in the naming of the gods (or their absence), the event of meaning that shines forth in the evocation (or denial) of the gods, wherein man is let into his own ("saved") and allowed to dwell.

By this account, then, we are also granted an account of why Heidegger can find not only danger but destiny in the world-night and destitution that has come upon us in the flight of the gods. Though the lack of God [Fehl Gottes] announces a certain misfortune [Unheil] and disappearance of everything wholesome [alles Heilsamen] and holy in beings, such that even the traces of the gods and the holy become obliterated and we fail to notice the lack, this darkness nevertheless leaves all beings in the unnative [Unheimischen] and gives us something to think about. The lack of God directs us to the abyss, to the hidden fullness of what has been [Ge-wesenen] and what, thus gathered, is presencing in the old gods as fled. Their flight does not mean that divinity and holiness have also vanished. Their flight demands a renunciation of them (lest our thinking become a mere wishful thinking), a renunciation that is only possible if they are seized upon in their divinity, i.e., how it is that they once showed themselves as divine. The endurance of this renunciation thereby becomes a preservation of divinity, for it remains near the origin that gave them as gods. Hence the sorrow and pain of this renunciation, which leaves us wandering apart in the night, is holy. The night in which we wander is not a desperate gloom but a holy night with its own clarity and stillness. It shelters the past divinities and conceals those coming. It calls on us to become more watchful, thoughtful, to awaken and thereby await the original word that calls forth divinity. Though the gods remain far off, the holy appears; we are even as a silence unaddressed by the gods and in the absence of their hints (EHD 27-28, 109-10, 136, 184, 190; HW 271-72; GR 70, 87, 93ff; N II 394-95; US 64ff, 71-72; VA 183).

This is no mere variation of negative theology; indeed, this understanding of divinity (which suggests duplicity on the part of the divine) is most unlike our traditional Western understanding of God and divinity (which is undoubtedly why Heidegger once said that he believed "being [presence] can never be thought as the essence and ground of god ..."[20]). The fact of the matter is that Heidegger's account of divinity perhaps finds its only parallel in the understanding of divinity revealed in tragic literature -- an understanding that, like Heidegger's, is perplexing to ontotheological thinking. In tragedy (Greek or otherwise), the gods are responsible for both good and evil and are therefore strangely duplicitous, as they are with Heidegger in their presencing and absencing. This is not contradictory, nor can it be explained away with a self-certain affirmation of meaning above and beyond human being by, e.g., invoking the mystery and unintelligibility of God to finite human minds. Instead of justifying the gods and

thereby giving some sort of theodicy that tries to still the
question of the meaning of existence, Heidegger and tragedy
reveal the mystery and duplicity of the gods in order to
initiate the question and *abide with the question* of being and
what is divine. When questioned, the gods become significant;
questionable, the gods are question-*worthy*. And by questioning the gods, the question of being is raised, whereby human
being may be sighted/sited. The duplicity of the gods is a
function of the uncertainty and questionableness of being,
which leads us back to our own selves and our questioning
existence.[21]

Thus there may be dwelling in the holy in the time of need
as well, in the no-more of the gods that have fled and the
not-yet of the god(s) that is (are) coming. More *uncanny* and
strange than the advent of the god and gods in the sights of
the familiar may be that the place of the god and gods remains
empty. Heidegger names the quadrant of the divinities -- not
to assert the existence of a god, but -- to open our thinking
to the divine and holy aspect of what is shown to us and what
may yet be thought. Thus to think the lack of God is a
"religious" thinking too, and no mere atheism. For mortals
dwell in that they both "wait for hints of their [the gods]
advent *and do not mistake the signs of their absence*" (my
emphasis). In such dwelling is there a turn in our thinking,
a reaching into the abyss and the holy, which decides beforehand about gods and men, whether they are, and who, how, and
when they are. Whether the god lives or remains dead will
only be decided from within this dwelling in being (EHD 76; HW
255, 271; TK 46; VA 151).

> In order to arrive at what you are not
>   You must go through the way in which you are not.
> And what you do not know is the only thing you know
> And what you own is what you do not own
> And where you are is where you are not.[22]

NOTES

1. Williams, *Philosophy of Religion*, p. 121, says that Heidegger "is
using the terms 'holy', 'gods' and 'God' with reference to the poetry of
Hölderlin and not to theology or religion," without ever defining theology
or religion and without taking note of those instances in which Heidegger
talks about gods and the holy outside his elucidations of Hölderlin.   See
Jonas, "Heidegger and Theology," p. 219, for the characterization of
Heidegger's thinking as "paganism"; see also Martin Buber, *The Eclipse of
God* (New York: Harper & Row, 1952), pp. 21ff, for objections to Heidegger's juxtaposing gods with God.   See Charles Wei-hsun Fu, "Heidegger and
Zen on Being and Nothingness: A Critical Essay in Transmetaphysical Dia-
lectics" in *Buddhist and Western Philosophy: A Critical Comparative Study*,
ed. Nathan Katz (New Dehli: Sterling, 1981), pp. 184-85, for the characterization of Heidegger's thinking as "quasi-onto-theo-logical".
2. See André Schuwer, "Nature and the Holy: On Heidegger's Interpretation of Hölderlin's Hymn 'Wie Wenn Am Feiertage'," *Research in Phenomenology* 7 (1977), pp. 228-32; F. Joseph Smith, "In-the-World and On-the-
Earth" in *Heidegger and the Quest for Truth*, p. 186; Vycinas, *Earth and
Gods*, pp. 126ff, 168f, 205, 209ff, 297.   The latter two essays are particularly interesting for their discussion of *chaos* and its relation to
logos, *physis*, and being.
3. The adverb *einst* and the adjective *einstig* both have meanings of
past and future, depending on the context.   Rather ingeniously, Heidegger
often calls nature and the holy *das Einstige*, to capture the "once and
future" character of the holy without (as in Hölderlin's case) having to
resort to misleading metaphysical terms such as "eternity" and "the eternal".
4. Contra Francois Fédier, "Heidegger et Dieu" in *Heidegger et la
Question de Dieu*, p. 44, Macquarrie, *Principles*, pp. 115-22, Orr, *The
Meaning of Transcendence*, p. 143, and Williams, p. 118, who say, respectively, that God is not subordinated to Being, that a different order of
Being belongs to God, whereby God is to be equated with ("holy") Being,
that the Being of God cannot be spoken of because it cannot be understood
in terms of the Being of beings, or that God is not determined by Being.
These misinterpretations seem to be tainted by an onto-theo-logical,
Christian understanding of God (revealingly capitalized in all three
cases) that does not take heed of how Heidegger understands the god and
gods "of *Occident* and Orient".   See the exposition that follows.
5. See Danner, *Das Göttliche und der Gott*, p. 128; Gethmann-Siefert,
Die Verhältnis/Philosophie und Theologie, p. 113; Perotti, *On the Divine*,
pp. 88, 101-102; Orr, p. 113. See Vycinas, pp. 171, 187-88, 213ff, for an
elucidation of gods as worlds and modes of *physis* and *logos*, and especially Walter F. Otto, *Homeric Gods*, trans. Moses Hadas (1954; rpt. New York:
Thames and Hudson, 1979) (on whom Vycinas by and large depends), who
stresses that "the divinities become figures of reality in which the
manifold being of nature finds its perfect and eternal expression" (p.
39), such that *being*, and not the gods themselves, are what is most
important, manifest in the selflessness and withdrawal of the personali-
ties of the gods before specific goals (e.g., pp. 237-39).

6. Cf. Danner, p. 129, who stresses that 'the god' is not the singular of 'the gods', but is the 'divine god' who presences out of the dimension of the godhead [*Gottheit*], of which the gods and divinities are but messengers, and Perotti, p. 102, who stresses that the god is 'a highest being' of whom the gods are but messengers and not to be confused with him. Both interpretations seem to want to leave room in Heidegger for *the* God, but it is a bit more complicated than that; presumably, 'the gods' are also divine, since they too presence out of divinity.

Our interpretation is based on the recognition of the Greek experience of Zeus and the Greek use of the singular "the god" (*theos*) in conjunction with "the gods" (*theoi*). "The god" named the divine realm in general, as opposed to the mortal realm, and was often associated with Zeus. Hence "the god" was both a being (the highest being, the king of the gods, Zeus) and a dimension, the epitome of the divine and the divine sway in general. See Otto, *Homeric Gods*, pp. 42, 171ff, 283. See also Vycinas, pp. 170, 189ff. This seems to more adequately cover the way Heidegger talks about "the god".

7. See Heraclitus, Fragment 32 ("The One, which alone is wise, does not want and yet wants to be called by the name of Zeus", among other translations). See Otto, *Homeric Gods*, pp. 263ff, and Vycinas, p. 170, for discussion of the relation between gods and fate.

8. See also Richardson, *From Phenomenology to Thought*, p. 590.

9. See Krell, "Nietzsche and the Task of Thinking," pp. 216-218, who points out the play on words between "measuring" and "missing" implied in Heidegger's discussion.

Note that since man too belongs to the holy (as will be elucidated below), it is misleading of Orr, p. 114, to characterize only the place of the gods as the Holy.

10. With regard to this often cited character of the poet in Heidegger, the following question was raised by Erling W. Eng at a symposium on Heidegger in 1969: "Is Heidegger's conception of the poet, like Hölderlin's, not a prophetic one that has more in common with the ancient Hebrew prophets and psalmists than with the Greek poets? Furthermore, is this not in accord with Heidegger's efforts to replace the metaphysics of light, so very Greek in character, with an 'archaeology' of the word?" (Cited in Werner Marx, "The World in Another Beginning: Poetic Dwelling and the Role of the Poet" in *On Heidegger and Language*, p. 243 n.28). The question, at the very least, indicates the latitude we must give to Heidegger's conception of the poet, and the extent to which references to the Greeks to illuminate Heidegger's thinking should not be taken as limitations on the applicability of Heidegger's insights.

11. See Paul Ricoeur, "Religion, Atheism, and Faith" in *The Conflict of Interpretations*, p. 467.

12. Cf. Otto, *Homeric Gods*, pp. 138-139, 145, and "Die Zeit und das Sein" in *Anteile: Martin Heidegger zum 60. Geburtstag* (Frankfurt: Klostermann, 1950), p. 15, who stresses that for the Greeks the dead were past magnitudes, significant in their abiding form. This is in accord with antique religion in general, which saw in death the greater, solemn being, a divine presencing raised up into an absolute perfection and truth, that demanded devotion.

13. "Pain" is a word that arises in Trakl's poetry and is taken by Heidegger to refer to the strife, tension, and difference between revealing and concealing, being at home by not being at home (being a stranger and wanderer) and the like. It has nothing to do with physical sensitivity. See US 61ff.

14. See Otto, "Zeit und Sein," pp. 11–12.

15. A recent example is Peter Berger's call for the inductive possibility in *The Heretical Imperative: Contemporary Possibilities of Religious Affirmation* (Garden City, N.Y.: Anchor Press/Doubleday, 1980), pp. 114ff and *passim*, but it is the common approach of "liberal Protestant theology" from Schleiermacher to Tillich and, we might add, of phenomenology of religion from Rudolph Otto to Mircea Eliade and others.

16. In a short but thought-provoking epilogue to his *Religion in Four Dimensions* (New York: Reader's Digest Press, 1976), pp. 466ff, Walter Kaufmann wonders about the extent to which landscape and religion interact, noting specifically the ties between monotheism and the desert, the mosque in Isalm as a stylized oasis, and Taoism and the Chinese landscape.

17. Besides the application this has to this study (e.g., Chapter 2), I am thinking here of those instances in which persons not particularly fond of the Christian (and/or Jewish) tradition dismiss religion *in toto*; those who have dealt with professional philosophers, or have asked students in undergraduate courses to write down what they think of religion, know what is meant.

18. E.g., Bernard Welte, "God in Heidegger's Thought," *Philosophy Today* 26 (1982), pp. 85–100. See also notes 4 and 6 above, and the theologians mentioned in Chapter 2, for other examples.

19. "Zeit und Sein," pp. 7–28.

20. "Dialogue avec Martin Heidegger," 6 November 1951 (Comité des conferences des étudiants de l'Université de Zurich), tr. J. Greisch, in *Heidegger et la question de Dieu*, p. 333.

21. See my "Beyond Theodicy: The Divine in Heidegger and Tragedy," *Philosophy Today* 29 (1985), pp. 110–120.

22. T.S. Eliot, "Four Quartets," p. 127.

CHAPTER 5

RELIGION AS RESPONSE: THE CALL OF BEING

> *These are only hints and guesses*
> *Hints followed by guesses . . .*
> T.S. Eliot

1. THE PROBLEM -- A NON-METAPHYSICAL THINKING

Thus far, in our last three chapters, we have been working our way toward uncovering the nature of the thinking that Heidegger undertakes in order to prepare for a reorientation of religious thinking.   In Chapter 2, under the guidance of Nietzsche's proclamation of the death of God, we undertook the task of mapping out how Heidegger's thinking is not a "theological" thinking, i.e., not a thinking to be based or founded on the certainty of either faith, God, revelation, or the subject, and is not involved in apologetics and justification of any particular system of signs and symbols.   Since such "abysmal" thinking "begins" with the loss of the traditional issue for thinking -- i.e., the transcendent-transcendental basis on which thinking is secured -- our attention shifted in Chapter 3 to characterizing the issue or matter [*Sache*] of Heideggerian thinking.   Here reflections on truth and world led to a "topological" thinking, a situated thinking that takes place and comes-to-pass within an opening region in which truth "happens" -- within which thinking takes place and is appropriated in an event of meaning [*Ereignis*] in which thinking comes into its own.   This gave us a means of avoiding a dilemma fostered by theological thinking -- namely, the problem of the plurality of religions and religious "truth-claims" -- and thereby gave us a glimpse of the significance Heidegger's thinking could have for religion.   This vision was expanded on in Chapter 4 with an elucidation of the event of meaning as the holy in which the gods show themselves and man learns to build and dwell on the earth by becoming mortal and sparing the fourfold.   Thus the thinking that lets us into the play of the world was further characterized as a dwelling, building, and sparing.
    Now,   however, it seems incumbent upon us to take a closer look at what Heidegger says about thinking, that we might get a better grasp of its ramifications for religious thinking and might better grasp whatever religious character Heidegger's thinking itself might have.   Such is the concern of this chapter.   Toward that end, our discussion divides into three sections.   First, we will expand on the themes of the last two chapters by taking a closer look at the "relation" between being and man -- man's building and dwelling *in* and sparing

the fourfold -- and reflecting on the call and response motifs Heidegger uses to characterize such thinking. Second, in light of the emphasis on the "poet" and his relation to the gods in the last chapter, we will address the matter of the "poetic" character of thinking and the relation of thinking to poetizing. This will help lead us into the final section in which we can reflect on the possible "religious" import of thinking -- the "piety of thinking", if you will -- and what bearing that has on our understanding of "religious" thinking.

2. THINKING -- RESPONDING AND CORRESPONDING

It is common in our tradition to coordinate man and thinking; man is the being who thinks, the rational animal. Indeed, thinking is what distinguishes man and constitutes his essence. But as soon as we say essence of man, we have named being. An inquiry into thinking, then, would seem to necessarily involve us in the question of the "relation" between man and being.

How are we to think these two, man and being? How do they belong together? Customarily -- and that means, metaphysically -- we would think these two in terms of some sort of unity, such that man and being are two things given on the one hand and the other and then coordinated, combined in some sort of system or mediated through some sort of synthesis (ID 16). Thinking is then seen as either "subjective" (i.e., coordination of man and being beginning with man and going out toward being) or "objective" (i.e., coordination of the two beginning with being and going back to man). However, Heidegger notes that to begin with one or the other, man or being, is to arrive too late: as soon as I say 'essence of man' I have said relatedness to being, and as soon as I say 'being of beings' I have said relatedness to the essence of man. To think otherwise is to have missed the whole point in *Sein und Zeit* that man is not a worldless subject but being-in-the-world, already comporting toward beings in their being (i.e., as they show themselves). The "relation" itself, then, already lies in each of the members of the relation. Their *belonging* to one another -- i.e., what makes it possible for both to be disclosed and shown as they show themselves -- is what is first of all at stake. Only in that they are first appropriated [*übereignet*] to each other can we talk of man and being in the way that metaphysics does.[1] However, by thinking man and being in terms of this appropriation, they lose the qualities with which metaphysics has endowed them. Speaking from the matter at stake, there are no longer members of the relation, nor the relation as such. Rather, speaking from the matter at stake, the appropriation of the two, their *belonging*-together, we name *Ereignis*, that realm in which each achieves its *own* essence and in which thinking therefore always already moves (ID 19, 26; SZ 266ff; WD 74; cf. WM 407-409).

Now, as we have seen, in naming *Ereignis* we name the *Es gibt*; being and man, then, belong to one another in the giving, granting, and sending of being -- in the reaching and extending of being toward man. Being presences [*west*] insofar as it bears-upon and concerns [*an-geht*] man; being 'is' an issue for man (cf. the definition of Dasein in SZ 16). We are given to be, and therefore must consider what it means to be. What makes one think ["gives to thinking" -- *zu denken gibt*] is the withdrawal and denial in the giving of being, that being *is* not, but *es gibt* as the unconcealing of presencing. The mystery of this giving and clearing of being which is near yet withdraws, the mystery of the difference between being and beings -- this is what draws forth, calls forth, and claims thinking, constantly and everywhere, as what is to be thought (AED 77; ID 19; N II 372; VA 242-43, 280; WD 55, 58-59; ZD 6, 10, 24-25).

By this analysis, being is a call to man; in Dasein's *everyday interpretation* of itself, this call is that of conscience (SZ 356). To call [*heißen*][2] means to set in motion, to get something underway -- to bid, not in the sense of commanding and ordering, but of commending and entrusting. Finding ourselves already submitted to world (being) in our thrownness, we are commended and entrusted with the opening and clearing of being which such thrownness provides, bringing us out into the open and disclosing our possibilities 'out there' in the open, giving us to understand our ownmost potentiality-for-being ourselves. Calling, then, is a possible abode, already stemming from the place to which the call goes out (from ourselves, our being, to ourselves, as *das Man*), "which, in calling to and calling upon, in reaching out and instructing, directs us toward doing or letting" and thus brings us to our*selves* in our possible comportment toward beings (HW 74; SZ 356-59, 362-64; WD 80, 82-83, 152-53).[3]

Of course, we are wont to take calling as a mode of discourse, conversation, and language. But that does not mean that the call of being is a vocal utterance. Indeed, by Heidegger's analysis, the call, as a giving and a directive to thinking, does not report anything, but calls without uttering. "The call discourses in the uncanny mode of *keeping silent*," calling one back into the reticence of one's existent potentiality-for-being. The 'voice' [*Stimme*] of being is a soundless voice which attunes [*gestimmt*] us to the shock of the abyss, i.e., the groundless clearing and granting of being (SZ 360-61, 368; WM 306-307).

Such a silent call is in keeping with Heidegger's understanding of the essence of language as Saying [*Sage*], i.e., showing [*Zeige*]. Language gathers together, relates [*verhält*], maintains [*unterhält*], and shelters [*hütet*] the realms of significance in which we abide and from which we

speak. In other words (recalling our discussion in Chapter
3), world emerges into language; language discloses world, and
is that through which world comes-to-presence. Our speaking
originates from out of the unspoken contexts of meaning and
ways of being concealed and sheltered within language (concealed and sheltered, but obviously not as constant presence;
the world that emerges into language is nothing). Language
can therefore be said to speak as the "peal of stillness", for
its soundless voice -- its showing what is unthought and
unspoken -- lays claim to our thinking and speaking and addresses us, beckoning us toward the matter of thinking (the
clearing, granting, and giving of being) and therefore unob-
trusively attunes [stimmt] and determines [bestimmt] us in our
essence (PT 45; SG 91; US 30, 214, 251, 254; WM 476).
So far we have been considering what gets thinking underway, what sets it into motion, i.e., the call and appeal of
being. But this call and appeal speaks just so long as there
are men who hear it; thinking only prospers when we have an
ear for the word, i.e., only when there is hearing [hören]
(AED 77, 89). "Indeed, hearing constitutes the primary and
authentic way in which Dasein is open for its ownmost potentiality-for-being" (SZ 217), a potentiality granted in the
clearing of being in which man belongs [gehören] to being.
Thinking, then, is what it is, according to its essential
origin, as "the belonging to being that listens [das hörend
dem Sein Gehörende]" (WM 316).
Now since the call is not essentially vocalization, such
hearing as Heidegger is talking about here is not a matter of
picking up soundwaves with the ear. Indeed, we do not hear as
long as we only listen to the sound of the word or the expression of a speaker (i.e., to what is said); hearing only is in
belonging to [gehören] that which is spoken to in the speaking. Hearing is attending to the saying of what is said, that
is, what is shown in what is said -- the possibilities, the
projection, and potentiality-for-being given in our already
being submitted to a world and the traditional way in which it
is interpreted. Hearing is then attending to the concealed
and withheld realms of meaning sheltered in what is said (by
not being said) that called forth what is said and which still
calls forth to us from what is said. Hearing, we could say,
is attending to the "original" conversation between being and
man, attending to the soundless address of what is to be sent
to man that he may dwell in his proper place (EHD 124; VA 213,
215).[4] Thus Heidegger, in an early attempt to translate noein
(the Greek word usually translated as thinking), talks of
apprehending [vernehmen], which harbors a twofold meaning of
accepting [hin-nehmen] and letting something come to one, and
to hear and question (a witness) and so establish how a matter
stands (EM 145-46). Thinking, then, does not merely accept
what is said as if it were some passive experience. Thinking,
as apprehending, has the sense of letting what shows itself

come to one by *bringing* it forth and *bringing* it to stand out
in the open from out of what is said.   It is in this sense
that we should think the hearing of being.

If in hearing Dasein is open to its ownmost potentiality-
for-being, hearing must belong to the disclosedness of Dasein
and its constitution as thrown projection.   In existing, Dasein is the basis from which its possibilities are projected,
i.e., it is its thrownness, its past, its heritage, and the
situation to which it is delivered over and has to be.   Dasein
is the basis that is thrownness, but only *from it* and as *this
basis*, i.e., it has *not* laid this basis and can *never* have
power over this ownmost being that is granted to it.   This *not*
of thrownness indicates the nullity [*Nichtigkeit*] of Dasein,
that is, that Dasein is held out into the nothing and must
reach into the abyss, wherein its possibilities are disclosed.
Projection, then, is also shot through with this nullity.   In
having a potentiality-for-being, Dasein stands in one possibility and is thus constantly *not* other possibilities.   In
being freed for its possibilities, Dasein's freedom (its being
set out into the open) is the choice of one possibility and
hence tolerating *not* having chosen others and *not* being able
to choose them.   The not, the nullity, the nothing, determines
Dasein, not as a privation which could somehow be made up, but
as the way in which it is, the way being presences and comes
to be disclosed (SZ 179 note a, 196-97, 376-81; WM 110, 115,
121).[5]   Furthermore, we are attuned to the nothing (the silent
call of being) in anxiety, the basic disposition [*Befindlich-
keit*] in which we find ourselves, i.e., in which we discover
the uncanniness of thrown projection and are thrown back upon
our ownmost potentiality-for-being (cf. SZ 249-51, 333-34,
392).   Such anxiety robs us of speech; self-assurance and
arrogance are stifled.   One is denied any counter-discourse to
the call of being.   Thus hearing is constituted by keeping
silent, a reticence in which the soundlessness of uncanniness
calls forth, calling Dasein back to the stillness of itself
and appropriating it to the peal of stillness that is the call
of being (SZ 393-94; US 32; WM 112).

As we have seen, Heidegger calls such disclosedness [*Er-
schlossenheit*] resoluteness [*Entschlossenheit*] (SZ 393).   Such
resoluteness becomes authentically what it can be in being-
towards-the-end, i.e., anticipation of death (SZ 405).   This
is because facing one's own mortality is a way in which one's
uniqueness is revealed.   The *individual*, in the face of death,
sees that certain possibilities are called for on his part
because he is unique.   But, since "*anticipation discloses to
existence that its uttermost possibility lies in giving itself
up*" (SZ 350), resoluteness cannot be the subjective willing of
a man rigid and firm in his convictions (i.e., resolution in
the traditional sense).   Rather, resolution means "the opening
up of Dasein, out of its captivity in beings, to the openness
of being" (HW 55; cf. G 55).   In other words, rather than

fleeing into the fugitive concealments of *das Man* in which
Dasein understands itself in terms of the world (i.e., beings
and others around it), one steps back, as it were, from
beings, from the fact that they are as they are and not otherwise. We *question* beings, wondering, astonished that they
are, and thereby ask after being. One's security in beings
and others is thereby shattered, and one is opened up to the
current factical possibilities given by "resolutely" maintaining oneself in what is disclosing (EM 6, 23-24, 53, 89; SZ
350, 407-408; VA 259; WP 38-40; WM 307). Thus the wanting-
to-have-a-conscience (wanting to hear the call) that characterizes this resoluteness is no mere willing, wishing, and
striving. Instead, it "wants" to know what is coming (i.e.,
being) and is thereby willing to know and submit to what is
granted to it. Resolution is willing to be appealed to,
standing in a knowing readiness for the affiliation [*Zugehör-
igkeit*] with destiny (the gathered sending of being) (EHD 86-
87; G 30-31; SZ 382; US 100). Its questioning then is no
enforcement of some set procedure from question to answer but
an entrance into harmonic concordance with that which is being
questioned. It thereby lays itself open to what is being
questioned and becomes the permeable space of its disclosure.[6]
Resoluteness, the character of the authentic thinking and
hearing of man, is thus openedness ["un-closedness"; *Entschlossenheit*].

In other words, in resoluteness (openedness) we contem-
plate meaning [*Sinn*] which holds sway in everything that is.
We venture after sense [*Sinn*] and thereby attain to reflection
[*Besinnung*] or meditative [*besinnliche*] thinking that does not
cling one-sidedly to a single idea or a one-track course of
ideas, but makes the truth of our own presuppositions and
goals most worthy of question. We release [*loslassen*] ourselves from our will to secure and control beings by grasping
[*greifen*] or attacking [*angreifen*] them with concepts [*Begrif-
fen*]. Instead, we let beings be, which is not easy, for it is
not mere indifference and passivity in which one weakly allows
things to slide by and drift along. In letting beings be,
thinking acts, turning toward beings and thinking about them
in their being (the play of the fourfold which they gather).
Thinking thus accomplishes not only an engagement by and for
beings, but by and for the truth of being. We are released
[*gelassen*] to being, whereby thinking can be characterized as
a releasement [*Gelassenheit*][7] to the giving and granting of
being, a resolution for essential truth. Steadfast and composed in maintaining itself within the disclosure of being,
such *Gelassenheit* is a thinking-within-anxiety that holds open
the place of the nothing that being may come-to-presence[8] (G
passim; HW 16, 75; VA 68; WD 127-28; WM 313-14).

Through reflection so understood, we attain to a place (VA
68). Hence situation belongs to openedness, as disclosed by
the fact that thrownness and death mark off a region of possi-

ble choices. The situation is not a mixture of circumstances
and accidents present-at-hand; it is the *Da*, the place in
which being is lit up and disclosed in resoluteness (openedness) (SZ 396-98).   In openedness, one stands out (ek-sists)
in the clearing of being (N II 358), bounded by the nullity of
the being of Dasein, but thus granted possibilities (being).
The call of being, then, calls forth into a situation, the
opening of essential possibilities that takes place [*sich
ereignet*] in the granting of being.   Resoluteness is then a
topological thinking, an openedness to the situational character of the truth in which it stands -- to the *topos* of being
that is its sending and granting.[9]

Addressing us while withdrawing and thus gathering together and holding apart past, present, and future, being clears a
place and puts us in a place, installing us in the place that
is cleared.   Hence to resoluteness belongs the moment (of
vision) [*Augenblick*] that is the authentic present.   With the
in-flashing [*Einblitz*] of being, insight [*Einblick*] takes
place, with man being the one who is caught sight of [*Erblick-
ten*].   "In the experience and recognition of the meaningful
moment, the peculiar [*eigen*] essence of man is consummated,"[10]
decisively composed [*zusammennimmt*] and steadied in his full
disclosedness. We thus sight/site ourselves in hearing the
call of being (HW 348-49; N I 312; SG 108-109; SZ 194-95,
508ff, 516-17, 542; TK 43-45; VA 255).

In openedness, we attain to the open realm of the clearing
of being.   But this means that thinking, which begins in
openedness, is a corresponding [*entsprechen* and *Entsprechung*]
to the clearing openness of being which addresses man and
calls forth his thinking (SG 88; TK 41; WD 1).   Thinking and
being are the Same, as Parmenides has told us, or, as
Heidegger translates Fragment 5, thinking and being belong
together in the Same by virtue of the Same (ID 14).

In order to elucidate what this means, Heidegger turns to
another great thinker of early Greece, Heraclitus, who he
finds also attests to this corresponding of thinking.   In
Fragment 50, Heraclitus talks about authentic hearing in terms
of *logos* ("the laying that gathers", as Heidegger translates
it; the laying which brings all beings together in their
being) and *legein* ("laying by letting-lie-before").   The proper hearing of man is a *legein* as *homolegein*, a letting-lie-
before us whatever already lies together before us as laid and
gathered in *logos*; proper hearing lets lie the Same (*homon*).
Proper hearing therefore corresponds to the *logos* (VA 215-17;
cf. WD 171, WP 21).   Heidegger goes on to say that

> As such, the proper hearing of mortals is in a certain way
> the same as the *logos*. At the same time, however, precisely
> as *homolegein*, it is not the same at all. It is not the same
> as the *logos* itself. Rather, *homolegein* remains a *legein*
> which always and only lays or lets lie whatever is already,

as *homon*, gathered together and lying before us; this lying
never springs from the *homolegein* but rather rests in the
laying that gathers, i.e., in the *logos* (VA 217).

In other words, man as Dasein is the clearing, but does not
produce it, but only *is* in corresponding to the openness of
the clearing, striving to remain within it.[11] There is a
difference in the corresponding to being, a difference from
which the corresponding emerges and in which it resides as it
lays out what lies before it and has been granted to it.
Hence the corresponding Heidegger talks of here is no mere
one-to-one match of things present-at-hand, but more like the
corresponding that is an exchange of letters, a dialogue that
opens up possibilities for thinking.

This saying of Heraclitus also points out something else:
homolegein, for all its allowing, is still an action, a *laying
out*; the gathering together of the *logos* calls forth a corresponding *disclosure* on the part of mortals to "complete" the
gathering called for. If mortals merely mimicked what has
been granted, there would be no corresponding, no movement, no
emergence of possibilities and hence no "completion" of the
gathering of the *logos* (for that gathering lays out world, and
hence possibilities for being). Hence corresponding demands
responding [*ent-sprechen*]; there must be a reciprocity to the
call of being in the "matching" and corresponding of thinking.
Customarily, speaking and hearing are divided into separate
capabilities, and indeed, put in opposition: one speaks, the
other listens; one is active, the other passive. But the
ability to hear is itself adapted to the possibility of language and making use of it. Thus Heidegger sees speaking and
hearing as belonging to an original unity, co-essential in the
original conversation that is the call and correspondence of
being to man. Being able to hear, then, is going to involve
an original re-saying [*Wiedersagen*] (but not a parroting
[*Nachsagen*]) of what was heard (as already implied in the
sameness [but not identity] of thinking and being) (EHD 38-39,
124; GR 71; VA 245).

In other words, we correspond to the call of being in a
twofold way that is one: receiving the call, and replying to,
responding to, the call. Speaking is itself a hearing; hearing is itself a speaking. In our speaking, we say again the
Saying we have heard; we lay out and thus interpret [*aus-
-legen*] the meaning-fullness of being which has been granted
and in which we dwell. We speak by way of language, whereby
our speaking is itself a saying, a manifold showing of that
which hearing (i.e., heeding what appears) lets be said. The
corresponding that is attuned to the voice of being is itself
a speaking in the service of language (PT 43; US 32, 254-55;
VA 26, 182; WP 44; cf. VA 243-44).

We have already seen that hearing is constituted by a
reticence, a keeping silent. Now, however, hearing, as corre-

sponding and responding to the call of being, is to be a speaking. This makes sense only if we are clear as to what keeping silent and speaking *are*, and what they *do*. Keeping silent may indeed entail keeping quiet and not uttering a sound, but if authentic, it is still a saying (SZ 218-19). As an example, one may think of Zen masters who sometimes remain silent in response to the queries of a student. Attuned to the task of enlightening the student, and to the bearing of the student revealed in his questions, such silence can be telling; it *says* something to the student. But what we must realize is that even when speaking we keep silent. Our speaking and naming makes known; it is a saying and hence a showing which opens up as *what* and *how* something may be experienced and held in its presencing, a calling which bids *things* and *world* to come forth. But in bringing them forth, they remain distant; the thing is not completely brought forth and disposed by our naming, and the world withdraws and remains unspoken, even while granting presencing and granting the word to name what is present (EHD 188; US 21-22, 28-31; WD 85). Thus one "who speaks sparingly, in veiled pronouncements, which first of all withhold" (N I 266), and "who is capable of letting the unsaid appear, and indeed, as such, in his saying and directly only through this saying" (EHD 189), is also silent. Instead of trying to control, the authentic word, "breaks up", so to speak, even as it is spoken, returning to what Saying has shown and granted us (US 216) and thereby accomplishing the indeterminateness and indeterminableness (i.e., the revealing *and* concealing) of the happening of the truth of being.[12] Thinking, then, responding and corresponding to the call of being, "un-speaks" [*ent-sprechen*] even as it speaks; its answer [*Ant-wort*] does not still the genuine question, but first unlocks it, maintaining what is questioned in its question-worthiness. Hence answers, e.g., the sayings of thinkers, are not terminations but beginnings [*Anfangen*] which seize on [*fangt an*] the *Ereignis* of being. Answers are only as long as they are rooted in questioning, the movement of the call, and remain questionable-questionworthy-questioning sayings (HW 58; VA 119, 219; WD 141, 163-64; WP 32; cf. HW 64, & note b, VA 48).

That naming, even while calling forth and revealing, veils and conceals (by keeping silent) indicates the ambiguity [*Mehrdeutigkeit*] of language, and hence also its capacity for duplicity [*Zwei-deutigkeit*]. Language is duplicitous insofar as both the common and the extraordinary are something said; hence there are no guarantees as to the essentiality of the word. Indeed, it seems that language plays with our speech such that it drifts away into the more obvious meanings, the common talk which we all are, even in our venturing forth (and why we must venture forth) to disclose being. This makes responding an always precarious affair that risks going astray even while it attempts to pay heed to the withdrawal and mystery of the granting of being (EHD 36-37, 188; GR 61-62, 71; US 74; VA 185; WD 83; cf. EM 169-70, 180-81). But such duplicity should not tempt thinking to force saying into the rigid groove of a univocal statement, for the ambiguity of language is not lax imprecision or equivocation, the residue of an unachieved formal-logical univocity. It is instead a gathering and unison [*Einklang*] that plays in language -- plays, not haphazardly, but most strictly , according to a concealed sway as thinking responds and corresponds to what is to be thought. Thinking, if it is to be strict and rigorous, must enter into this ambiguity, this greater meaning [*Mehr--deutigkeit*], that being may come-to-presence, though it thereby risks confusion with the vagueness and equivocation of those who do not heed the call (WD 68; US 75, 167; WM 423).

Likewise, the danger and difficulty of language should not make us so suspicious and questioning that we shun the trouble and risk of speaking by falling completely silent; responding, as responding, must lose the character of questioning (in the sense of a cynicism that continually doubts everything granted in what is said) and become simply saying, lest we lose our essence (being). For the being of man is grounded in language and conversation, taking place out of the speaking of language. Man is a sayer, *the* sayer, compelled to bear witness to what he may be (since being is an issue for man) (EM 88; EHD 36, 38-39; US 11, 301; VA 70) Man is behooved [*gebraucht*] to speak from language, for being needs to use [*braucht*][13] the essence of man to come-to-presence; being needs and compels [*be-nötigt*] accommodation for its presencing, and thus appropriates and claims man in its coming (HW 373; G 62-64; N II 390-91, 482-83; Sp 209; US 149; WD 85). Such accommodation are we in responding and corresponding through original saying, i.e., naming, which opens up the being of beings in its gathering, thereby gathering again and preserving what was originally gathered (EM 131). Placed before and open to being, we remain referred to and corresponding to being, and thus authentically are as this reference of corresponding (ID 18). Said another way, we are in the draw of the self-withdrawal of being, making us signs [*Zeichen*] which point out and show [*zeigt*] that which withdraws itself (being). Referring [*deuten*] into the withdrawing, we are signs without significance [*deutungslos*], our only task being to seek the word out of which the truth of being comes to language (WD 5-6, 52, 95-96; WM 311, 313).

In our pointing and showing through the word, we look after, take heed [*in-die-Acht-nehmen*] of, being, letting it presence as it comes. In the giving of being we are therefore bidden to the guardianship of being, which is nothing like the protection of something present-at-hand, but is a vigilance for the has-been and coming destiny of being. Through the openedness of Da-sein, man protects and preserves being, defending himself against semblance and disguise in order to assure its unconcealment ever anew, holding open the place of the nothing that being may come to presence. Man is therefore the shepherd of being for whom it is ever a question of finding what is fitting and proper [Schickliche] in his essence which corresponds to the destiny [Ge-schick] of being. Man comes to stand in "relation" to being in standing-out into the clearing of being, resolutely sustaining and enduring [aussteht] it, taking it upon himself in care, whereby care names the being of Dasein (HW 348; SG 146; SZ 255-56, 294; WD 124, 172; WM 330-32, 418-19). This says not only that being is safeguarded and preserved, but that man becomes free for his ownmost possibilities. As the one needed and used, man is allowed to enter into the ownness of his essence and is held and kept there. Man is beheld [er-äuget] in the in-flashing of being, gathered into his own [ge-eignet] and made appropriate [vereignet] for the Ereignis of truth, that he may attest to this truth, sounding the word that brings the soundless Saying to language. "Hence, man's essence is discovered as the thinking-speaking response that both builds and finds a dwelling place in the house of Being"[14] (ID 26; SZ 264; TK 45; US 122, 125-26, 200; VA 40; WD 1, 119, 168).

But this "house", of course, as we have seen, is no object, no enclosure, but something like a region [Gegend] which,

> as that which counters [das Gegende], is the clearing that gives free reign [freigebende Lichtung], in which what has been cleared, along with that which conceals itself, attains the open [Freie]. The freeing-sheltering of the region is this way-making movement [Be-wëgung] in which those ways which belong to the region arise [sich ergeben] (US 197).

The region offers ways, not by effecting [bewirken] us and thus conveying us up and down paths already there [vorhandenen Wege], but in that it moves by giving way [be-wëgt], i.e., it withdraws, and draws us into the draw, forming a way and keeping it ready in the forming. Thinking therefore abides [halt sich...auf] in that region in that it walks the way of the region, and therefore moves in bringing-forth and being the way (US 178-79, 197-98, 261). What is crucial then in thinking is not a doctrine, topic, or position, but following and executing each particular step on the way, for "that which remains in thinking is the way" (EM 91; US 99; VA 13). This way, however, is not a method to be staked out according to a plan like a road or traced from one place to another (e.g., as in a series of propositions), for in pursuing the matter at stake it can happen that thinking changes on the way, and indeed, needs to speak in the language most opportune for each of the stations on the way. No, it is the going, the movement, which allows a way to arrive. Thinking is not determined by an external, remote goal such that it is a way into

alien distances, but is determined only by the going, which is
its arrival and homecoming. Hence thinking is a curious --
one might almost say wondrous -- way-building in which what is
built does not remain behind but is built into the next step
and projects forward from it. Thinking may therefore be
characterized as an enactment or performance of what it is
about, a way both built and followed. In corresponding it
follows what has been granted and sent; in responding it
builds, lays out, projects, brings-forth, the possibilities
(being) granted. Thinking discloses the "there" of being, the
placing and clearing of᾽ being that is thrownness and projection. In thinking we attain to where we already are; in
being, we attain to being in which we already are. Thinking
is both a building *and* a dwelling that lets being come to
shine in the clearing (cf. AED 82; ID 9; HW 74; US 110; WD
164-65; WP 34-35; ZD 2).[15]

3. THINKING AND POETIZING

It is noteworthy that insofar as Heidegger has sketched out
thinking in terms of a hearing-speaking response and correspondence to the call of being such that it presences in the
manner of a way, thinking has been disengaged from any necessary connection to the rule of logic and *ratio* -- and the
standard of theoretical and/or natural-scientific representation and statement -- that have held sway throughout the
history of metaphysics. This, of course, does not mean that
Heidegger has abdicated thought for "experience" (in the sense
of the German *Erlebnis*) in which the objective is referred
back to the subjective, in which life and lived experience are
referred back to the "I" (US 129-30). Thinking in Heidegger's
understanding is always a showing and laying out -- and in
this sense a demonstration -- and not an argument based upon
some privileged standpoint. Mysticism (and criticism of
Heidegger having a "mystical" element) is thereby also ruled
out, since mysticism assumes some "inner" experience that
serves as the basis and foundation of all "outward" expression
and speculation, making it an essentially metaphysical possibility.[16] The disengagement from logic and *ratio* simply means
that the latter are no longer privileged and that thinking
therefore may be manifest in many ways, as many ways as there
are "happenings" of "truth". Indeed, since language (when it
comes to thinking in a truly fundamental way) is now first and
foremost an evocative and creative articulation of meaning
that reaches out into an open future (rather than a metaphysical proposition and representation of beings as being constantly present), thinking takes on a "poetic" character,[17] as
critics of Heidegger have been quick to point out with regard
to his own thinking. And indeed, for Heidegger, "all reflective thinking is a poetizing [*Dichten*], all poetry, in turn, a

thinking" (US 267). Throughout his writings there is talk of the poetic character of thinking, that "thinking is the poetizing of the truth of being" and therefore "primordial poetry" (AED 84; HW 328-29, 372). Likewise, as early as *Sein und Zeit* (216) and thereafter, thinking is said to go on in poetry, and Heidegger's characterizations of poetry (e.g., "a saying in the manner of the making manifest that shows," hearing, corresponding and responding, the topology of being) parallel his characterizations of thinking (AED 84; EHD 55, 127; GR 30; PT 44; US 70-71, 164). Finally, insofar as language is primordial poetry [*Urdichtung*], such that even pure prose (which we might consider to be thinking's mode of expression) is poetic (EM 131; US 31), thinking and poetry seem to converge, or at least draw very close. Alike in their care of the word and therefore in the same "neighborhood" (the Saying of language), thinking must even sometimes talk with poetry to learn what is its own (US 38-39, 173, 238; WD 155; WP 45).

Yet Heidegger also notes that the thinker and poet "dwell near to one another on divided mountains," to quote Hölderlin's *Patmos*, such that thinking and poetry are like neighboring trees that remain unknown to each other (AED 85; WM 312). Philosophical thinking is never poetry [*Dichtkunst*], nor the work of a poet philosophy. The sayings of thinker and poet are not identical, but remain distinct, such that there is a luminous but abysmal difference between the two (EM 28; N I 329; VA 193; WD 8-9, 154).

How are we to comprehend all this? Does Heidegger indeed identify thinking and poetry, for all intents and purposes, such that his thinking too is "poetic", and thereby perhaps a bit muddled? Or does Heidegger give us some measure for establishing the difference between thinking and poetry that is less figurative than talk of "divided mountains" and "neighboring trees"?

The question is of no little importance, of course, but it is even more pressing for our study in that we found in the last chapter that it was the "poet" who was bound to the signs of the gods and not the thinker. Is this then where the distinction between thinking and poetry is to be made, as Heidegger himself apparently makes it when he says: "The thinker says being. The poet names the holy" (WM 312)? On this view, the poet, bound to the signs [*Winke*] of the gods, whereby the poetic word acquires its power, takes his measure from the holy, from divinity [*Gottheit*]. Here he stands bound by holy compulsion to attest to the holy, naming the gods by intercepting their signs and passing them on to his people. The poet's "imaginings", far from being fancies or illusions, are "visible inclusions of the alien in the sight of the familiar", i.e., testimony to the nearness of the god and therefore the belonging together of man and god, whence man receives the measure for his dwelling (EHD 41, 45-46, 69, 71-72, 187-89; GR 30-31; HW 273; VA 196, 198-201). It is this responding to the claim of the holy and the divine which the thinker (supposedly) cannot pretend to do.[18]

But to what extent does this constitute a difference between the thinker and the poet? As others have pointed out,[19] naming the holy and uttering being would seem to come down to the same thing, i.e., naming the essence of things and transmuting the world into word. Indeed, Heidegger says just that: the poet, too, names being. His poetry does not soar above the earth and get lost in the clouds on some flight of fancy, but "founds" and "establishes" the dwelling place of man, the topology of being, on the earth. In other words, poetry too is a saying of the unconcealedness of beings, a projective saying that opens up and originates being, truth, and history (EM 153; EHD 41, 76-77, 90-91; GR 33, 67, 69-70, 109; HW 60-63; VA 190, 192; WM 339). In this it is no different from thinking, even if it does speak of the holy. Furthermore, Heidegger, who is presumably a thinker and not a poet, talks of the gods and the presencing and absencing of the gods, sometimes (as in his essays "*Das Ding*" and "*Bauen Wohnen Denken*") without any reference to a poet. In the end, this distinction does not seem designed to bar the thinker from naming the gods and the holy, but only to suggest that his talk is not tied to such matters,[20] and may pose special problems due to the way thinking comes-to-presence. Indeed, Heidegger's reluctance to grant the saying of the gods and the holy to thinkers seems to be based by and large on the fact that their sayings, despite various attempts at deconstruction, show themselves in the form of statements and assertions rather than "song". Such an appearance might mislead us to understand the god and gods as explanations and assertions, which they are not. However, since Heidegger has tried to show that *all* saying, no matter how concealedly, is primordially disclosive rather than assertive, it appears that the naming of the gods and the holy cannot be absolutely denied the thinker and thinking. That means that this distinction is insufficient to distinguish thinking and poetry.

This last point, that the thinker may also speak of gods and is in that sense not essentially different from the poet, might be countered by pointing out that thinkers speak of the gods only subsequently, *after* the poet has spoken of them. Such a suggestion would be based on the discussion of "the others" named by Hölderlin in his poem *Heimkunft* -- the deliberating and slow ones who hear the poetic saying and are bound to its care, whereby they are the kindred of the poet (EHD 29f). This suggests that the poet is the chosen one, the *only* one who can tell us of the mysterious holy. The thinker, then, is the one who heeds this saying and *only* comments on and reaffirms the poetic word; his task is in *preserving* the truth of the poet. In this way the thinker and the poet are distinguished.[21]

However, this way of distinguishing the two, beyond the fact that it relies on construing poetry as the sole projective saying of the topology of being (which we have already discounted by virtue of Heidegger's characterization of thinking), overlooks two points. First, "preservation" and "creation" become highly ambiguous in a Heideggerian scheme of things, given the uncanny essence of Dasein as thrown projection. Who does the job of setting (bringing) "truth" into work, the "creator" or the "preserver", is undecided, since both creation and preservation belong to the one who "creates" and the one who "preserves". The "creator" is preserving the truth of being by (in the case of poetry and thinking) saying the word; the "preserver" is creating by bringing movement and happening to the word. Both can be called the creative preserving of the truth of being in the word, for both preserve the coming of what has been. The author of the word is not important, only the "happening" of truth. Both creator and preserver belong equally to the word, and "disappear" in its movement (cf. HW 58-59, 74).

Second, to divide poet and thinker in this way assumes a linear view of time which mistakes Heidegger's meaning when he says, for instance, that the poet "originally founds" the truth of a people. Origin does not refer to some fixed first point at the beginning of some chronological order [Zeitenfolge] that can then be calculated. The origin is the inception of the truth of being that is always coming, the inception of the enduring granting of being. "The powers of poetry, of thinking, of creating states, especially in the era of unfolded history, operate forwards and backwards and are generally not calculable" (GR 144).[22]

Is then everything in a hopeless muddle regarding thinking and poetry? No, but we must attend to two points. First, Heidegger talks about thinking and poetry (or "poetizing", "composing" -- dichten) in different ways in different contexts. For instance, on the one hand, both may be used by him to talk about the "narrower" areas of traditional philosophy and poetry (or poesy [Poesie], as Heidegger sometimes calls the latter). By and large, these would clearly seem to manifest themselves in different ways; beauty and "singing" pertain to the poetic word, whereas the word of philosophy is rarely picturesque or charming (cf. HW 60-61; US 195; VA 229). On the other hand, Heidegger talks about poetizing and thinking in a wider, one might say, essential sense. For instance, poetry, Dichten, encompasses the fact that truth, the clearing of being, happens in being composed [gedichtet], and can thus be claimed as the essence of art (HW 59-61) or man ("man dwells poetically", to quote Hölderlin; see VA 187ff). In this sense, thinking, however construed (as philosophy or otherwise), poetizes, composes, is "poetic", in that it opens up the clearing and concealing of being. Likewise, thinking in the wider sense of a responsive opening up and bringing

forth of beings in their being may be accomplished by poetry,
poesy, for the latter often transforms the way in which we see
the world.

Seen in this light, it begins to become clearer that the
question here is not whether, for instance, Hölderlin was a
philosopher or Kant a poet, or whether there is no telling the
difference between the poet and the thinker. What is con-
founding and question-worthy is that each, in their own way,
in difference and not indifferently, say the Same, i.e., each
opens up and contributes to the clearing of being. Here there
seems to be no clear position, as Heidegger admits:

> Poetizing [*Dichten*] moves in the element of saying, and so
> does thinking. When we reflect on poetizing, we find our-
> selves at once in the same element in which thinking moves.
> *We cannot here decide flatly whether poetizing is really a*
> *kind of thinking, or thinking really a kind of poetry.* It
> remains dark to us what determines their real [*eigentliche*]
> relation, and from what source what we so casually call the
> 'real' really stems (US 188-89; my emphasis).

We remain in the dark because we are still prone to look for
the "real" in some fixed, timeless *position*. Hence we have
the literal/metaphorical distinction which, rooted as it is in
metaphysics (SG 88-89; US 207), secured a distinction between
philosophy and poetry, and indeed, secured philosophy as the
guardian of thinking and the "really real" with its literal
language of statement and assertion, over and above the metaphor as the emotive or simply abbreviated statement of the
literal. But by this time, and this becomes our second point,
it should be clear that Heidegger is not trying to formulate a
position (regarding thinking vis á vis poetry, or anything
else for that matter), but to execute a movement, indeed, a
leap [*Sprung*] that is itself a thinking, immersed as it is in
the Saying of language. This leap of thinking, so called
because it brings us abruptly (as if at the edge of a chasm)
to where everything is different and strange, is a leap away
[*Ab-sprung*] from representational, metaphysical thinking and
an abrupt entry into that belonging from which man and being
have been assigned to each other and reach each other. It is
therefore a leap away from being as ground into the abyss [*Ab-
grund*] that enigmatically gives us measure for our being, but
which we cannot seize and grasp through calculation and measuring out from ourselves (ID 20-21; SG 159, 185; WD 48). In
this region, we are confounded, for the constraints and security of our scientific and philosophical traditions, and their
distinctions (e.g., between the literal and the metaphorical,
the rational and the emotional, etc.) have become questionable, which is as Heidegger wants it. He wants us *to think*
how it is that thinking and poetry are different ways in the
Same, and thus how one may be both poet and thinker in an

original unity, and thus ultimately a third, moving within
another thinking (N I 313).   But why think about the distinction at all if it has become so questionable and one is
looking to another thinking?   Because the movement of thinking, the leap away, does not abandon the region from which it
leaps away.   For one thing, nobody could in one single leap
take one's distance from the tradition whose well-worn tracks
of thinking fade into realms where they can hardly be seen (US
130).   But in addition, as movement and transition, such a
thinking will always speak of what it leaves behind in parting
as well as of that to which its departure submits (US 74).
What happens in the leap away is that region from which it
springs first becomes surveyable in the leap, and surveyable
in another way, such that it appropriates it in a "more original" [ursprünglicher] way.   In other words, the leap away is a
disruption, dislocation, and differing that breaks up the
rigidity and closure of that region "left behind" such that
meaning emerges and is brought forth; and it is the meaning of
being, the event of meaning in which being is given and granted, that is "more original" than any set meaning and to which
the leap of thinking attains.   Hence the leap of thinking does
not spring forward into another region separated from itself
nor away from out of the region from which it springs.   That
would be like the acorn jumping out of the ground in order to
become an oak tree, or the oak reaching up by uprooting itself.   No, the leap of thinking, like the oak, abides, abides
in a recollecting forethinking [andenkende Vordenken] (SG 107,
158-59) that reaches ahead by reaching back, that thinks what
is unthought in what has been as what is to be thought; it recalls and re-collects possibilities of being gathered [ge-]
and presencing [-wesen] in what has been [Ge-wesen].   Hence
the thinking of Heidegger is always on the way, in this case,
from within thinking and from within poetry in their established separateness, toward a wording that is simply Saying,
and thus heeding the separateness in the overcoming.   His
"other thinking", whatever it may be, is not realized except
outward from within rational exposition and the distinctions
and performances he wishes to overcome, and not once and for
all, but constantly, repeatedly.   In this way, the thinking of
Heidegger, as with all thinking, remains ambivalent, only
slowly, tentatively gaining insights into the implications of
questioning and trying to overcome the traditional modes of
thinking.   In this way, too, his remains a thinking and not
poetry.[23]
     In the end, if we remain puzzled before the matter of
thinking and poetry, this is as it should be.   We then take up
the task of thinking, which is not to make things easier with
simple answers, but to make them more difficult, allowing
ourselves to be challenged and thereby open up paths and
perspectives from which we may think what is granted, and

therefore promised, to our thinking. Our task is to see the
riddle, and abide in it (EM 12-13; HW 67; WM 372).

4. THANKING -- AND THE PIETY OF THINKING

The characterization of thinking in terms of a hearing-speaking responding and corresponding to a call has certain religious overtones, and suggests that there may be a religious
dimension to the thinking of Heidegger to be considered. Such
a suspicion is given added weight when we note two points.
First, two of the historical "happenings" of truth Heidegger
mentions (and to which we would expect there to be corresponding ways of thinking) -- namely, "experience" of the divine
("the being that is most in being") and sacrifice (HW 49) --
have religious overtones. Second, poetry, which dwells in the
same neighborhood as thinking and which thinking must sometimes consider, is linked by Heidegger to the naming of the
gods and the holy, as we have seen. We might then very well
expect to find a religious dimension in the thinking of
Heidegger and, correspondingly, some help in understanding
religious thinking and religious phenomena. It will be our
task to take up these points in this final part of the chapter
by re-emphasizing some basic points about Heidegger's thinking
in order to let this religious dimension of his thinking
appear more fully.
      We have already seen that thinking, in keeping with the
character of the disclosedness of Dasein as thrown projection,
may be characterized as a recollective forethinking which
considers the unthought in what is said, in what is having
been, as what is to be thought. Thinking then is memory
[Gedächtnis], remembrace, recollection, a thinking that recalls [andenken] being. Memory here does not involve retaining facts, reporting past opinions, tracing influences, or the
like (N II 483; WD 92, 97). Instead, memory "names the whole
disposition [Gemüt] in the sense of a steadfast intimate
concentration upon what essentially addresses us in all meditation," an unceasing, gathered abiding with what is coming-
to-presence [An-wesen] (WD 92). Memory is a retaining and
holding onto [be-halten] what holds us in our essence, i.e.,
the giving of being. Memory thinks about [denkt...an] what
remains in what is having been, and hence what is coming,
i.e., the giving and granting of being. Remembrance thinks
what is having been as what has not yet unfolded; it therefore
thinks ahead to the origin, i.e., the inception of the truth
of being, and therefore thinks history as advent. Memory is
the gathering of thinking, gathered, concentrated, on what is
at once present and past and to come. Thinking as memory and
remembrance keeps that which is to be thought about, and
thereby is the keeping [Verwahrnis] which retains it and which
it inhabits. Memory thinks about the original site, the

source from which it springs and in which it abides, recalling
and catching sight of itself as given in the coming-to-pass
and taking place of truth (AED 82; EHD 100, 143, 149-50; N II
481-82, 490; WD 1,7, 92-93, 97, 157-58; WM 411, 416). Holding
to and keeping what remains to be thought, memory means as
much as devotion [An-dacht], a word with the special tone of
the pious and piety, for it denotes the all-comprehensive
relation of concentration and gathering on the holy and the
gracious. Indeed, judging from what we found in Chapter 4,
such is the case: thinking devotes itself to the preservation, keeping, and looking-after (sparing) what calls forth
thinking, devoting its thought to and remembering [denkt...zu
und an] what is to be thought and what from the beginning
demands remembrance [Andenken] -- the giving and granting of
being in the midst of the play of the fourfold that is the
holy (cf. WD 92, 94-95, 125, 157-58)
     Through such remembrance and devotion in which thinking
preserves the truth of being that is the holy, thinking assumes the character of sacrifice. Sacrifice here is not to be
thought in terms of expediency and some effort to gain something for oneself; thinking is, in fact, quite "useless" (EM
9; ZD 1). Instead, characterizing thinking in terms of sacrifice points out that thinking is thinking only when it abandons those things by which we usually define the self and in
which we thereby try to obtain security (e.g., material possessions, ideologies, spiritual possessions and achievements
such as faith and being "born again"). In that sense, thinking is a sacrifice of ourselves for the sake of being and the
richness of possibilities -- the holiness -- given to us in
the play of the world. Sacrifice in thinking points to its
opening up, its freedom from constraint whereby man is allowed
to expend himself for the preservation of the truth of being
and what is one's own.
     Yet there is more.

> In sacrifice there occurs [sich ereignet] the hidden thanking
> which alone appreciates the grace wherewith being has con-
> veyed [übereignet] itself to the essence of man in thinking,
> in order that he may take over the guardianship of being in
> relationship to being (WM 310).

Thanking [Danken] then is also of the essence of thinking.
How are we to understand this? At the beginning of this
chapter we found that, for Heidegger, thinking is sent on its
way by the giving and sending of being. In other words, we
are capable of thinking only insofar as we are gifted or
presented [beschenkt] with being; man receives the presencing
that Es gibt as a gift. The giving provokes thought, makes us
think and therefore gives us to thinking [gibt...zu denken],
whereby our essence (thinking) is bestowed upon us. Being
favors [mögen] us, bestowing essence as gift [das Wesen

schenken] and thereby enabling [*vermögen*] us to be, making our being possible [*möglich*]. In thinking, then, we are gifted with being and thus with our essence, receiving being and thinking as gift (WD 2, 51, 85-86; WM 316; ZD 12-13). Devoting [*zu-denken*] itself to what is to be thought [*zu-Denkende*] by thinking back and recalling [*Gedenken*] that to which we owe thanks [*verdanken*] for the endowment of our essence, our thinking thanks. Our thinking is thanks-giving, for it thinks of itself as beholden [*hörig*], thinking out of a devotion that hears [*hörenden Andacht*]; it recalls its indebtedness to what provokes thought -- the call of being. Through such thanking, we think what and how we are, giving thought and re-calling where we are gathered and where we belong -- in the giving and granting of being. Thanking is thus no recompense, no repayment of a gift with a gift, but is nevertheless an offering [*Entgegentragen*] whereby we allow being, which provokes thought, to come-to-presence, by thinking. Thinking as thanking therefore does not thank for something, but only thanks for being allowed to thank (think) -- by thinking (G 64-65; WD 93-94, 158-59; WM 310).[24]

If the province of thanks-giving in our lives is construed as our religious activity, then Heidegger's account suggests a description of religion and religious activity in terms of a thinking-speaking-devoted response and recollection of one's way to be. In such a scheme, religion could no longer be seen as an assertion of what is, affirming and uncovering what is already there, but must be viewed as a destructive-creative-preserving activity which makes and lets appear what has not been seen before. Men of "faith" would not be believers who hold onto and believe in a *credo* which religion has already established, but a glorification and extolling of place which it helps open up, annihilating the rigid structures of the old and creating the structures of the new, not just at the "beginning" of a religious tradition, but throughout. For instance, the peculiar activity of prayer, even where apparently a mere affirmation ("Hallowed be they name"), might perhaps be seen as a creative activity that helps out what was into what will be, i.e., as a contribution to the future that helps shape what will be by letting it be (e.g., the Lord's Prayer as bidding: "Hallowed [will] be thy name, Thy kingdom [to] come, Thy will [to] be done ..."). Acting with faith, that faith may come to one, as the counsel of some Christians goes, or saying the name of Amida Buddha in Pure Land Buddhism -- these are other examples of prayer or religious activity contributing to the future by rising up from what has been. In this way, the man of "faith" is one who "thinks", i.e., one who comes to an understanding and into understanding, corresponding and responding to a claim put on him in which he recognizes and catches sight of his way to be.[25] By this understanding, religion would no longer be seen in terms of dogmas, creeds, institutions, or a master plan, but would be seen first and foremost as a going, being on the way and therefore being a way. Consequently it would be senseless to pass judgment on religion from the "outside" (or the "inside", for that matter) concerning the "objectivity" or "utility" of something it holds to be true and asserts. Instead, one would have to go along the way with religion and enter into "conversation" with it, not to empathize but to think about and ponder what its activity and saying discloses -- i.e., the meaning and significance that religion opens up, the claim which it reveals and which speaks to us as well.

Note that this view does not limit us to personal or "prophetic" religion versus institutional or "priestly" religion. Instead, it breaks up such a dichotomy and forces us to look at the dynamic in the institutions, sacred writings, "creeds" and "dogmas" of a religion, and the constancy, the steadiness, of even the most radical devotee, such that religious activity and institutions embody a way that reaches forward and back, bestowing and closing off, gathering together in the Same (though not the identical). In fact, given the differing and strife constitutive of the responding and corresponding that are thinking, our Heideggerian account of religious thinking calls for a radical rethinking of what constitutes religious traditions. Tradition may no longer be thought of as a "thing" to be grasped, defined, and maintained (i.e., a whole, a totality), but must be thought as a creative process in and through which an understanding of the world is brought-forth, ventured, and revealed in and out of differing from other understandings "within" the tradition, and in and out of differing from other traditions as well. Tradition becomes a series of rifts, tears, and transgressions from which meaning emerges, a compilation of glosses that does not gloss over into an ever-present Meaning. As a way or path, a tradition would not be a completely ordered totality (authored by God), but a meaning that is realized as it is laid out and interpreted, with a resultant shifting and wandering of meaning from age to age, interpretation to interpretation, text to text. We would perhaps thereby come to a better understanding of those traditions that claim no attachment to a canon (e.g., Mahāyāna Buddhism, in which "scriptures" and the lack thereof have proliferated) and those traditions in which "authoritative" texts and commentaries proliferate, though under the guise of being anchored in the true revelation of a book or person (e.g., Judaism, Hinduism).[26] In all, Heidegger's scheme forces us to look at what still calls forth to be thought in what is said and done in religious traditions, and thus to look at the bounty of what is disclosed.

Religion as thinking-speaking-devoted response and recollection of one's way to be would also effect another matter in religious thought and thinking about religion: time. The peculiar stasis of some religious traditions, particularly so-called "primitive" or traditional religions, has opened reli-

gion to the charge of being ideology, lacking thought, and
even being plain stupid. Some have not even tried to puzzle
out this peculiar stasis, but have insisted (and glorified to
the point of nostalgia) that religions, particularly in their
archaic forms, wish to overcome the terror of history and
"abolish time" (at least as we know it), as evidenced by the
myths of "eternal return".[27] But the peculiar stasis of (archaic) religions, according to a Heideggerian way of thinking,
need not be due to a wish to abolish time or to a lack of
thought, but may point to the richness of the tradition and
their myths which, as sayings, call forth "thought" again and
again in new and novel ways, bestowing and projecting and
holding open a future, even while gathering man back to the
place in which he is. Walter F. Otto, in harmony with a
Heideggerian understanding of time and history, has pointed
out that comportment toward the gods and other religious
activity in ancient and "primitive" society reaches out and
happens through past, present, and future and should not be
misconstrued in terms of the Platonic-Christian disjunction
between the eternal, divine, timeless realm and the temporal,
earthly, transitory realm that makes the latter meaningless.[28]
The myths of the birth of the gods -- which hold out the
promise and bounty of the future and the wonder of origin --
the remembrance of the past and what has been in festival and
cult through which the past is consecrated, raised up, and
transfigured into a higher order (e.g., eternal form) which
calls forth devotion, and the release of body and soul from
the fetters of utility and goals and what is familiar in these
cults and festivals in the present, whereby one is given up to
the splendor of the present and is caught sight of (perhaps by
a god) -- all this points to a thoughtful "consideration" of
man's being taking place in time. The so-called myth of the
eternal return does not abolish time but immerses man in time,
along a way, looking ahead to the origin in which he abides.
With this view, the traditional distinction between historical
and traditional-archaic religions falls away, or at the very
least becomes highly questionable, for all religions -- as
thoughtful, responsive ways of being -- carry themselves out
as ways that gather together in their happening.

The above points to the fact that myth is another area
that demands rethinking in light of our Heideggerian scheme.
As Heidegger notes, *mythos* is the saying, the saying word, and
bound up for the Greeks with *logos* (VA 248; WD 6-7). We might
then say that myth shows us a world; it is a saying, a saga
[*Sage*], that lets us in on the presencing of the divine and
the holy and what calls for thinking. If that is the case,
religious thinking does not need to "demythologize" so much as
"re-mythologize", i.e., re-say and re-call what is shown and
what is possible in an original appropriation of what has been
given and said in the myth.

These considerations give us other directions in which we
would have to change our understanding of religious thinking
given a Heideggerian understanding of thinking. For instance,
since the essence of language is showing for Heidegger, we
could very well extend what Heidegger says about "language" to
include other actions that point out and signify a world
besides the working of the word. Rite and ritual also tell of
a world and sight man within a world, visiting man with a
sense of the divine and the holy that is the worlding of the
world. Rite, ritual, and worship then need not be reduced to
emotion and "experience" (again, in the sense of *Erlebnis*) but
may be considered as more intimately bound up with the whole
"thoughtful" response and correspondence that we are urging is
at the core of religion and religious thinking. Ceremony and
ritual would then be less important as emotional comforts than
as "works" that attempt to show the divine and the holy as
they reveal themselves to a people. What is tricky and dangerous here, as with language as word, is the tendency to fall
into the rigidity and formality of ceremony, leaving us to
consider in the future how exactly we might construe the
dynamics of rite and ceremony without leaping into this same
rigidity and formality.
       The consideration of actions such as ritual and ceremony
draws us on to a consideration of the larger question of
"ethics" in the thinking of Heidegger, and its significance
for religion. Here we touch upon a controversial subject in
Heidegger, largely because Heidegger left few if any clues as
to how we are to deal with ethics in the context of his
thinking. Because of this lack, Heidegger has been roundly
criticized in a variety of ways over the matter of ethics.[29]
William Barrett has even gone so far as to say that Heidegger's thinking (and hence our own, by implication) "cannot
enter the religious because it does not arrive at the ethical."[30] Yet such indictments seem too severe; careful reading
of the criticisms made of Heidegger regarding ethics and
practical philosophy shows that things are not as bad as the
criticisms indicate, and the possibility of the ethical in
Heidegger still remains.[31] In addition, we may note that
Barrett's claim simply takes too narrow a view of the relationship between religion and ethics; ethics is only occasionally the focal point of religious traditions around the world.
       Yet the issue is important, and eventually must be faced:
does the thinking of Heidegger suggest how one is to act in a
(religious) community? The problem here seems to lie -- at
least in part -- in the lack of any models for practical
action that are not in some way indebted to the Platonic,
ontotheological tradition criticized so extensively by Heidegger. This is what presumably confused Heidegger and left him
with virtually nothing "positive" to say in this area other
than to indicate that thinking -- attending to the *ēthos*, the
abode, of man -- is a kind of "original ethics" (WM 356).

Though the matter remains puzzling, we might hazard that there
is one "model" of practical action in our tradition that might
serve as an illustration of the sort of non-metaphysical ethic
that might be developed from the thinking of Heidegger, and it
is one we have already found to be consonate with Heidegger's
thinking: tragedy. Tragedy may be seen as a "critique of
virtue," that "assesses the implications of a particular form
of virtue" by acknowledging its significance even "while recognizing its inherent limitations . . ."[32] This is because
the tragic hero suffers -- not because of some fault, but --
because of his attempt to secure the world according to a
particular ideal or set of ideals that blinds him to the way
things are, making him act inhuman. The moral of such "dreadful" (i.e., causing anxiety [Angst], which leads to thought)
action as occurs in tragedy thereby seems attuned to the
bearing of the thinking of Heidegger: virtues and ideals must
be understood and recalled as hints [Winke] that beckon [wink-
en] us toward the world and how we may be. As hints, the
ethical ideals and virtues revealed to us by a god or gods
cannot be imitated or represented, but call for a thinking
that is a resolute openedness [Ent-schlossenheit] to the way
things are, a "releasement" [Gelassenheit] of all attempts to
calculate and manipulate. Such an ethical thinking that pon-
ders the abode (ēthos) of man -- i.e., the world, the giving
of being -- and is thereby the "original ethics", would have
to learn the complexity, ambiguity, and even duplicity, of
ethical virtue and action, and the difficult responsibilities
that this entails.[33]

Perhaps most challenging in Heidegger's account of thinking as hearing-speaking-responding-devotional-recollective
thanks-giving is the way in which it makes questionable and
questionworthy to what extent, and in what manner, thanking
may be separated from thinking -- indeed, from both thinking
and poetizing. It remains open how these three -- Denken,
Dichten, and Danken -- refer to one another and are at the
same time different (WM 312). Heidegger himself remains at a
loss for the word to characterize it; the best we can do, he
says, is to call it "another thinking" (Sp 209) that is "philosophical, religious and poetical at the same time."[34] If it
is philosophical in its unriddling, questioning, provocative
force, and poetical in its evocative, projective play, perhaps
it is "religious" in its "yielding to the holding sway and
safekeeping of truth," obedient and submissive [fugsam] to
what thinking has to think about, and in that sense pious
(promos) (US 175; VA 42). The thinker is a pious one who
holds himself open, mindful of and devoted to being by maintaining it in its questionworthiness, i.e., bringing being to
light in the esteem [Ansehen] standing within it and in which
it stands, and therefore respecting being in its coming-to-
presence (cf. SG 34). If such thinking as we have then in
Heidegger is "religious", if we may use that word, it is not

in producing a worldly wisdom or a way to the blessed life (ZD 1) but in its bearing [*Haltung*] as a thoughtful knowing, a thinking that *steps back*, renouncing the claim to a binding doctrine and valid cultural achievement or a deed of the spirit -- steps back from metaphysics and what has been thought (but in no way casting it aside presumptively) into the unthought, thereby cultivating the field of metaphysics and thinking toward being as advent and *promise* (HW 210-11; ID 400; N II 41, 369-70, 390; US 109, 173; VA 183-84). But it steps back from this promise *as well*, gaining distance from that which is about to arrive in order to allow it to arrive; it does not rush ahead and speak what cannot be said. Rather, it hesitates [*zögern*], in care [*Sorge*] for the word, and gathers its bearing in a gesture [*Gebärde*] which unites within itself what we bear to being and what it bears toward us. That gesture is a hint, born of shy reverence, which does not "capture" being but ensnares [*entziehen*] us, delighting [*entzücken*] us and carrying us away into the stillness of the call, beckoning us on, to and fro, in the opening region of being in which we are (US 107-108, 119, 141; ZD 32).

If we may call this thinking by any name that gathers together all its "elements" in one saying, it is perhaps by a word Heidegger used infrequently because it can be misleading: hermeneutics. The name recalls the god Hermes, messenger of the gods, who led the dead to Hades and others up to the light, the uncanny guide full of ingenuity, cunning, and deceit who could lead one to sudden profit or loss. This was in keeping with his mysterious, nocturnal nature, the night being full of danger and yet a benefit. He was the invisible god and guide whose entry into a room was marked by *silence* coming over the gathering therein.[35] It is these characteristics that mark the thinking of Heidegger, above and beyond the interpretive aspect implied in hermeneutics (i.e., bringing messages and tidings, and thus hearing a message as well) (cf. US 120-22, 135-37, 154). It is a playful thinking that listens to the stillness, that brings man back down from the heights of his self-illuminating subjectivity to his dark, provisional essence being held out into the nothing, back down to his mortality whereby he is brought into the light. Here arises a thinking, more difficult and more dangerous because it enters the unsure path of human finitude, a thinking which attends to the message and bears it out, unriddling and thereby philosophical, riddlesome and therefore poetic, submitting to the task of bearing the message of what is granted and therefore enduring and thereby "religious". It searches out what shows itself obliquely and shines and reveals itself from beyond the horizon of intelligible representation -- silent, mysterious, perhaps divine. All this marks the thinking of Heidegger as a considerate, devotional, responsive, poetic thinking-thanking that does not account for where we are, as onto-theo-logical thinking would, but beckons us on to where we already are yet to where we must go, into the clearing and corresponding to being.[36]

> These are only hints and guesses,
> Hints followed by guesses; and the rest
> Is prayer, observance, discipline, thought and action.[37]

NOTES

1. As Heidegger himself puts it concerning a classic metaphysical problem: "The question of whether there is a world at all and whether its being can be proved makes no sense if it is raised by *Dasein* as being-in-the-world; and who else would raise it?" (SZ 269).

2. Here we are following Heidegger's thinking in WD; earlier he had used the word *Rufen* to refer to the call of being. The change in words does not seem to be critical for what is being laid out, except that *heiβen* is perhaps more flexible in its meanings.

3. Note that Heidegger's use of the word 'conscience' in SZ to help describe this calling is not at all out of place in that we traditionally think of our conscience as our guide that gives us directions and "talks" to us, albeit "in our heads". Of course, the very appropriateness of the word 'conscience' is also its inappropriateness, for its traditional connotations direct us to an inner self or soul, which Heidegger does not mean to suggest (see SZ 363). Hence the absence of the word in Heidegger's later writings.

4. Cf. EM 138, and VA 225-26 (and this entire essay on *Logos*), in which Heidegger discusses Heraclitus' saying about tending, not to the mortal speaker and what he says, but to the *Logos*, the laying that gathers (as Heidegger translates it).

This account of hearing, we should note, helps clarify why Heidegger emphasizes the unthought and unsaid in his "method" of interpreting the speaking of others.

5. Heidegger characterizes the being-a-basis of a nullity that constitutes thrown projection as *being-guilty* (SZ 376ff), trading on the 'not' and 'having responsibility for' character of our everyday notion of guilt. Here, however, the notion of guilt excludes any ideas of present-at-hand lack or privation, as in the Christian conception of our guilt because of the Fall from a primordially pure state. Here, guilt, if we may use such a term (and Heidegger does not in later writings), is our tendency to secure ourselves on some ground, in beings (God or objects) or ourselves (e.g., reason), and thereby close ourselves off when we are essentially open and opening up (disclosing).

6. George Steiner, *Martin Heidegger* (New York: Viking, 1978), p. 55.

7. "Gathered-letting-be" [*Ge-lassenheit*] might be a better translation, but it is awkward; there is probably no better translation for *Gelassenheit* than "releasement" (but see the discussion in the next chapter). However, such a translation does have a tendency to mislead insofar as it suggests a passivity and mystical disengagement from things that is in no way Heidegger's meaning.

8. Cf. Caputo, *The Mystical Element*, p. 26, and especially Krell, "Nietzsche and the Task of Thinking," pp. 264n, 295, *"Schlag der Liebe, Schlag des Todes*: On a Theme in Heidegger and Trakl," *Research in Phenomenology* 7 (1977), pp. 243-44, and "Death and Interpretation," pp. 247ff, for emphasis on the fact that anxiety, "freedom unto death" and *Gelassenheit*.are not different comportments (the first two willful, the other notwillful), and thus the emphasis on the unity of Heidegger's thinking.

9. Cf. WD 64, and Otto Pöggeler, "Being as Appropriation," p. 93. See also Pöggeler's other essays: "Heidegger's Topology of Being" and "Metaphysics and Topology of Being in Heidegger".

10. Otto, "Die Zeit und das Sein," p. 25.

11. See Chapter 3, p. 69, note 7.

12. Pöggeler, "Heidegger's Topology of Being," pp. 114-15.

13. *Brauch* is the term Heidegger uses to translate *To chreōn* in the Anaximander fragment, and *es braucht* the phrase he uses to translate *chrē* at the beginning of Fragment 6 of Parmenides (see HW 366ff and WD 115ff, respectively); Heidegger also uses the verb *brauchen* elsewhere to try to express (as in the above examples) the presencing of what is present in another way. There are overtones here of "use" and "usage" (but not in the sense of utilizing a tool) and "need" (though not in any sense of lack and wanting, or of brute necessity and blind compulsion), in keeping with the German words *Brauch*, *brauchen*, and *gebrauchen*. Theodore Kisiel and Murray Greene, in translating Werner Marx's *Heidegger and the Tradition* (translator's introduction and pp. 126-27n) suggest the word "behoove" as a translation for *Brauch*, and it does in some sense capture the sense of fittingness, propriety, and necessity Heidegger is trying to bring to light as the "relation" between being and man.

14. Perotti, *Heidegger on the Divine*, p. 80.

15. Cf. Adamczewski, "On the Way to Being: Reflecting on Conversations with Martin Heidegger," pp. 18, 22; Mehta, *The Way and the Vision*, pp. 4, 47; Steiner, p. 20; Vycinas, *Earth and Gods*, pp. 82-83.

16. See my "The Inside and the Outside: Religious Experience and Religious Thought," *Auslegung* 12 (1986), pp. 122-133. I also deal with this issue in "Mysticism and Ontology: A Heideggerian Critique of Caputo," *The Southern Journal of Philosophy* 24 (1986), pp. 463-478.

17. Pöggeler, "Being as Appropriation," p. 100.

18. Cf. Pöggeler, "Metaphysics and Topology of Being," p. 23; Vycinas, p. 286.

Compare this account of the poet by Heidegger with Walter F. Otto's in *Homeric Gods*, pp. 195-96, 206, 213, and *passim*, in which Otto describes how in the thoroughly natural Greek religion it is left to the poets, the "most enlightened of all," to see through the natural course of events to their divine background, and thus show the miracle in the natural event.

19. Sandra Lee Bartky, "Heidegger and the Modes of World-Disclosure," *Phenomenology and Phenomenological Research* 40 (December 1979), p. 234, and Perotti, pp. 98-99.

20. ". . . the thinker's task is to be open to Being -- but not specifically Being as holy." Perotti, p. 111.

21. Such is Perotti's thesis, pp. 100ff.

22. Cf. Bartky, p. 222, in which she says she can find no evidence for a poet who brought the German people (one of the three "historical" peo-

ples Heidegger cites) its characteristic modes of thought and ways of grasping being, leading her to cast aspersions on Heidegger's "thesis" that the poet founds the truth of a people. Besides the possibility of taking "poet" too narrowly, the criticism assumes chronological order.

23. Bruzina, "Heidegger on the Metaphor and Philosophy," pp. 198-99 and *passim*. See also Kockelmans, *On the Truth of Being*, pp. 196-208, and Arion L. Kelkel, *La légende de l'être. Langage et poésie chez Heidegger* (Paris: Vrin, 1980), for a discussion of the relationship between thinking and poetizing.

24. Cf. Kockelmans, "Thanks-giving: The Completion of Thought" in *Heidegger and the Quest for Truth*, pp. 163-83; Zimmerman, *Eclipse of the Self*, p. 247.

25. Cf. T. R. Martland, "To Glorify: The Essence of Poetry and Religion," *Religious Studies* 16 (1980), pp. 413-23, who gives a variety of examples, from Hinduism, to Mariolatry in Catholicism, to the Buddhist declaration of emptiness, to Christian mysticism and Confucian moral action, to help illustrate the annihilative-creative nature of religious activity, in line with the corresponding-responding-unspeaking disclosure of Heidegger's thinking.

26. See my "The Inside and the Outside," p. 129-30.

27. Cf. Mircea Eliade, *The Myth of the Eternal Return* (Princeton: Princeton University Press/Bollington, 1954), in which he insists that "interest in the 'irreversible' and the 'new' in history is a recent discovery in the life of humanity" and that on the other hand "archaic humanity defended itself, to the utmost of its powers, against all the novelty and irreversibility which history entails" (p. 48), and thereupon goes on to glorify the "paradise of archtypes and repetition" of archaic man *vis á vis* fallen, historical man.

28. Otto, "Die Zeit und das Sein," pp. 7-28.

29. Caputo, *The Mystical Element*, pp. 254-57, finds ethics disappearing in Heidegger into either "cybernetic" or the vague and undefined "original ethics". Marx, *Heidegger and the Tradition*, pp. 249-50, likewise claims that Heidegger does away with ethics, morals, and politics. Reiner Schürmann, "Questioning the Foundation of Practical Philosophy" in *Phenomenology: Dialogues and Bridges*, ed. Ronald Bruzina and Bruce Wilshire (Albany: State University of New York Press, 1982), pp. 11-21, argues forebodingly that Heidegger's thinking deprives ethics of its legitimating ground. Cf. his *Le principe d'anarchie. Heidegger et la question de l'agir* (Paris: Seuil, 1982).

30. *Illusion of Technique*, p. 251.

31. See, e.g., Gregory Schufrieder, "Heidegger on Community," *Man and World* 14 (1981), pp. 25-54, and Kockelmans, *On the Truth of Being*, pp. 250-74.

32. John D. Barbour, *Tragedy as a Critique of Virtue: The Novel and Ethical Reflection* (Chico, CA: Scholars Press, 1984), pp. ix, 154.

33. I have attempted to carry these reflections further in my paper "Heidegger, Tragedy and Ethical Reflection" (unpublished).

34. Vycinas, p. 2.   35. Otto, *Homeric Gods*, pp. 104ff.

36. Cf. Krell, "Nietzsche and the Task of Thinking," pp. 199, 211, 307; Raschke, "Religious Pluralism and the Truth," p. 41.

37. T.S. Eliot, "Four Quartets," p. 136.

CHAPTER 6

WAITING: THE FUTURE OF RELIGION
AND THE TASK OF THANKING

I said to my soul, be still, and wait without hope
For hope would be hope for the wrong thing . . .
T.S. Eliot

1. THE PROBLEM -- HOPE AND NOSTALGIA

Having now considered the thinking of Heidegger with respect
to truth, the gods, and the response that thinking itself is,
and having attempted to bring this to bear on religion and
religious thinking, we are left with an important question and
criticism of the thinking of Heidegger which is of no little
consequence for our understanding of religious thinking. That
question is one of hope and nostalgia, of whether Heidegger's
thinking is nothing but a foolish longing for a paradise lost,
for that primordial origin to which we must return if we are
to save ourselves from destruction in this nihilistic age.
The criticism has been raised in a number of different ways.
On the one hand, one may point to Heidegger's "critique" of
science which, combined with an apparent degeneracy theory of
history (i.e., metaphysics since the Greeks as the oblivion of
being culminating in Nietzsche and today's nihilistic, technological world), seems to ally Heidegger with a romantic tradition that wishes to escape the modern world and return to some
rustic idyll, free of technology. Examples which Heidegger
occasionally gives to illustrate the point of his thinking,
plus personal essays like *Der Feldweg* and *Warum bleiben wir in*
der Provinz?, laden as they are with idyllic recollections of
the life of the peasant and farmer, reinforce this criticism.
Then there is the "Heideggerian hope" which Jacques Derrida
sees in Heidegger's thinking, that tell-tale metaphysical
element which longs for safety and security and is betrayed by
Heidegger's wish to repeat the origin with "the proper word
and the unique name." Finally, there is the "faint, modest
and inarticulate" hope (as Richard Rorty puts it) in Heidegger
that seeks what is worst in the tradition -- namely, the gods
and the holy -- and through such mystifications covers up the
pressing socio-political problems of the day.[1]
   All of this is of course most important for our attempt to
understand religious thinking in a new way in light of Heidegger's thinking. Religion is often at the forefront in pointing out the nihilism of the modern era dominated by science
and technology, and that, combined with its eschatological and
soteriological hopes, leaves it open to criticism of being
nostalgic and/or hopeful to the point of "wishful thinking".

If religious thinking still harbors a disdain for modern science and technology and hopes for paradise, even after a Heideggerian transformation, we suspect that very little may have been gained by our exercise. On the other hand, if the thinking of Heidegger can provide a way for religious thinking to draw near to science and technology without disdaining them, we strengthen our resolve to look at the significance of Heidegger's thinking for religion. Hence we must now more fully address a problem we have only vaguely sketched so far -- the problem of the direction religious thinking may take in a technologically and politically dominated world. Addressing that problem in this chapter, we will 1) look at Heidegger's "critique" of science and technology and its relation to his thinking, and what that might mean for the interplay between religion and science, 2) reconsider the overcoming of metaphysics and the thinking of the origin of which Heidegger speaks, and then finally 3) consider the coming of the god or gods and what that means for (religious) thinking.

2. SCIENCE AND RELIGIOUS THINKING

The matter at stake here begins to unfold if we turn with Heidegger to modern science and ask how it *is*. Undoubtedly few would argue with Heidegger's provisional definition: science (understanding science here always as modern science) is the theory of the real (VA 46). But what exactly does that mean? What, for instance, is the real [*das Wirkliche*]? The real is the working, the worked [*Wirkende, Gewirkte*], with roots in the Greek word for work (*ergon*) and its sense of "bringing *hither* -- into unconcealment, *forth* -- into presencing [*bringen her* -- *ins Unverborgene, vor* -- *ins Anwesen*]." However, Heidegger finds that what is decisive for our modern understanding of the real is not the Greek understanding of *ergon*, but the Roman translation (interpretation) of *ergon* into *operatio* as *actus*. The real thereby becomes that which results from *operatio*; it is the consequence or outcome brought about by a circumstance [*Sache*] that precedes it, i.e., by a cause [*Ur-sache*] (thought in terms of *causa efficiens*). In other words, the real is the circumstance [*Sache*] that has been brought forth in a doing [*sich . . . herausgestellt*], that which follows from a doing [*Tun*] -- the factual [*Tat-sächliche*]. This word today means the same as assurance -- what is certain and sure. The real as factual is thus something which has come to a secure *stand*; the real shows itself as object [*Gegen-stand*, that which stands over against]. Objectness [*Gegenständigkeit*][2] characterizes the essence of the real in modern science (VA 49ff).
   The character of the real in modern science becomes clearer when we see it in light of what theory is. For the Greeks, *theōria* meant a beholding that watches over truth, a reverent

heeding of the unconcealment of beings (VA 53). But again Heidegger sees the decisive turn for our understanding of theory in the Roman translation of *theōrein* as *contemplari* and *theōria* as *contemplatio*. These translations, with their root meanings of partitioning off and enclosing sectors (e.g., Latin *templum* is a sector cut out of the heavens or the earth), direct the understanding of theory toward a seeing that compartmentalizes. Heidegger adds to that a consideration of the German translation of *contemplatio* -- *Betrachtung* (view, observation) -- and its roots in the Latin *tractare*, to manipulate, to work over or refine [*bearbeiten*], and the German *trachten*, to strive, to work oneself *toward* [*sich* zu-*arbeiten*] something, to pursue and entrap it in order to secure it. "Accordingly, theory as observation would be an entrapping and securing refining [*nachstellende und sicher-stellende Bearbeiten*] of the real" (VA 54ff).

What this means is that theory, corresponding to the way in which the real shows itself (objectness), secures a region of the real as its object-area, ordering [*stellt*] it into an interacting network [*Ge-wirk*, a gathering of that which works and is worked], setting beings in place [*gestellt*] in a sur-veyable series of related causes whereby they can be calculat-ed in their future course or verified in their past. Theory maps out *in advance* the possiblities for the posing of ques-tions, pre-setting and re-presenting [*vor-stellen*] that which things are to be taken as, i.e., what and how they are to be evaluated (as being or non-being). The theory sketches out in advance what *is*, such that any new phenomenon is refined and worked over into an object that fits into the normative objec-tive coherence of the theory. In other words, every event must be seen in the ground plan [*Grundriß*] stipulated by the theory. From this characterization of theory we can under-stand two qualities of modern science. We can understand, first, the axiomatic character of modern science. *Axiom* means evaluation in Greek, and that is exactly what theory in modern science does: it evaluates the "reality" of things according to its plan. Secondly, we can also comprehend why modern science is mathematical, for *ta mathamata* for the Greeks was that which was known *in advance* in observation and intercourse with things (numbers simply being the most striking example of what is already known). The mathematical indicates the funda-mental position we take in theory by which we observe things as already given and as they should be given, and thus lies at the heart of modern science (FD 66-68,73-76, 92ff; HW 78-79, 86-87; VA 56-57).

Modern science therefore sets upon [*stellt*] the real, and because it strives after the real in its theory, its entrap-ping-securing procedure (i.e., its *method* of striving) becomes of decisive importance. Indeed, method (technique) is of such importance that it is not just a mere instrument serving the sciences, but rather presses the sciences into its own ser-

vice. The theme of science is set up [gestellt] by, set up
within [hereingestellt], and remains subordinated to [unter-
stellt] method, such that the victory of scientific method,
rather than the victory of science, can be said to distinguish
our age.[3]   Methodology is that through which the object-area
comes into representation; it is a reckoning up [Berechnen],
meaning that in reckoning [rechnen] with things as set up in
representation, they are reckoned on, counted on, set up as
objects of expectation (i.e., as already known). This is done
by means of explanation, accounting for an unknown by means of
a known and at the same time confirming the known by means of
the unknown. The best example of this is the experiment in
natural science in which rules and laws are represented according to the ground-plan of the object-area, setting up the
conditions by which, e.g., a series of motions can be followed
in their necessary sequence, and that means, controlled in
advance by calculation (HW 79-81; US 178; VA 58).
    The more exactly and rigorously the ground-plan of nature
is projected by the method, the more exact and rigorous becomes the possibility of experiment, and thus the more certain
[gewiß] and sure [sicher] we are of beings as beings. Truth
becomes this bond between projection and being, the certainty
of representations that secures beings by positing the grounds
(reasons) by which things are. Thus there arises a continuous
call for the ground to be rendered according to which the
judgment that something is has justification, i.e., is proven
correct when it is right in relation to some secured ground.
Thus does the principle that "nothing is without ground", the
principle of ground or reason [der Satz vom Grund], hold sway
in modern science. The principle demands the universal calculatability of objects, for according to it things are considered as being [seiend] only when they are secured and certi-
fied as calculable objects, i.e., as things that can be
explained according to reasons. The principle of ground
drives man to become subject (subiectum[4]), the fundamental
certainty and absolute ground (fundamentum absolutum et inconcussum) that does not depend upon a relation to something
else; only thinking thinking itself, with a knowledge that
knows itself, is absolutely mathematical and certain. Thus
the principle of ground also drives science into an ongoing
activity [Betrieb] in which methodology continually adapts and
arranges [einrichten] itself in a new procedure until everything is arranged into a world picture [Weltbild], a struc-
tured image [Gebild] and system of beings in their entirety
that are first being and only in being to the extent that they
are set up by man who represents and sets forth [durch den
vorstellenden-herstellenden Menschen gestellt ist] (FD 103-
105; HW 83, 87-94, 100-101, 109, 238, 243-44; N II 422, 428-
29; SG 59-60, 193-98, 206).
    The projection of theory, developed by means of a corre-
sponding methodology that adapts and establishes itself at any

given time in ongoing activity and rigorously secures itself by binding itself to the project-area, constitutes the essence of modern science and transforms science into research (HW 86). At the heart of research is the method, the procedure, the technique, which secures the object-area. This securing demands specialization, a delimitation and localization of the object-area that results in greater precision (and makes our age an atomic age in more than one sense). In addition, the ongoing activity by which methodology adapts itself requires institutionalization, for if a science (actually its method) becomes an institution, this secures the ongoing activity of that method and insures the precedence of methodology over beings (i.e., that things will be seen from a [sociological, economic, religious, etc.] perspective; cf. the inertia of academies and institutions). Science becomes a business (busyness) chasing after results and calculations, its representative the research worker "who presses forward in the way characteristic of technologists in the essential sense, constantly moving, negotiating at meetings, collecting information at congresses, contracting for commissions." In all of this, the technical interpretation of thinking (calculative [rechnende] "thinking") which reckons with given conditions that are put [stellt] to a specific purpose and counts on definite results, becomes the norm; reason and logic, the "invention of schoolteachers" (with emphasis here on "school"), rule (EM 129; G 12-13; HW 77,83-85,97; VA 59; WM 303, 308-309, 314-15, 317).

This analysis suggests that we need to go one step further with Heidegger in understanding modern science, and ask about this uncanny rule of method and technique at the heart of the sciences. In other words, we need to ask about the essence of modern technology or technique [Technik].[5] Yet this is not a question confined to philosophy of science. Heidegger realizes, perhaps more than any other thinker, the extent to which technology has pervaded our lives, such that it holds sway not only in the natural sciences but in the business of culture, politics, ethics, economics, and even religion. No matter how important the questions in these other areas may be, this matter of technology is the most important, for in technology Heidegger sees the decisive way in which everything presents itself to us today and has any being at all. Heidegger saw this as early as Sein und Zeit -- the stated purpose of which is an inquiry into the meaning of being -- in which a central issue is the knowing consciousness that serves as the ideal type in the method of natural science and the emphasis placed on the present-at-hand [Vorhanden] rather than what is ready-to-hand [Zuhanden].[6] Modern technological science is therefore not merely another cultural activity that we can dispense with at will as just another viewpoint, for technology has altered the whole of the earth and man with it. Even the once pre-eminent role of philosophy in the realm of thinking has

been brought to a close by modern science (which is one reason
why Heidegger calls the sciences the completion and end of
philosophy and metaphysics), so that we now look to science
and believe that thinking is subject to the jurisdiction of
science. We need only look around us at the proliferation of
the social sciences, human sciences, historical sciences, in
addition to the natural sciences, and the extent to which
philosophy today tends to cater to them (e.g., as their "theoretical" arm), to see what Heidegger means. Far from expendable, this question of technology shows itself as what is most
worthy of thought. Properly understood, the question of technology is the question of being, of what it means to be in a
scientific-technological world (FD 13-14; HW 75-76; Sp 206,
209; VA 45, 80-81, 118-19; WD 53, 55; ZD 13, 65).

What this means is that we must recognize that there is a
meaning that is not invented or produced by us in the technical processes (including technical thinking) which lay claim
to what we do and how we *are*. Technology is no mere means or
application of the sciences, but a mode of revealing (and
concealing) in which the presencing [*Wesende*] of truth takes
place [*sich ereignet*] and holds sway in the sciences themselves. Thus in asking about technology, Heidegger is seeking
to find out *how* technology holds sway over our world; he is
asking about, and trying to understand, the *essence* [*Wesen*,
presencing] of technology, which is nothing technological, but
the prevailing truth of being at work in modern science and
technology that lays claim to the way we *are*. In such questioning, Heidegger is trying to prepare for a decision whether
science and technology are the measure of our knowledge and
thinking in which the ground and limit (and thus the genuine
effectiveness) of science and technology are determined (FD
10; G 23-24; Sp 206; VA 20-21, 41; WD 53, 142).

What does technology reveal? We can see it in the analysis of modern science given by Heidegger: "the revealing that
rules throughout modern technology has the character of setting-upon [*Stellens*], in the sense of a challenging-forth
[*Herausforderung*]" (VA 24). Nature (among other things) is
set upon and challenged to produce [*herstellen*]; earth is to
put out coal and ore, agriculture becomes a mechanized food
industry, rivers become sites for damming and hydroelectric
power. A regulated system of unlocking, transforming, stor-
ing, and distributing powers and energies from things secures
what is challenged from things, and constitutes a part of the
revealing of technology. Everything is ordered [*bestellt*] to
stand by, present-at-hand for further regulating, securing,
and ordering. Whatever is so ordered is standing-reserve
[*Bestand*],[7] a word designating the way in which anything
comes-to-presence that is so challenged-forth. Heidegger
gives the example of an airplane on a runway taxi strip,
revealed and standing there *in order* to ensure the possibility
of transportation. Standing-reserve, as the way things come-

to-presence in modern technology, even takes precedence over
subject and object such that subject and object are now stand-
ing-reserves in the purely "relational", i.e., ordering, character of the subject-object relation.   Hence even man is
sucked up into a standing-reserve under the sway of the challenging-forth of modern technology.   The forester commanded by
profit making in the lumber industry, or the often heard talk
of human resources, are just two examples of this latter point
(VA 22-25, 61).

     This last point is of no little importance, for though
ultimately (at least not yet) man is never transformed into
mere standing-reserve -- because he drives technology forward
and takes part in the ordering of technology -- the fact that
man is shown to be under some kind of claim in technology
indicates that the unconcealment of technology within which he
moves is never a piece of human handiwork.   In other words,
modern technology is no mere doing, but a claim put on man
that challenges him to approach nature as an object of research and gathers him into ordering it as standing-reserve.
This claim that challenges and gathers man to order what is
self-revealing as standing-reserve is called Ge-stell by Heidegger.   With this word (which might be translated as "Enfram-
ing"), Heidegger tries to evoke the gathered (note the Ge-
prefix) modes of challenging-revealing that lie at the heart
of technology: the representing [Vor-stellen] which sets upon
[stellt] the real, entrapping, securing, and ordering [nach-
stellen, sicherstellen und bestellen] it into a stable pool of
standing-reserve, re-presenting the real as pre-set [vor-
stellt].   However, this does not mean that Ge-stell is a genus
or essentia, a whatness under which all things are arranged.
Ge-stell is no thing, but the way of revealing that holds sway
in the essence (presencing) of modern technology.   Challenging
us to reveal the real as ordered in a standing-reserve such
that we stand in its essential realm, Ge-stell concerns us
everywhere, immediately, and not as something we can take up a
relationship to subsequently.   As in every case of essence
(presencing), Ge-stell sends man into a way of revealing and
is thus a sending of destiny [Schickung des Geschickes] that
holds sway throughout our being (ID 22-24; VA 26-28, 31-32,
38).

     However, Ge-stell is an insidious destiny, for it is a
self-perpetuating and self-intensifying revealing in which man
moves further away from seeing himself as under the sway of a
claim the more things are understood as a standing-reserve at
the command of man.   Ge-stell, in its presencing and revealing, i.e., in its claim as destiny, remains veiled and concealed, entrapping its own essential truth [Wesenswahrheit]
with oblivion, and disguising such oblivion.   Ge-stell, as a
matter of being (presencing and revealing), fails to be
thought by the challenging-forth of technological "thinking"
(which is concerned with beings).   The result is that other

possibilities of revealing are driven out, and technological "thinking" stays to one side (i.e., it is "one-sided"), though it puffs itself up in such a way as to appear quite natural and harmless, the way of seeing that can see things from *all* sides. Under the sway of technology, the essence (being) of things is forgotten, i.e., things are not dealt with *as* things, but things are annihilated and re-presented *as* object. And with such oblivion of being, the four "voices of destiny" (earth, sky, mortals, and divinities) fall silent, for with everything fixed [*gestellt*] at calculated distances in an unbounded calculatability that views all things in an identical way, there is an absence of distance, with everything becoming equal and *indifferent* (EHD 178; HW 292; ID 21-22, 24; TK 37, 44; US 212-13; VA 35, 168; WD 57-58; WM 414).

Put another way, science does not think. Moving within a domain of truth already opened up, apprehending and confirming what shows itself to be correct within that domain already opened up, science fixes on the *one* way in which whatever is of concern to it (nature, man, history, language) comes-to-presence [*anwest*] and *does not think* about anything else. For example, the physicist, as physicist, does not concern himself with the way in which nature shows itself to the artist, or to the farmer, and thus does not even think about the fact that the way in which nature shows itself to him (as object) is a showing and only one way that things may be shown; all this is *nothing* to him, as it should be if he is to be what he is. Science as science, then, does not have access to its essence, i.e., *does not think* about being, but deals with beings, and therefore does not think about the inconspicuous state of affairs -- the concealed claim of *Ge-stell* -- holding sway at the heart of the sciences (EM 28; HW 49-50; VA 61-67; WD 4, 57, 154; WM 105f, 303-304, 309, 420-21).

Under the sway of *Ge-stell*, the being of beings is now the will to power and the will to will, for things now *are* only insofar as they are products of human willing, produced by the self-assertion of man. Under the sway of *Ge-stell*, man has been transformed into a laboring animal (worker), rising up into the subjectness of his essence and thereby entering into insurrection against the earth, occupying an ultimate position beyond the earth from which to establish control over it, mimicking the God in whose image he is made. Thus is man uprooted from the earth: the earth is now an object of assault and production, man now the laboring animal that produces things. In the end, since everything everywhere *is* only insofar as it is a construct of human willing, it seems as though man everywhere and always only encounters himself, i.e., his own technological thinking thinking itself. All observation of and teaching about the world change into a doctrine of man (anthropology) which is finished with philosophy and sets it aside (e.g., Dilthey's disavowal of metaphysics) in favor of an evaluation and explanation of all things

in their entirety in terms of their relation to man. But in
this technological age which shows itself as the end, completion, and fulfillment of the history of metaphysics, man in
fact does not encounter himself. Instead, man loses what is
his own [eigen] and becomes inauthentic [uneigentlich], the
anonymous, uniform Man that is anesthetized by the giddy whirl
of products secured to meet all his needs. He verges on
becoming standing-reserve, standing by as a consumer for the
goods produced for him. The resultant lack of need plunges
human action into meaninglessness. There is no longer any
truth and openness to things standing in reserve, such that
man is unconditioned [unbedingt]; being is nothing, empty,
abandoned. Man no longer hears the call of being, is no
longer open to possibilities, and therefore no longer thinks.
Intelligence becomes something cultivated, an organized clev-
erness in examining and calculating given things that is an
asset, or an ornament (cf. the professor who has gone to
another country on his sabbatical to "experience" another
culture), but ultimately simply the organization of a lack.
Nihilism descends upon man. Thus does Ge-stell show itself as
the supreme danger to man.[8]
    This however does not serve as an indictment of technolo-
gy, just as Heidegger's remark about science not thinking is
no reproach. Despite the sarcasm and venom in some of his
observations, Heidegger is in no way seeking to pass judgment
on the utility and worthiness of science and technology and
thereby to replace or reform them. As Heidegger notes, reac-
tive negations of the age and flights into tradition that seek
salvation in the restoration of what is past lead to blindness
and self-delusion concerning what is at stake in technology --
namely, Ge-stell, which names being itself and the claim it
puts on us. Romanticism, as much as a scientific and technological thinking which thrusts technology forward as the road
to a happier life, remains bound within technological thinking. Attempts at passing judgment and evaluating the present
age, whether in terms of decline and loss, catastrophe and
destruction, or in terms of human happiness and a better
tomorrow, are all technological behavior which fail to glimpse
the worthiness of questioning our present metaphysical position. Both advocates and opponents of technology see it in
terms of a human fabrication, in terms of things (machines,
tools, instruments) which, given an appropriate moral constitution or grounding on the rock of ages, could be mastered or
controlled or disposed of by man at will. They fail to see
technology in terms of its essence (presencing), which is a
matter of being itself and which therefore cannot be mastered
or overcome by man (since being lays claim to our thinking and
enables it to be). Only by thinking beyond what is simply
present-at-hand and asking about the essence and presencing of
technology do we respond to such a claim and discover the
possibilities of thinking that spring from being itself and

transform us in our relationship to technology (G 17, 22; HW 95-97; ID 29; SG 41; TK 38, 45-46; VA 13, 33, 35-36; WD 14, 154-55; WM 392).

In other words, as Heidegger quotes Hölderlin: "But where danger is, grows/The saving power also." The salvation -- and here saving again means being let into one's own essence -- which both the technologist and the romantic seek (each in their own way) only comes from within the danger (Ge-stell), for the danger is a matter of being itself which lets man into his essence. Thus the ambiguous nature of all revealing and truth -- that the concealment and oblivion of being also serves as a safekeeping [Wahrnis] and guarding of being -- once again emerges in the context of the essence and presencing of technology. In this case, being becomes questionable in a technological age (being is nothing, a vapor and fallacy), but is thereby questionworthy. Things still are, and we begin to wonder how we are to think essence (being) in a more suitable way (than as substance). Science concerns itself with beings and beside that nothing, and thus shows its own limitation to one way of presencing (objectness), and thus makes this and other modes of presencing (ways of being) worthy of questioning (e.g., what is the unity of these manifold ways of being?). And Ge-stell, the danger, drives all planning and calculating and securing to the incalculatable, the infinitesimally small and extraordinarily large, beyond representation and therefore beyond the ordinary understanding of thinking, which now becomes questionable. Thus does Ge-stell not only name a danger, a setting-upon [Stellen] in the manner of technological thinking that threatens to block every view of the Ereignis of truth and being, but also a promise of a placing and presenting [Stellen und Dar-stellen] which lets what is present come into unconcealment and recalls the original unity of technē and poiēsis in Greek thought. In Ge-stell lies a strange ownership and appropriation [Vereignen und Zueignen] that is a revealing, sending, and destining of being, granting man entrance to the truth of being. Concealed in Ge-stell lies a hint of Ereignis, the taking place and coming-to-pass [sich ereignen] of being that claims man and brings him into his own. Thus does the turning from technology to another thinking take place from out of the danger, from man's openness to understanding the essence of technology and thereby taking over the freeing claim of technology (HW 95-96, 112-13, 373; ID 24; WD 57; WM 105ff, 415).

Ge-stell then serves as a kind of "prelude" to Ereignis, but this way of putting it, as well as Heidegger's talk of a turning and change in destiny to another beginning, should not lead us to think Ge-stell and Ereignis (with its gathering in the Geviert and corresponding "poetic dwelling") as historically disjunctive, thereby once again raising the spectre of romanticism.[9] Getting over and surmounting [verwinden] a particular destiny of being -- in this case, Ge-stell -- does

not allow itself to be construed logically, historiographical-
ly, or metaphysically as a sequence belonging to the process
of history. In the turn, technology would not be done away
with, struck down, and absolutely destroyed. Instead, the
mere dominance of *Ge-stell* would turn into a more original
appropriating [*anfängliches Ereignen*] that would take back the
world of technology into service in the realm of *Ereignis*.
That is to say that man would achieve an appropriate relationship to the essence of technology by letting it come to its
appropriate place, in its proper limits -- within the clearing
of being -- and thereby achieve its real "movement" [*eigent-
liche >›Bewegung‹‹*] (ID 25; Sp 214; SZ 13; TK 37-39). A new
image of science might begin to emerge, one that thinks (which
Heidegger considers the leading atomic physicists of his day
to be doing; FD 51) or is perhaps more "poetic" in conception, given the aesthetic qualities of simplicity, symmetry,
and elegance that seem to go into making up scientific theory.
Indeed, a Heideggerian conception of science could help develop a more historical and topological form of "objectivity"
(*Sachlichkeit*) and a more hermeneutical and less mathematical
notion of rationality by laying stress on discovery and the
dynamics of truth interpreted within a finite, language-bound,
holistic context. In addition, a Heideggerian conception of
science could very well aid recent attempts to rethink science
in the philosophy of science (e.g., Thomas Kuhn, but probably
not Paul Feyerabend). Finally, such a Heideggerian conception
of science would also correspond well with the new cosmology
that has arisen in the sciences by themselves, particularly
the conception of reality in the physical sciences -- i.e.,
reality conceived as a system of indeterminately inscribed
processes which lack a hard-core foundation, a fluid and
ephemeral constellation of events which appear under different
circumstances at different times.[10]
But with the emergence of such a new image of science, the
"conversation" between science and religion, long a bitter one
in the West, changes as well. We could very well cite the
onto-theo-logy of both traditional science and religion as the
source of their conflict. That is to say, the dispute between
science and religion has been over where the *foundations* are,
the success of science without the postulates of religion in
modern times weighing heavily in favor of science, even for
religious persons (who have been systematically retreating in
their assertions about much of the world ever since the Church
versus Galileo).[11] But if both science and religion are now
considered anew in light of Heidegger's thinking as dealing
less in assertions and foundations and more in terms of parti-
cipants in the conversation of mankind that is open to thinking and dwelling on the earth, the matter changes. For one
thing, since it deals in but one way in which things may show
themselves, the dictatorship of science comes to an end, with
consequences of no little importance for the strategies of

both sides. For instance, the invocation of Western science as the sole arbitrator of the facts by cultural anthropologists in passing judgment on "primitive" religions (and, one suspects, by implication, on other religions as well) as irrational is unwarranted, for Western science is no more rational than "primitive" religion given the standards set up by such anthropologists (e.g., Western scientific facts are also theory-laden, there is also a tendency to avoid anomalies, etc.). Likewise, a sort of "cognitive bargaining" with modern scientific consciousness on the part of theology and religious thinking, such that religion is shown to have a meaning or utility for scientific consciousness on the latter's terms (e.g., it fulfills a "need") is unwarranted, for it gives an undeserved authority and certainty to that ordinary, modern scientific consciousness. But now, just because we cannot reasonably presume Western science and the modern scientific consciousness as a certain ground against which religious thinking must be gauged, neither are we allowed to assert just anything at all on the part of religion. "Primitive" religion is not made "right", or just as "right" as Western science, given its own standpoint; nor does some neo-orthodox reassertion of tradition become correct either. Such talk, as we have noted, stays within the context of scientific-technological thinking and ends up being as absurd as it sounds. Hence, though the supremacy of scientific truth as final judge comes to an end, religious advocates are denied the security of retreating into the assertion of their own paradigm based on their own privileged experiences which we must enter according to certain procedures (e.g., affirming faith) if they are to be understood. Religious thinking, if it is to have any bearing on the world, must try to sight its way in and through the technological world, learning to dwell at home in *this* world in conversation with science and technology, since science and technology have been successful in evoking new meaning and possibilities by letting beings show themselves in other ways. Religion cannot make believe that science and technology do not make a difference. Likewise, it will not help, as Heidegger says, to take over Zen Buddhism or some other Eastern experience of the world in order to turn around the sheer dominance of technology. The turn eastward would then be no better than a neo-orthodox reassertion of tradition or a retreat to the experiential self common in liberal Protestant thought. What must be recognized is that even in the turn eastward in the search for new possibilities for (religious) thinking (which we are in no way denying), the "conversion" sought must still be done with the help and with a new appropriation of the European tradition from whence technology springs, for to make an Eastern tradition understandable we must think about -- must think in, through, and out of -- the technological thinking in which we dwell and which gives us the possibilities for understanding the East.

This undoubtedly holds true not only for Westerners but for those of other traditions who lament the Europeanization of the earth and man at the expense of other traditions. Insofar as such an encroachment has taken place, it will not do to simply (re)assert one's own tradition and brush technology aside selectively. One cannot fly around the world in jet airplanes advocating a return to traditional ways without appearing both reactionary and absurd. Thinkers of other traditions might do well to think along with Heidegger and first try to understand the nature of scientific-technological thinking and its *essential* danger. Such understanding might then yield authentic possibilities for developing one's own tradition. Thus, ironically, Heidegger might be found to have a universal significance in the very Europeanization of the earth which he lamented.

But even beyond these considerations of traditional problems between the two separate concerns of science and religion, a Heideggerian rethinking of both science and religion draws them both closer together in much the same way that we found thinking, poetizing, and thanking drawing near in Heidegger's general reconsideration of thinking. Science takes on a certain "religious" character not totally unfamiliar among scientists; the religious emotion that shows itself in some of Einstein's thoughts about the universe is but one example of this tendency on the part of scientists. Of course it may be a bit hard to swallow that "the overcoming of metaphysics drives science to the frontiers of the unspeakable and holy mystery" and "toward the gateway to the universe's inmost 'holy of holies',"[12] but if religious thinking means going out into the world and learning to think and dwell within that world, science is going to be a part of or partner to it, and religious thinking a part of or partner to science. This does not mean that either one or the other must rearrange its doctrines in order to include the other; indeed, this is precisely what should *not* be done. Such rearrangement either reduces religious doctrine to scientific doctrine for the sake of desperately holding on to those religious doctrines (in whatever form), or it willfully narrows the vista science opens up for us for the sake of faith. Instead, each must be aware of and perhaps draw on the other in a spirit of conversation in order to draw out new possibilities for thinking. And this not unexpectedly goes back to what first started science on its way with the Greeks. With the Greeks, the world was their temple, and a knowledge of the divine emanated from the vitality and movement of that world. The divine was the sanctity of the natural itself and could be sought, experienced, and received by the pious soul and great heart who went out and thought about the world. Hence the scientific investigation could be one with their "spirituality", not as an apologetic for their "spirituality" but as a way in which man discovered the unfathomable and ineffable possibilities

open to him and let him be who he is. The result, at least
for a time, was that their "spirituality" harmonized with
their experience of the natural world. Perhaps a further
rethinking of science and religion after Heidegger could yield
a similar accord.

3. DECONSTRUCTION AND RELIGIOUS THINKING

As we have already noted, the issue of nostalgia in Heidegger's treatment of the matter of modern science and technology is but one way the problem of nostalgia and hopefulness
arises in the thinking of Heidegger. Talk of repetition, the
step back, the possibility of the restoration (salvation) of
man by asking the question of being, of understanding the
Greeks (and others) "more originally", of destroying ancient
ontology and overcoming metaphysics (presumably for something
better), of the truth and house of being -- all this sounds
like a longing for a new age in which one can *finally* repose
in the fullness of being brought to presence. Looking at this
array of Heidegger's own phrases, one can easily see why
Jacques Derrida might criticize Heidegger for "logocentrism"
and for still being caught up in a metaphysics that longs for
the absolute and final presence of being. The very questionableness of these formulations in a thinker such as Heidegger
who wants to get over metaphysics makes his thinking all the
more thought-provoking and question-worthy, giving us the
opportunity, if not indeed compelling us, to further clarify
Heidegger's thinking and its "religious" dimension.
   To address this problem of hope and nostalgia in Heidegger
in general, it seems best to take up once again this matter of
nihilism and the oblivion of being which Heidegger associates
with metaphysics and which is somehow to be "overcome". Specifically, we turn to Heidegger's essay "*Zur Seinsfrage*",
which addresses the problem of "the line" that marks the zone
of completed nihilism and which we must presumably cross over
in order to get from our nihilistic, technological age and its
forgetfulness of being to an age in which being emerges anew
and nihilism is overcome. However, in considering the zone of
this line, Heidegger does not talk so much about crossing over
the line (*trans lineam*) as he does about the zone of the line
itself. Why? We need only recall a saying by Heidegger in
Was ist Metaphysik?: Dasein is being held out into the nothing (WM 115). In other words, as we have seen over and over
again with Heidegger, the nothing belongs to the essence of
man, and not accidentally, as something added. This means
that if, in nihilism, the nothing attains dominance in a
special way (i.e., being in its oblivion is nothing), then man
has an essential share in nihilism and must be said to belong
to the essence of nihilism and its completion -- and this at

the same time as he helps make up the region of being.   Man
himself then,

> but not he for himself and particularly not through himself
> alone, *is* this zone and thus the line.   In no case is the
> line, thought of as a symbol of the zone of completed nihil-
> ism, like something impassable lying before man.   Then the
> possibility of a *trans lineam* and its crossing also vanishes
> (WM 412).

What this means is that Heidegger's talk of overcoming metaphysics (nihilism), though sometimes expressed in metaphysical
terms (especially early along his path of thinking), does not
have a traditional, metaphysical "aim".   The goal of overcoming appearances and mistakes in order to affirm some secure
foundation and/or *telos* is not what Heidegger seeks.   This is
because nihilism (metaphysics) is not something diseased which
we can claim to cure by cutting it out and putting it aside.
Nihilism belongs to the essence (being) of man and is therefore, in a certain sense, unavoidable.   Overcoming metaphysics
must be thought instead in terms of abandoning the metaphysical interpretation of metaphysics, i.e., it must be thought in
terms of getting-over [*Verwindung*] metaphysics (N II 367-68,
370; US 116; VA 79; WM 386-87, 411; ZD 25).
     To understand this we might once again consider the char-
acterization of man as the line, being held out into the
nothing.   Such a characterization suggests the image of man
standing at the edge of an abyss,[13] at the limit of what is
and hence on the threshold -- between what is familiar and
strange, what has been thought and unthought, at the often
indeterminate boundaries of language and thought (tradition).
Our (metaphysical) impulse is to turn away from the abyss, to
turn around and turn our backs on the abyss and find secure
ground, for the edge is dizzying and dangerous; or, in what
amounts to the same thing, we see the abyss and feverishly
attempt to fill it in (we *plan*) so that we make progress and
drive it away.   Overcoming metaphysics means getting-over the
fear and trembling (Heidegger likens it to getting-over grief
or pain; TK 38) at the edge of the abyss that leads to our
flight forward or back.   Overcoming is a call to step-back to
the edge, back to where we already and always *are*, for it is
only from out of the limits and boundaries that we are allowed
to be.   It is a call to step back near the origin [*Ur-sprung*,
or *An-fang*, or *Her-kunft*], into that fateful moment that marks
the boundary, the conflict between what is familiar and
strange, the cutting edge between past and future.   Origin as
Heidegger invokes it has nothing to do with a fixed point in
some chronology, but has to do with the emergence of the
enduring granting of being that takes place in thinking the
tradition.   The word "origin" reminds us of our sense that the
beginning is somehow the strangest [*Unheimlichste*] in that the

future opens up in ways not seen before (unthought) and still
not clearly grasped, with new ways of being *emerging* and
taking shape. At the edge, near the origin, man peers into
the dark mystery [*Geheimnis*] and question that is the essence
of man, and from which *springs* [*springen*] a wealth of possibilities to be seized [*fangt*] (cf. EM 149, 154, 164; HW 1, 44-
45, 64; US 190; WM 412).

Thus homecoming -- becoming at home in nearness to the
origin (nearness to being) and thereby coming to know the
mystery as mystery (EHD 24; WM 337-38) -- does not constitute
a return to what has been (metaphysics), but is a step back
out of this metaphysical heritage to the *essence* of metaphysics. Metaphysics is renounced [*verzichtet*]; we deny [*versag-
en*] its claim to safety and security. In this renunciation it
is "destroyed", disassembled, deconstructed, such that it no
longer has determining power. However, in this renunciation,
beyond denying the claim of metaphysics, we deny ourselves to
the claim that we once willed in metaphysics, and are transformed. The renunciation is itself a saying [*Sagen*] by which
what has been said is *drawn again* to the edge of the abyss and
re-peated [*wieder-holen*; both drawing again and repeating] by
laying it *out* and *interpreting* [*aus-legen*] it in such a way
that it is recalled to its origin (thought "more originally"
than by everyday thinking). Metaphysics, now for-given [*ver-
ziehet*, related to *verzichten*], is taken up and "incorporated"
(*verwinden* has this sense as well) in the projective saying
that fore-goes [*ent-sagt*] the former claim and instead commits
[*sagt . . . zu*] itself to being, going forth to that place at
the edge of the abyss in which we *are*. Metaphysics is not
restored in our getting-over, for-giving, and "incorporating"
it, but it forms the "nutrition", so to speak, for our thinking by giving-forth possibilities of our building and dwelling
where we are, in much the same way as the crops of a field --
cleared and plowed under -- provide the nutrition and possibility for new growth to emerge. Renunciation of metaphysics
gives the "promise" [*Zusagen*] of a saying which is attuned to
the abyss and therefore to being (cf. AED 90; EM 42; HW 100;
ID 41-42; N II 365, 368; SZ 30-31; US 99, 168, 222-23, 231ff;
VA 72, 79; WM 335-36, 367, 405, 416, 423).

What must be recognized, contra Derrida, is that despite a
tendency sometimes to overinterpret and thereby seemingly to
make a claim for *the* interpretation of a text, Heidegger is
not the usual hermeneutician in the manner of, say, Paul
Ricoeur. Heidegger does not see hermeneutics in terms of a
two step process of suspicion and deconstruction first and a
reconstruction, exegesis, and reconciliation second, under-
pinned by an overabundance of constantly present meaning that
assures rejuvenation, as is the case with Ricoeur's eschatological hopes of reconciliation in the Sacred.[14] With Heidegger, the two "movements" of destruction and reconstruction are
fused in the one act of thinking and therefore ultimately do

not even apply. Metaphysical promises are renounced along
with metaphysical destructions and overcomings such that
Heidegger denies us to the claims of metaphysics and holds
open the determination of the essence of man as a question.
With Heidegger, being withdraws, the nearness and origin that
are the granting of being remain distant even in drawing near.
Such distance in drawing near means that being and origin
remain as coming -- this is the "promise" -- and yet remain as
oblivion -- this is the "danger". Oblivion and safekeeping of
being, danger and salvation, remain one and the same. We find
ourselves in a twilight zone of ambiguity that has yet to be
decided, augering a new dawn -- or a new night. Beginning and
end, origin and future, converge and vanish here, leaving us
to experience the peculiar revealing and concealing of being
that does not know whither it is going except in the going,
that knows the danger, uncertainty, and indeterminacy of the
path of thinking, but knows it also as more promising than any
locale yet conceived in the West. Here we are neither opti-
mistic nor pessimistic, as if man and being were a business
transaction to be settled as successful or unsuccessful. Urging an anticipatory restraint that holds itself open to being
(as both "hope" and "hazard") by renouncing metaphysics and
thereby renouncing both flights into tradition and flights of
fancy into the future, Heidegger calls on us to hold, respond,
and correspond to the difference in which we dwell and
sight/site ourselves along the path of thinking (and poetizing, and thanking) -- along the line that traces the boundaries of language and tradition and thereby outlines the possibilities of thinking that transform and perhaps restore man to
his proper essence.[15]

As it stands, Derrida and his deconstruction, in its often
self-conscious recollection of Nietzsche (and perhaps Hegel),
seems much more susceptible to a Heideggerian critique than
Heidegger does to a deconstructive critique. Deconstruction
offers a constant critique through an endless proliferation of
signs, but no apparent point to the critique other than the
critique itself. Even if one avoids charging that this mirror-play of reflections is an example of "bad infinity" or
Kierkegaardian "aestheticism", one cannot help but see this
"free play" as a reflective method for *manipulating* various
signifiers in a system of signs and thus a willful dissemina-
tion of fictions and constructs that remains bound to the
Cartesian/metaphysical tradition of rendering man the master
of the world. Deconstruction, like Nietzsche, would seem to
covet the immortality of Dionysus, the *technician* and *spectator* -- but *not* the *mortal participant* -- in the play of the
world. Deconstruction flies above the earth, without gravity
(indeed, comedically), taking its revenge against the earth
(for its lack of absolutes) by deconstructing it and itself to
pieces, rather than dwelling on the earth, measured out between earth and sky. Such a view is strengthened when we see

how deconstruction and theology have taken to one another as of late. Some have likened Derrida and deconstruction to the "religious stage" in Kierkegaard, turning deconstruction into an iconoclastic version of the Protestant Principle in which an antisystematic, death of God a/theology can become a radical Christology, and the death of God can mark the omnipresence of God and the eschatological event that brings history to a close. Thus, instead of tragedy, we get the farce of a divine comedy.[16]

Rather than the security of metaphysics, whether negative or not, Heidegger practices that thinking-within-anxiety that is *Gelassenheit*, "released" from beings and open to the mystery, a combination of suspicion and innocence that resolutely holds to the path of thinking on the outskirts of language and thought, walking a tightrope between the dark yet revealing abysses that are both past and future. Here is that reaching into the abyss -- the way a tightrope walker maintains his balance, reaching out in both directions -- whence Heidegger finds the possibility of a turning of man in his essence and thus one's proper balance on the path of thinking. Here one is gathered together, collecting oneself and concentrating, anxious yet calm, daring and venturesome in one's openness, yet discreet in one's awareness of concealment (e.g., one's dependence on the onto-theo-logical character of Western language). The openness and willingness to know and to learn that characterizes such thinking never becomes a will to know and with that a will to power; it restrains itself and knows to let beings be, to know and allow the concealedness as well as the openness of things, to say "yes" and "no" to beings and to ways of being, to engage oneself with beings and allow oneself to be conditioned [*be-dingt*, be-thinged], but in that, heed the openness and truth of being and let that, not beings, hold sway. There is a rest and stillness to the balance thus struck, but movement as well, as thinking resolutely holds to the possibilities of thinking that spring forth *on the way*. Such thinking waits in that it waits on (tends to) being and thereby opens itself up to possibilities that are sent and given to us (that are coming to us) in our destiny. But such waiting is not passive and inactive; it engages itself with beings, thinking beings in their being and bringing them to appearance, thereby thinking forward without prophetic claims into the coming time in terms of those traits in the present age that have been scarcely thought through and yet in which being calls to us (cf. EM 23; G 45, 51, 71 and *passim*; HW 55, 71, 297-98; Sp 214; SZ 447; WM 111, 117-18, 188).

Such thinking is as much comportment [*Haltung* or *Verhalten*] and bearing as anything else -- an "attitude" that is gracious and considerate and abides in holding [*halten*] to the wonder and mystery of being. Jean Beaufret has even thought to consider *Gelassenheit* as *désinvolture* -- a graceful bearing and demeanor[17] which allows itself to embrace and be embraced by being, thereby overcoming *l'esprit de ressentiment* and revenge which Nietzsche found (and Heidegger finds) in Platonism (metaphysics).   It is here we have sought hints of religious thinking, for such thinking is only possible if there is an attentive openness for the holy, i.e., a reverent paying heed to the whole of being (i.e., the ambiguous revealing *and* concealing of being).   It thinks about [*denken . . . an*] this origin in awe and shyness [*Scheu*] -- awe before the vastness and mystery of the "promise" of being, shy and discreet in its attentiveness to the withdrawal and concealing of being.   In thinking about the origin, it clears and unfolds that region of the essence of man in which one remains [*bleibt*] at home in the abiding [*Bleibende*], that site and source that is the heart and spirit [*Gemüt*] of man.   Such thinking must have courage [*Mut*], but not a courage of one's convictions; it must be a courage to attack one's convictions, a questioning, a *sacrifice* which gives itself up in order to expend itself for the preservation of the truth of being and what is its own, abandoning those fugitive concealments by which it tries to secure itself.   Such courage slays the dizziness at the edge of the abyss, giving thinking an equanimity and calm [*Gleichmut*] that allows one to endure the nothing and thereby recognize that region of being whence every being returns into what it *is* and *may be*.   Such thinking also shows forbearance and patience [*Langmut*], not rushing ahead to secure itself but lingering, waiting, being drawn [*anmuten*] to what is noble in one's essence, having a presentiment [*Vermuten*] of the noble mind [*Edelmütige*], i.e., coming to know what is one's own. Though marked by a certain poverty [*Armut*] in its sacrifice of what it has, it is thereby rich in possibilities, willing to be rich by surpassing itself, overflowing in order to flow back to itself, back to the simple, onefold origin that is one's own [*Eigen*] and one's first and only "possession" [*Eigentum*].   Bearing a certain gentleness [*Sanftmut*] and grace [*Anmut*], poorer, simpler, tenderer yet tougher, quiet and economical of speech (reticent), calm, patient and self-sacrificing, thinking about being and therefore what is one's own, one leaps over all despair and sadness to a knowing cheerfulness [*wissende Heiterkeit*] in which one receives hale [*Heil*] and a boundless steadfastness through in-dwelling [*Inständigkeit*][18] in that which regions [*Gegende*], *Ereignis*, the holy (cf. AED 81, 89; EHD 94, 118, 122, 131-33; HW 360-61; G 59-61, 64; WD 67, 124; WM 118, 184, 307-308, 311, 342).   Put succinctly, one's thinking becomes gracious in its for-giveness of what has been and in receiving the gift of being that has been granted to it, giving thanks for the "message" and "meaning" given in the gift of being by giving forth and laying out what has been received in interpretation.   Thus do we attain to what is our own, becoming whole, holy, and saved.

4. FAITH AND RELIGIOUS THINKING

Of course, such a noble, high-minded [*hochgemute*] man as sketched above is not the usual "ideal" of the religious man and religious thinking. The usual responses to Heidegger by theologians (whether negative or positive) show this in their wish to overcome the thinking-*within*-anxiety that characterizes the thinking of Heidegger (see Chapter 2). The lamentations of John Caputo at the end of his study on the "mystical element" in Heidegger epitomize such a theological attitude. Caputo complains of the danger of Heidegger's path (as compared to Meister Eckhart's!), in which virtually all possibility of hope has been undermined. Heidegger's is a "finite hope" which is never insulated from despair, bound up as it is with a "finite" being that is "permeated with negativity" and the waiting of which acknowledges the possibility of a final disappointment. Heidegger's eventual reference to "a god" who is not the lord of history, rather than to "God Himself" who governs the missions of being with loving care, is for Caputo final proof of Heidegger's transposition of *Gelassenheit* into a non-religious setting where we are divested of God and worlds apart from "the absolute hope of the religious man."[19]

This complaint is interesting not only because it draws a very clear picture of how religion and religious thinking have traditionally been construed in the West -- a picture against which we have been arguing with the help of Heidegger throughout this work -- but also because this complaint runs counter to Richard Rorty's "pragmatic" critique of Heidegger. Rorty's complaint is that the invocation of the holy and the gods by Heidegger is a faint and inarticulate quest for what should no longer concern us (i.e., otherworldly matters) when we have pressing matters within the "real" world ("between beings and beings") to concern us.[20] Both complaints (which are theistic and atheistic respectively) place the other and its bearing on Heidegger's thinking in question, leaving us to discern 1) to what extent we are "divested of God" or waiting and hoping for a god in the "religious" thinking that we have been developing with the help of Heidegger, and 2) of what good, of what use, is the religious thinking we have been developing, whether we are seeking a god or God Himself or not?

To approach these questions it is important that we come to an understanding of Heidegger's own characterization of his thinking as "god-less". Though it is true that in later works he talks about the divine, the holy, the god and gods, we have seen that none of this has anything to do with the foundationalism usually associated with such talk, i.e., gods are not something to be believed in, providing foundations for arguments or constituting fundamental points of departure for making assertions about the world (see Chapter 4). In fact, the god and gods have much more in common with the nothing which mortal man must confront on the path of thinking in

coming into what is his own.   In this vein, what is perhaps
most striking in the later works of Heidegger is the extent to
which he talks about the absence of or lack of the gods and
god, or the extent to which he does not talk about the gods or
god at all, and remains silent.   Heidegger himself notes this:

> Someone who has experienced theology in his own roots, both
> the theology of the Christian faith and that of philosophy,
> would today rather remain silent about God when he is speak-
> ing in the realm of thinking.   For the onto-theological
> character of metaphysics has become questionable for think-
> ing, not because of any kind of atheism, but from the exper-
> ience of thinking which has discerned in onto-theo-logy the
> still *unthought* unity of the essence of metaphysics (ID 45).

To this we might add that the questionable character of metaphysics has not come about because of any kind of theism
either, despite talk by Heidegger of "the divine god" elsewhere (ID 65).   Thinking is as little theistic as it is atheistic (WM 352), for such things as the affirmation or denial
of God belong to metaphysics, which Heidegger is trying to
overcome.   Such overcoming is a rethinking (a questioning) of
all theological constructions, both theistic and atheistic,
and a "return" to the ontological *primordium* (i.e., the clearing of being and event of mean-ing) antecedent to either
theistic or atheistic hypotheses, whereupon these traditional
categories do not apply.[21]
   We can see, then, that Heidegger's silence concerning
theism or atheism is not nothing, nor does it mean that he
knows nothing of the divine, nor that he lacks the strength to
name God.[22]   This silence is something else, which we begin to
discern in the following passage:

> With the last stroke [i.e., midnight] the stillness becomes
> yet more still.   It reaches out even to those who have been
> sacrificed before their time in two world wars.   The simple
> has become simpler.   The ever Same astonishes [*befremdet*] and
> unleashes [*löst*].   The address of the pathway is now quite
> clear [*deutlich*].   Is the soul speaking?   Is the world speak-
> ing?   *Is God speaking?* (AED 90; my emphasis)

To this we might add a passage from an "autobiography" that
Nietzsche wrote at the age of 19, and of which Heidegger takes
special note (WD 75):

> Thus man grows out of everything that once embraced him; he
> has no need to break the shackles -- they fall away unfor-
> seen, when *a god bids them*; and where is the ring that in the
> end still encircles him?   Is it the world?   *Is it God?* (my
> emphases)

There where the ring encircles man, where the simple, silent abysses that are the past and future encircle the moment (of vision) [*Augenblick*] in which man is going, tracing the boundaries of language and thought that circumscribe the possibilities of thinking open to man -- there, *God is a question*; the divine becomes what is questioned [*Gefragte*] and called upon [*Gerufene*] as a possibility to be thought. (Recall that, after realizing that 'God is dead', Nietzsche's madman begins to ask questions, and "seeks" God.) Heidegger's silence is a questioning, not only because any sort of "being-towards-God" must be left open and without decision in recognition of the obscurity of the gods and the holy in the present age, but also in recognition that perhaps the divine is more godly in mortal questioning than in the self-secure certitude of onto-theo-logy (N I 324). The suggestion is that the holy and the divine only intimate themselves when we *think* about the mysterious and indeterminate *events* that befall us in our going along the path of thinking. Heidegger's silence responds and corresponds to the lack or absence of God that is the possibility of a god; it responds and corresponds to the silence of the gods and the silent call of being that bids man get underway, to go down and return to the poverty of his noble essence from which springs forth a wealth of possibilities. God and gods become possibilities and, as possibilities, "more powerful than any sort of reality of fact" (N I 393).[23]

Put another way, the god and gods, as possibilities, are close-by [*zu nah*] and affecting [*nahegehende*] us (and in that sense "present" [*gegen-wärtige*] gods), but only as still coming and arriving and therefore coming near [*zu nahe*], not easy to grasp because not some constant presence. The "religious" thinking that corresponds to such an arriving is thereby both a renunciation and a waiting: against [*gegen*] the old gods which are renounced by our no longer wanting them or asking them favors, waiting [*warten*] for the coming gods in the lack and absence held to by the renunciation (for the gods can only come if they are absent) (cf. EHD 184, 186-87; GR 97). Of course, to those standing about in the marketplace peddling relevant ideas and absolute hope (indeed, peddling God), the one who thinks in such a way, "seeking" a god, is quite the madman. His renunciation is a divesture of God and thus a cause for despair; his waiting is poor consolation and concern with what is not real. But we should not await [*erwarten*] consolation, expecting solutions to cosmic riddles or useful practical wisdom, for such results are only where there is an attempt to secure oneself in the face of the nothing. Awaiting represents and plans and closes off possibilities such that only what is present is real; there is thus no longer any openness. But then where can there be the *possibility* of a turning? A change can come only from one who is de-ranged [*ver-rückt*] and therefore dislodged [*ausrückt*] from man hitherto. Such a person is released from beings and open to the

mystery, surpassing himself, beside and outside himself [aus-
ser sich] and therefore away from the sheer oppression of what
is only presently present, to what is absent. Only he is able
to deal with what is presently present, for what is present is
always only something that arrives in the course of a coming
and going (i.e., is something coming-to-presence) and therefore only understood from out of what is absent -- from the
whole of being, whereby it is understood as whole and holy.
Only where there is a reaching into the abyss is there a turn
in the age and the salvation of man possible (cf. G 35, 42; HW
266-67, 347-48; N II 85; SZ 446; WD 161).
    Mention has been made previously of tragedy as a possible
illustration of the sort of "attitude" revealed by Heidegger
with regard to the gods (Chapters 4 and 5). The demeanor of
the tragic hero likewise shows itself here as a good example
of the religious thinking evoked by Heidegger. Like the
noble, "high-minded" man that is suggested by Heideggerian
thinking, the tragic hero has seemed dangerous to our theological tradition -- an arrogant, amoral hero who is justly
punished. The "failure" of the tragic hero would also not
measure up under the pragmatic, utilitarian scrutiny of Rorty.
Yet the grace and bearing of the tragic hero in the face of
ruin tells us of the nobility and worthiness of human being,
giving us a message and meaning that is salvific and "religious" in its own way. The tragic hero, devoted to the ideal
or dictates of a god, suffers and oftentimes is destroyed.
Through such action, the tragic hero (and the audience) comes
to be attentive to both what is revealed and concealed in
divinity and in the play of the world, and thereby comes to
realize the ambiguous and questionable nature of existence.
The tragic hero (and the audience) thus comes to think about
and question the mysterious and indeterminate events that
befall us, rather than providing and asserting pat answers (as
the tragic chorus does so often in the early stages of the
play). Thinking, questioning -- even questioning (challenging, indicting) the gods -- the tragic hero becomes human,
knowing his limitations, but then also what is revealed within
the confines of those limitations. What is possible and not
possible in the ideals (and/or gods) he follows comes to be
acknowledged and accepted, leading to a resolute openedness
[Ent-schlossenheit] to one's own path and destiny, and that of
others. Tragedy thereby offers no worldly wisdom or promise
of a blessed life, but shows the redemption (the salvation) of
the hero in his becoming human, a mortal wanderer who comes to
know his place amidst the play of the world.[24]
    Thus the emphasis in the "religious" thinking we have been
developing, and in the the thinking of Heidegger, on the
preparation of the site in which we dwell, thinking about
being and reaching into the abyss on the way whereby a glimpse
of a god or the holy may be found. The turning of the age
cannot take place by some new god, or the old one renewed,

bursting into the world, for where would he turn on his return if men had not prepared an abode for him by taking care of that place (the clearing of being) in which a god or gods may arrive (HW 270)? Or remain absent. This is not properly heeded by many who consider Heidegger: we must, by thinking, poetizing, and thanking, prepare for the appearance *or the absence* of the god, for either may bring us into the holy. Indeed, Heidegger's stress on the death or lack of God in our time suggests that we may long abide in the no-more of the gods that have fled and the not-yet of the gods that are coming (Sp 209; WM 338).

Such thinking as this is religious in that it knows of the gods and the divine (whereby it is able to wait and renounce) and, knowing that, pays (reverent) heed to the whole of being, to the fourfold in their intimate interplay that is the world-ing of the world, whereby man comes into his own. Of course, this thinking cannot effect the wholeness and holiness that will "save" man; it lacks the presumption that thinks it can force a god to arrive (Sp 209; WD 34). Such thinking as this has no result, no effect; in this sense it is quite "useless". Yet what is useless can still and all the more have force, for it holds to the matter of thought, gathering together meaning and trying to stand in the openness and clearing of being (EM 10; GR 36; WM 311, 358; ZD 66). Thus does it change the world, "changes it in the ever darker depths of a riddle, depths which as they grow darker offer promise of a greater brightness" (VA 229).

> I said to my soul, be still, and wait without hope
> For hope would be hope for the wrong thing; wait without love
> for love would be love of the wrong thing; there is yet faith
> But faith and the love and the hope are all in the waiting.
> Wait without thought, for you are not ready for thought:
> So the darkness shall be light, and the stillness the dancing.[25]

NOTES

1. See Gründer, "Heidegger's Critique of Science," trans. William Kramer, *Philosophy Today* 25 (1963), pp. 21, 26–27; Derrida, "Différance," pp. 159–60; and Richard Rorty, "Overcoming the Tradition: Heidegger and Dewey," in *Heidegger and Modern Philosophy*, p. 256, for these criticisms. Also, for other, similar criticisms of Heidegger by Derrida, see *Of Grammatology*, trans. G. C. Spivak (Baltimore: Johns Hopkins University Press, 1976), pp. 18–20, *Positions*, trans. Alan Bass (Chicago: University of Chicago Press, 1981), pp. 54–55, 111, and *Spurs: Nietzsche's Styles*, trans. Barbara Harlow (Chicago: University of Chicago Press, 1978), p. 81 and *passim*.

2. *Gegenständigkeit* is not to be confused with *Gegenständlichkeit* (objectivity); it is a coinage by Heidegger meant to indicate the kind of presence [*Anwesenheit*] of beings that appears in the modern age, i.e., the way in which being shows itself and endures as constant presence when things show themselves as object.

3. Cf. Nietzsche, *The Will to Power*, #466: "It is not the victory of *science* that distinguishes the 19th century, but the victory of scientific *method* over science."

4. Heidegger often uses this Latin term and a German cognate (*Subiectität*, subiectity) in describing the "subject" in modern metaphysics so that we do not reduce Descartes' *ego cogito* to something "subjective", i.e., an incidental quality of just this particular human being (FD 85); such only happens after being is understood as will, will to power, and will to will. See also "Metaphysics as the History of Being" in N II.

5. *Technik* may be translated as either technology or technique, and both meanings are meant by Heidegger. For simplicity, "technology" is used to translate *Technik* in the rest of the chapter.

6. Cf. Gründer, pp. 18–19.

7. William Lovitt, in a note to his translation of this essay (p. 17) in an essay on Heidegger and science ("A 'Gesprach' with Heidegger on Technology," *Man and World* 6 [1973], p. 60 n.12), tells us that this word, carrying the connotations of the verb *bestehen* and its dual meaning of "to last" and "to undergo", ordinarily denotes a store or supply or stock that is on "stand-by". It is also of considerable interest (to Heidegger) that the verb *bestehen* often simply replaces the verbs "to be" and "to exist" in modern German.

8. We could make hundreds of citations here, but we will only direct the reader to some of the key texts: the first essay in G; "The Age of the World Picture" in HW; the essays on metaphysics and nihilism in N II; SG, *passim*; SZ 170ff for a discussion of inauthenticity and *das Man*; "Overcoming Metaphysics" in VA. See also Chapter 2, which discusses these matters largely in terms of the history of metaphysics (onto-theo-logy) rather than in terms of the fulfillment of metaphysics (technology) as we are doing here.

9. As Werner Marx, for instance, tends to do; see *Heidegger and the Tradition*, pp. 174ff, and "The World in Another Beginning: Poetic Dwelling and the Role of the Poet," pp. 235ff.

10. See Theodore Kisiel, "Heidegger and the New Images of Science," *Research in Phenomenology* 7 (1977), pp. 162–81, and Rouse, "Kuhn, Heideg-

ger and Scientific Realism," pp. 269-90, and "Heidegger's Later Philosophy of Science," *Southern Journal of Philosophy* 33 (1985), pp. 75-92, for greater elaboration on the continuity between Heidegger and the most recent work in philosophy of science. Particularly interesting is Rouse's attempt to bolster the thesis of Thomas Kuhn's *The Structure of Scientific Revolutions* by correlating Kuhn's descriptions of normal and revolutionary science with Heidegger's description of the everyday/inauthentic and authentic modes of being.

See also Carl Raschke, "The New Cosmology and the Overcoming of Metaphysics," *Philosophy Today* 24 (1980), pp. 375ff, for further elaboration on the correlation between the new conception of reality holding sway in the physical sciences and the anti-foundationalist thinking of Heidegger.

11. For a short history of this retreat and the consequences it has had for theism (and atheism), see MacIntyre, "The Fate of Theism," pp. 3-29.

12. Raschke, "Overcoming," pp. 344, 386.

13. See Nietzsche, *Zarathustra*, III, 2:1: "... and where does man not stand at the edge of abysses?"

14. See *Conflict of Interpretations*, especially "The Hermeneutics of Symbols" I and II, pp. 287ff, 315ff, and "Freedom in the Light of Hope," pp. 402ff; and "The Critique of Religion" in Ricoeur, *The Philosophy of Paul Ricoeur*, ed. Charles E. Reagan and David Stewart (Boston: Beacon Press, 1978), pp. 217, 219. See also *Interpretation Theory: Discourse and the Surplus of Meaning* (Fort Worth: The Texas Christian University Press, 1976), in which the idea of the "surplus of meaning" is expanded on (e.g., symbol systems as "a reservoir of meaning", p. 65).

15. Cf. EM 186; G 66; HW 325-26; ID 42, 65; SG 84; TK 39, 41, 44, 46-47; US 32-33, 169; VA 78, 99, 108, 183; WM IX, 175, 368; and David Farrell Krell, "Results," *The Monist* 64 (1981), pp. 473, 475.

16. See Karsten Harries, "Meta-Criticism and Meta-Poetry: A Critique of Theoretical Anarchy" in *Studies in Phenomenology and the Human Sciences*, ed. John Sallis (Atlantic Highlands, N.J.: Humanities Press, 1979), pp. 70-72; Krell, "Results," p. 276; Raschke, *Alchemy of the Word*, pp. 45-46; David Couzons Hoy, "Forgetting the Text: Derrida's Critique of Heidegger," *Boundary 2* VIII (Fall 1979), pp. 223ff; John D. Caputo, "'Supposing Truth to be a Woman ...': Heidegger, Nietzsche and Derrida" in *The Thought of Martin Heidegger*, ed. Michael Zimmerman (New Orleans: Tulane University, 1984), pp. 20-21, for criticisms of deconstruction and deconstruction *vis á vis* the "hermeneutical" thinking of Heidegger. See Raschke, "The Deconstruction of God" in *Deconstruction and Theology* (New York: Crossroad, 1982), pp. 29-30, for the link between deconstruction and (the Nietzschean) Dionysus, and in the same volume, Mark C. Taylor, "Text as Victim," p. 70, and Thomas J.J. Altizer, "History as Apocalypse," pp. 147ff, for characterizations of the death of God in terms of a radical Christology and in terms of the omnipresence of God. See also, Taylor, *Erring: A Postmodern A/theology* (Chicago: University of Chicago Press, 1984).

See *Hermeneutics and Deconstruction*, ed. Hugh J. Silverman and Don Ihde (Albany: State University of New York Press, 1985), for recent discussion of the issues between Heidegger and Derrida.

17. Jean Beaufret, "Heidegger vu de France" in *Die Frage Martin Heideggers*, ed. Hans-Georg Gadamer (Heidelberg: Carl Winter Universitätsverlag,

1969); translated by Bernard Dauenhauer as "Heidegger Seen from France," *Southern Journal of Philosophy* 8 (1970), p. 437.

18. *Inständigkeit* is perhaps best translated as "instancy" (as Richardson does in *From Phenomenology to Thought*), capturing the "momentary" character of man's standing in the clearing of being (i.e., that man stands in the moment [of vision]), but the *standing-in* character obviously meant by Heidegger is lost.

19. Caputo, *The Mystical Element*, pp. 246-54.

20. It should be noted that Rorty's essay on Dewey and Heidegger, in which this complaint is lodged, is primarily concerned with scrapping the whole of the Western tradition in favor of getting something practical done today, and therefore finds Heidegger's concern with thinking and philosophy wanting. For an excellent criticism of Rorty from the side of Heidegger, see Caputo, "The Thought of Being and the Conversation of Mankind," *Review of Metaphysics* 36 (March 1983), pp. 661-85.

21. Cf. Krell, "Results," pp. 470, 478 n.15; Perotti, *On the Divine*, pp. 4, 94-95, 116-17; Raschke, "Overcoming," p. 385.

22. As Perotti, p. 94, and Karsten Harries, "Heidegger's Conception of the Holy," *The Personalist* 47 (1966), p. 185, claim respectively.

23. Cf. Danner, p. 3; Krell, "Nietzsche and the Task of Thinking," pp. 162, 174-75; Perotti, p. 75; Raschke, "Overcoming Metaphysics," p. 386; Gadamer, "The Religious Dimension in Heidegger," p. 206.

24. Cf. my "Beyond Theodicy: The Divine in Heidegger and Tragedy," pp. 110-20.

25. T.S. Eliot, "Four Quartets," pp. 126-27.

CHAPTER 7

A PAUSE ON THE WAY

> *We shall not cease from exploration*
> *And the end of all our exploring*
> *Will be to arrive where we started*
> *And know the place for the first time.*
> T.S. Eliot[1]

We have travelled a long and twisting path in our reconsideration of religious thinking in light of the thinking of Heidegger. We would do well at this point to pause on our way and take stock of the changes in horizon that we have wrought -- of where we have been and of where we are going.

Our thesis has been that with Heidegger's reconsiderations of thinking and being that leave thinking far richer and more complex than any particular logic or *ratio*, religious thinking might once again flourish. In suggesting this, we have sought, first and foremost, to align religious thinking with that *openedness* that Heidegger finds essential to all thinking. Such a resolute openedness pays heed to the situatedness of the essence and presencing of being and man revealed in the event of meaning. This event of meaning is the whole complex of significations and relations in which man abides; it is the worlding of the world, the interaction and mirror-play of the fourfold -- the closure of earth, the openness of sky, the hinting of divinities, the responding of mortals. Returning to the earth, standing out in time, abiding with things that gather the fourfold and thereby bringing-forth the whole as one conditioned (be-thinged) and mortal, man is provided with his potentialities-for-being and therefore made whole -- i.e., brought into what is his own and thereby healed, saved. The event of meaning, the worlding of the world, in which man takes part, is the holy. Man abides in the holy in his sojourn on the earth.

But to abide in this whole is not so simple. One must submit to what has been given and shown to one, and in such submission there must be reticence, silence, and openedness to hear the message of being sent. Yet to submit there must be a saying and responding that lays out and interprets what has been given to thinking, that it may correspond to being (the mirror-play of the fourfold). One must give thanks, for only by what is given (what is revealed *and* concealed) is one able to be; yet to give thanks is not a passive acceptance of what is past, but also a thanks for the future and thus a *venture* out into the world that responds to what calls for thinking, re-saying and re-calling what has been given and sent. Religious thinking, like all thinking, must question, finding what

has been granted questionable and therefore question-worthy.
In this way the holiness and meaning-fullness of world and
thing are brought-forth and revealed.   Here there is the
unriddling of the philosopher (destroying the idols that have
been handed down), the evocation and celebration of the poet
(re-calling and calling forth the message that has been
granted and sent) and the thankfulness and piety of the religious man (submitting to what has been granted, and giving
thanks for it, as the gift that grants man his essence, to
think).   Such thinking is "hermeneutic" thinking, not bent on
a· willful assertion of a position but a grace-full and meaning-full and for-giving bearing of tidings that re-calls the
call of being that belongs to what has been and what is coming, that is hinted by the gods and the poet and lets man into
his own.
     Giving himself up to be drawn back to himself, man is
healed and made whole, let into his own, let into the event of
meaning that gives him to think and which he thinks.   Bound
back to himself and his world through such thinking, man is
"saved".   The bearing of such thinking, its sighting meaning-
fullness in all things as a gathering of the fourfold, its shy
reverence, its hesitiation and care, its thankfulness for
being by thinking what needs to be thought -- all this suggests a "religious" character in the essence of the authentic
man.   In all of this, such thinking we have described here
indeed seems religious. Here, in choosing to call such thinking "religious" we not only respond to what is suggested in
the description of thinking in terms of thanks and "submission", but we also heed the promptings of the word itself:
religion, Latin *religio*, *re-ligare*, to bind back, to be bound
back, in this case, to be bound back to that origin of world
and thing that is both the "heart" and "soul" of man and the
disclosure of world. Heeding the word itself, and what has
been disclosed by Heidegger, the "definition" of religion that
emerges here, then, concerns a return to who we are, to our
proper place in the cosmos. Whether one comes to see oneself
in a situation in which one is a partner with God, or a True
Self in a place outside *samsāra*, or a no-self in place amidst
the impermanence of things, or in a family that constitutes
the childern of God and the body of Christ, religion and being
religious seem to come down to this: re-placing ourselves,
and being replaced, in that situation whereby we attain to who
we are in our essence, whereby we are made whole and therefore
holy.[2]   Here lies the suggestion that there can be no more
"religious" task than for man to find his place amidst the
fourfold -- the whole and holy -- which lets us know who and
what we are as we site/sight ourselves in the midst of a
mysterious revealing and concealing that shows promise of the
divine.
     We may note at this point that two lines of thought are
woven together in this text, two paths of thought that may be

followed from here, separately or together. The first path
concerns the way in which religious phenomena are better
understood or illuminated through the understanding of religion that has been disclosed in dialogue with Heidegger. We
have attempted to shed some light along these lines throughout
our study in the following areas:
1) The entire concept of a religious tradition demands to be
   rethought at this point, for -- as is clear from Heidegger's analysis of truth, world, and meaning -- tradition
   can no longer be seen as a simple unity that *centers* on a
   particular theme, goal, object, set of doctrines, or beliefs. The complex dynamic of truth at which Heidegger
   hints with the word *Ereignis* suggests that a tradition is
   characterized by the differences, the rifts, and the transgressions that *take place* through the interpretations that
   are laid out concerning whatever is considered to be at
   stake. A tradition is wandering meaning, a shifting and
   sliding of meaning that emerges from the rifts that occur
   from text to text, interpretation to interpretation. Such
   a view, on closer examination, could shed light on the
   proliferation and plurality of authorities within any number of religious traditions. But such a view also suggests
   that traditions are not simply and easily comparable -- let
   alone reducible -- given the historical particularity of
   the meaning(s) that emerge(s) "within" a tradition and
   "between" traditions. The plurality of religions is thereby less a problem to be solved than an opportunity for
   thinking, for possibilities that may yet open up in the
   conversation of mankind.
2) With religious traditions de-centered we are led away from
   attending to the "objects" (or other such goals) of worship
   to an awareness of the space that is opened up (and closed
   off) by the naming of the god or gods (or their lack) --
   i.e., "what" is hinted at and disclosed through the advent
   or withdrawal of the gods. Herein lies the *Sache* -- what
   is and is not possible within the ever-changing boundaries
   that serve as the "ground" of a tradition's disclosure --
   of a tradition, whereby traditions (or better, the various
   moments of traditions) may be compared. And this lends
   "God-talk" -- talk of the gods and talk from the gods -- a
   curious character, a puzzling, questionable character that
   calls for thinking.
3) Hence the refashioned understanding of religious thinking
   that has been sketched above, a thinking that is *an enactment of what it is about* -- neither rational discussion
   based on faith, nor prereflective, naive experience, but
   both, and more. Here "simple" faith, theology, prayer, and
   ritual (among other religious phenomena), are all interpretations, attempts to lay out and bring-forth a world in
   which man seeks to find himself and thereby understand
   himself. Such interpretations *take place* in conjunction

and in competition with other interpretations, be they
"religious", "philosophical", "poetic", or "scientific",
and none of which may claim authority by means other than
the insight they provide.

Some of these matters have never been dealt with before
from a basis in Heideggerian thinking; others have been dealt
with tentatively, and rarely in a thoroughly Heideggerian
fashion. For example, in the past, theologians and philosophers of religion have taken to analyzing such phenomena as
religious language and religious tradition using the "philosophical hermeneutics" of Hans-Georg Gadamer and Paul Ricoeur,
relying on these two as spokesmen for Heidegger. Yet we
should not be misled: Gadamer and Ricoeur appropriate Heidegger to their own ends -- ends that are "safe" and traditional
and thereby tend to obscure the originality and radicality of
Heidegger. Gadamer, for instance, in his appropriation of
Heidegger to Hegel, is interested in stressing continuity with
our tradition and our belonging to some universal essence of
language and reason, whereby (religious) meaning may be found
in the ineffable depths of our culture and tradition.
Ricoeur, likewise, is interested in maintaining continuity
with our metaphysical tradition and its methods and positing
some ineffable surplus of meaning to which (religious) symbols
point. Both Gadamer and Ricoeur thereby serve the ultimately
nihilistic goal of *asserting* or *justifying* a particular religious standpoint or tradition -- a goal at odds with
Heidegger.[3] Much therefore needs to be done to see to what
extent a Heideggerian understanding of religion will prove
fruitful in understanding religious phenomena, and where criticisms against Heidegger will have to be made.

The other path of thought that emerges from this study is
the pursuit and development of the "religious" dimension in
the thinking of Heidegger as a unique instance of religious
thinking to be compared and contrasted with the sorts of
thinking that emerge from other religious traditions. This
previously has been the area of greatest confusion concerning
Heidegger's significance for religious thinking. Here we have
suggested that the religious dimension in the thinking of
Heidegger has the most in common with, and can perhaps best be
understood in terms of, the religious "attitude" exemplified
by tragedy and tragic literature. In this regard, it is
helpful to note the following points:[4]

1) For both Heidegger and tragedy, the play of the world and
   the meaningfulness of that world are situationally and
   historically determined. Meaning is brought forth by
   thinking and acting in and through time, on the earth,
   responding and corresponding to a situation in which one is
   given to be, destined to be, in a unique way. There is no
   meaning above and beyond the situation (above and beyond
   the world) -- i.e., no explanation and justification for
   how the situation came about in the past, no promise of

success or reward in the future -- which would grant the individual some solace and control over the situation. Such meanings are rejected as empty piety by the tragic hero, and as a product of the will to power and to securing permanence by Heidegger.

2) Relatedly, the historical nature of being means that concealing is essential to any revealing and unconcealing of being. The whole of the giving of being that is the play of the world -- and the play of tragedy -- involves the jointure that holds between the revealing and concealing of being. Both the authentic individual and the tragic hero are thrown into a situation he or she does *not* determine or control, and is called upon to act (to be) in the context of such a situation. History is thereby a burden that exerts a determining power on one's fate (i.e., how one may be) that cannot be changed. Likewise, in being, the authentic individual and the tragic hero stands in one possibility and thus is constantly *not* other possibilities. The closure of these possibilities determines us in the way we are, the way being presences and comes to be disclosed. This is shown best in the irresolvable tension that exists between mutually exclusive virtues in the tragic drama; in each instance, the virtue of the hero entails irredeemable loss (e.g., Oedipus cannot save both Thebes and himself). Shot through with nullity, meaning and significance in the play of the world and tragedy are "without why", groundless, emerging from the abyss.

3) This point bears on the part the god and the gods can have in the play of the world and the play of tragedy, for it is a strange, ambiguous, duplicitous part they play. On the one hand, the gods provide a measure for human being; human beings *are* who they *are* by living up to the measure that the divine provides. On the other hand, their measure is an abysmal one. For one thing, appearing as the highest, the god and gods are not the whole; their perfection is misleading, a limitation in the light of the holy (the whole of being). What is more, the god or gods are often present as absent, only appearing by virtue of the actions of human beings and therefore dependent upon the latter for their appearance. When they do appear, they are strange and unknown -- even demonic (as the action of tragedy makes clear) -- and remain strangers to men. In addition, the gods sometimes withdraw from a situation in which they were once present, and sometimes, called upon, they do not appear at all, and the place of the god and gods remains empty (e.g., in *King Lear*, or *Waiting for God[ot]*). Whether present or absent, the divine cannot be calculated, counted on, or reckoned with, but is a hint -- a hint of the duplicity (the revealing and concealing) of being.

4) Hinting calls for thinking; thinking calls for questioning. Questioning -- to ask after being, to ask the meaning of

being -- is the way in which human beings encounter the
divine (especially in tragedy) and are opened up to being
and the play of the world. Questioning, challenging, even
indicting and rejecting, the divine, the world in which
human beings dwell is opened up and we are able to
site/sight ourselves. Thinking, we come to ourselves. By
raising the questionableness of existence, even to the
extent of questioning the gods, Heidegger and tragedy save
us -- not with some aesthetic spectacle, some theodicy, but
-- by leading us back to our own selves and our questioning
existence. Such thinking is neither desperate nor despair-
ing, but a "knowing cheerfulness", as Heidegger puts it,
that gives thanks for what has been granted and withheld --
for one's uniqueness (and that of others), and the responsibilities incumbent therein.

The above comparison helps clarify why we have pursued the
religious dimension in Heidegger's thinking as clearly distinct from Christian faith and theology. Indeed, given their
insistence on being centered or secured upon some foundation,
we might clearly distinguish Heidegger's "religious" thinking
from the Western religious traditions in general (though Judaism's flexibility with regard to creed and belief might
prove the exception). The negative, dialectical, and mystical
theologies of these traditions -- which are closest to and
have been compared most often with Heidegger's thinking --
have a point and purpose that is ultimately incompatible with
the thinking of Heidegger. These theologies, like all theology, seeks to *secure* the transcendent and thereby ourselves by
asserting (implicitly or explicitly) some ultimate meaning
beyond our understanding, and thereafter to *justify* whatever
stand is taken *vis á vis* such ultimate meaning. Tragedy and
suffering, for instance, are dismissed in the name of the
original sin (or finitude, or some other such "fault") of man
and the goodness and righteousness of God. A "divine comedy"
results from the self-certain affirmation of a meaning above
and beyond the world of human being and stills the question of
the meaning of existence (being). On the other hand, as we
have seen, no such asserting, securing, or justifying is in
play in Heidegger's evocation of *Ereignis* or his talk of the
"divine" or "unknown" god. The word *Ereignis* does not point
to God or an Absolute, but "merely" attempts to show what is
going on -- what is at stake -- in thinking. *Ereignis* thereby
indicates that holiness and meaning-fullness do not lie in
pointing beyond to some greater reality and meaning but in
evoking, provoking, and bringing-forth meaning within the moment, within the situation, in which we find ourselves.

Further investigation of such parallels would certainly
clarify the popular practice of comparing Heidegger with Eastern thought, particularly Buddhism and Taoism.[5] Such comparisons are sometimes interesting, but they have a natural
tendency toward the superficial and have been hampered in the

past by their lack of clarification of the religious significance of Heidegger's thinking. This has led to a one-sided-
ness in the "dialogue" in which Heidegger is said to come
close -- but not quite close enough -- to being a Zen Buddhist
or a Taoist in the tradition of Lao-tzu or Chuang-tzu.[6] The
most recent example of this can be found in Steven Heine's
comparison of Heidegger and Dōgen on being and time.[7] Besides
beginning one-sidedly in seeking to critically evaluate only
Heidegger (pp. 29, 32), Heine makes an issue of the apparent
confusion in Heidegger concerning the "soteriological" dimension of thinking (pp. 148-49). Yet Heidegger's questioning
attitude (which is what Heine seems to indict as confusion) --
as we have hinted in comparisons with tragic literature -- has
its own salvific and "religious" import that might usefully
serve as an alternative to and criticism of Dōgen (or Heine's
interpretation of Dōgen). Heine, like others, lacking a clear
understanding of the "religious" dimension in Heidegger, ends
up failing to provide us with a *thoughtful* dialogue between
Heidegger and the East. Further development of the religious
dimension in Heidegger and its parallels with the tragic would
be a step toward uncovering the "real" issue between Heidegger
and the East.

There is then much to think about given the "foundation"
we have attempted to lay out concerning Heidegger's significance for religious thinking. Each of these two paths, promising richer possibilities for religious thinking, still call
forth for further thought. Such thinking, at this point, must
be left to the darkness of the future and the further quest of
finding our place amidst the whole.

NOTES

1. "Four Quartets," p. 145.

2. Cf. my "Mysticism and Ontology: A Heideggerian Critique of Caputo," pp. 472-73.

3. See, e.g., Gadamer, "Heidegger and the Language of Metaphysics" in *Philosophical Hermeneutics*, pp. 230, 239, and *passim*, in which Gadamer interprets Heidegger as a "renewal of the tradition" and finds East and West belonging together within the one universal essence of langauge and reason. See, e.g., Ricoeur, "Existence and Interpretation" in *Conflict of Interpretations*, pp. 1-25, for Ricoeur's quarrel with Heidegger's radicality, and our commments on pp. 139 and 143 n.13, above. For a characterization of both Gadamer and Ricoeur as nihilistic, see Hubert L. Dreyfus, "Holism and Hermeneutics," *Review of Metaphysics* 34 (1980), pp. 20-21.

4. See also my essays "Beyond Theodicy: The Divine in Heidegger and Tragedy," pp. 110-20, "Mysticism and Ontology," pp. 473-476, and "Heidegger, Tragedy and Ethical Reflection" (unpublished). Cf. Gelven, "Heidegger and Tragedy" in *Martin Heidegger and the Question of Literature*, pp. 215-28.

5. Comparisons with Hindu thought are rare, perhaps because, centered on *Brahman*, Hindu thought would prove as incompatible with Heidegger as Western thinking; see J.L. Mehta, "Heidegger and Vedanta: Reflections on a Questionable Theme," *International Philosophical Quarterly* 18 (1978), pp. 121-144.

Comparisons with Confucian thought also seem to be rare, though the interest of Confucianism and Heidegger in a creative thinking of the tradition would seem to make them ideal candidates for comparison.

6. E.g., Fu, "Heidegger and Zen on Being and Nothingness," and "The Trans-onto-theo-logical Foundations of Language"; John Steffney, "Trans-metaphysical Thinking in Heidegger and Zen," *Philosophy East and West* 27 (1977), pp. 323-335.

7. *Existential and Ontological Dimensions of Time in Heidegger and Dōgen* (Albany: State University of New York Press, 1985).

SELECTED BIBLIOGRAPHY

This bibliography is divided into three sections:

    I. Works by Heidegger (with English translations)
   II. Works on Heidegger
III. Other Works

Each section includes only those works cited in the text. For a more extensive bibliography of the literature concerning Martin Heidegger, see Hans-Martin Sass, *Martin Heidegger: Bibliography and Glossary* (Bowling Green, KY: Philosophy Documentation Center, 1982).

I. WORKS BY HEIDEGGER (with English translations)

Aus der Erfahrung des Denkens. Gesamtausgabe, Band 13. Frankfurt: Klostermann, 1983.
    75-86   "The Thinker as Poet." In Heidegger, *Poetry, Language, Thought*. Trans. Albert Hofstadter. New York: Harper & Row, 1971. 3-14.
    87-90   "The Pathway." Trans. T.F. O'Meara, and Thomas Sheehan. *Listening* 8 (1973):32-39.
Einführung in die Metaphysik. Gesamtausgabe, Band 40. Frankfurt: Klostermann, 1983.
    An Introduction to Metaphysics. Trans. Ralph Mannheim. New Haven: Yale University Press, 1959.
Erläuterungen zu Hölderlins Dichtung. Gesamtausgabe, Band 4. Frankfurt: Klostermann, 1981.
    9-31   "Remembrance of the Poet." Trans. David Scott. In Heidegger, *Existence and Being*. Ed. Werner Brock. Chicago: Regnery, 1949. 253-290.
   33-48   "Hölderlin and the Essence of Poetry." Trans. David Scott. In Heidegger, *Existence and Being*. 291-315.
Die Frage nach dem Ding. Gesamtausgabe, Band 41. Frankfurt: Klostermann, 1984.
    What is a Thing? Trans. W.B. Barton and Vera Deutsch. South Bend, IN: Indiana: Gateway, 1967.
Gelassenheit. Pfullingen: Neske, 1959.
    Discourse on Thinking. Trans. John M. Anderson and E. Hans Freund. New York: Harper & Row, 1966.
Die Grundprobleme der Phänomenologie. Gesamtausgabe, Band 24. Frankfurt: Klostermann, 1975.
    The Basic Problems of Phenomenology. Trans. Albert Hofstadter. Bloomington: Indiana University Press, 1982.
Hölderlins Hymen >>Germanien<< und >>Der Rhein<<. Gesamtausgabe, Band 39. Frankfurt: Klostermann, 1980.

Holzwege. Gesamtausgabe, Band 5. Frankfurt: Klostermann, 1977.

 1-74   "The Origin of the Work of Art." In *Poetry, Language,*
         Thought. 17-87.
 75-113 "The Age of the World Picture." In Heidegger, *The Question*
         Concerning Technology and Other Essays. Trans. William
         Lovitt. New York: Harper & Row, 1977. 115-154.
 115-208 *Hegel's Concept of Experience.* New York: Harper & Row, 1970.
 209-267 "The Word of Nietzsche: 'God is Dead'." In *The Question Con-*
         cerning Technology. 53-112.
 269-320 "What are Poets For?" In *Poetry, Language, Thought.* 91-142.
 321-374 "The Anaximander Fragment." In Heidegger, *Early Greek Think-*
         ing. Trans. David F. Krell and Frank Capuzzi. New York: Har-
         per & Row, 1975. 13-58.

Identität und Differenz. Pfullingen: Neske, 1957.
   Identity and Difference. Trans. Joan Stambaugh. New York: Harper &
      Row, 1974.

Kant und das Problem der Metaphysik. 2. Auflage. Frankfurt: Klostermann,
   1951.
   Kant and the Problem of Metaphysics. Trans. James S. Churchhill.
      Bloomington: Indiana University Press, 1962.

Nietzsche. 1. Band. Pfullingen: Neske, 1961.
 9-254   *Nietzsche, Volume I: The Will to Power as Art.* Trans. David
         Farrell Krell. New York: Harper & Row, 1979.
 255-472 *Nietzsche, Volume II: The Eternal Return of the Same.* Trans.
         David Farrell Krell. New York: Harper & Row, 1984.
 473-658 *Nietzsche, Volume III: The Will to Power as Knowledge and as*
         Metaphysics. Trans. Joan Stambaugh, David Krell and Frank
         Capuzzi. New York: Harper & Row, 1987. 1-158.

Nietzsche. 2. Band. Pfullingen: Neske, 1961.
 7-29   *Nietzsche, Volume III.* 161-183.
 31-256 *Nietzsche, Volume IV: Nihilism.* Trans. Frank Capuzzi. New
         York: Harper & Row, 1982. 1-196.
 257-333 *Nietzsche, Volume III.* 187-251.
 335-398 *Nietzsche, Volume IV.* 197-250.
 399-490 *The End of Philosophy.* Trans. Joan Stambaugh. New York: Har-
         per & Row, 1973. 1-83.

"Nur Noch ein Gott Kann Uns Retten." *Spiegel*-Gespräch mit Martin Heidegger
   am 23 September 1966. *Der Spiegel* (Hamburg), Nr. 26, 31 Mai 1976. 193ff.
   "'Only a God Can Save Us': The *Spiegel* Interview." Trans. William J.
      Richardson. In *Heidegger: The Man and the Thinker.* Ed. Thomas Shee-
      han. 45-67.

Phänomenologie und Theologie. Frankfurt: Klostermann, 1970.
 13-33   "Phenomenology and Theology." In Heidegger, *The Piety of*
         Thinking. Trans. James G. Hart and John C. Maraldo. Bloom-
         ington: Indiana University Press, 1976. 5-21.
 37-46   "The Theological Discussion of 'The Problem of a Non-Object-
         ifying Thinking and Speaking in Today's Theology' — Some
         Pointers to Its Major Aspects." In *The Piety of Thinking.*
         22-31.

"Preface" in Richardson, William J. *Heidegger: From Phenomenology to*
   Thought. viii-xxiii.

Der Satz vom Grund. Pfullingen: Neske, 1957.
   191-211   "The Principle of Ground." Trans. K. Hoeller. *Man and World*
             7 (1974):207-222.
Sein und Zeit. Gesamtausgabe, Band 2. Frankfurt: Klostermann, 1977.
   Being and Time. Trans. John Macquarrie and Edward Robinson. New York:
      Harper & Row, 1962.
Die Technik und die Kehre. Pfullingen: Neske, 1962.
   37-47   "The Turning." In *The Question Concerning Technology*. 36-49.
Unterwegs zur Sprache. Pfullingen: Neske, 1959.
   On the Way to Language. Trans. Peter D. Hertz. New York: Harper & Row,
      1971.
Vorträge und Aufsätze. Pfullingen: Neske, 1954.
   13-44   "The Question Concerning Technology." In *The Question Con-*
         cerning Technology. 3-35.
   45-70   "Science and Reflection." In *The Question Concerning Tech-*
         nology. 155-182.
   71-99   "Overcoming Metaphysics." In *The End of Philosophy*. 84-110.
   101-126   "Who is Nietzsche's Zarathustra?" Trans. Bernd Magnus. *Re-*
         view of Metaphysics 20 (March 1967):411-431.
   145-162   "Building Thinking Dwelling." In *Poetry, Language, Thought*.
         145-161.
   163-185   "The Thing." In *Poetry, Language, Thought*. 165-186.
   187-204   "... Poetically Man Dwells ..." In *Poetry, Language,*
         Thought. 213-229.
   207-229   "Logos." In *Early Greek Thinking*. 59-78.
   231-256   "Moira." In *Early Greek Thinking*. 79-101.
   257-282   "Alētheia." In *Early Greek Thinking*. 102-123.
Was Heisst Denken? Tübingen: Niemeyer, 1954.
   What is Called Thinking? Trans. J. Glenn Gray. New York: Harper and
      Row, 1968.
Was ist das -- die Philosophie? Pfullingen: Neske, 1956.
   What is Philosophy? Trans. William Kluback and Jean T. Wilde. New
      York: Twayne, 1958.
Wegmarken. Gesamtausgabe, Band 9. Frankfurt: Klostermann, 1976.
   79-101   "From the Last Marburg Lecture." Trans. John Macquarrie. In
         The Future of Our Religious Past: Essays in Honor of Rudolf
         Bultmann. Ed. James M. Robinson. London: SCM, 1971. 312-322.
   103-122   "What is Metaphysics?" Trans. David Farrell Krell. In Heid-
         egger, *Basic Writings*. Ed. David Farrell Krell. New York:
         Harper & Row, 1976. 95-112.
   123-175   *The Essence of Reasons*. Trans. Terence Mallick. Bilingual
         ed. Evanston: Northwestern University Press, 1969.
   177-202   "The Essence of Truth." Trans. John Sallis. In *Basic Writ-*
         ings. 117-141.
   203-238   "Plato's Doctrine of Truth." Trans. John Barlow. In *Philoso-*
         phy in the Twentieth Century. Vol. 3. Ed. William Barrett
         and Henry D. Aiken. New York: Harper & Row, 1962. 251-270.
   239-301   "On the Being and Conception of *Physis* in Aristotle's
         Physics B 1." Trans. Thomas Sheehan. *Man and World* 4 (1977):
         219-270.

303-312   "'Postscript' to 'What is Metaphysics?'" Trans. W.F.C. Hull
           and A. Crick. In *Existentialism from Dostoevsky to Satre*.
           Ed. Walter Kaufmann. Expanded ed. New York: New American Li-
           brary, 1975. 257-264.
313-364   "Letter on Humanism." Trans. Frank Capuzzi. In *Basic Writ-
           ings*. 193-242.
365-383   "The Way Back into the Ground of Metaphysics" ["Introduction
           to 'What is Metaphysics?'"] Trans. Walter Kaufmann. In *Exis-
           tentialism from Dostoevsky to Satre*. 265-279.
385-426   *The Question of Being*. Trans. William Kluback and Jean T.
           Wilde. Bilingual ed. New York: Twayne, 1962.
445-480   "Kant's Thesis on Being." Trans. Ted Klein and William T.
           Pohl. *Southwestern Journal of Philosophy* 4 (1973):7-33.
Zur Sache des Denkens. Tübingen: Niemeyer, 1969.
   On Time and Being. Trans. Joan Stambaugh. New York: Harper & Row,
      1972.

II. WORKS ON HEIDEGGER

Adamczewski, Zygmunt. "On the Way to Being: Reflecting on Conversations
   with Martin Heidegger." In *Heidegger and the Path of Thinking*. Ed. John
   Sallis. 12-36.
Bartky, Sandra Lee. "Heidegger and the Modes of World-Disclosure." *Philos-
   ophy and Phenomenological Research* 40 (December 1979):212-236.
Beaufret, Jean. "Heidegger Seen From France." Trans. Bernard Dauenhauer.
   The Southern Journal of Philosophy 8 (1970):433-438.
----------. "Heidegger et la théologie." In *Heidegger et la Question de
   Dieu*. Ed. R. Kearney and J. O'Leary. 19-36.
Biemel, Walter. *Martin Heidegger: An Illustrated Study*. Trans. J.L. Mehta.
   New York: Harvest, 1970.
Birault, Henri. "Thinking and Poetizing in Heidegger." In *On Heidegger and
   Language*. Ed. J.J. Kockelmans. 147-168.
Bruzina, Ronald. "Heidegger on the Metaphor and Philosophy." In *Heidegger
   and Modern Philosophy*. Ed. M. Murray. 184-200.
Caputo, John D. "Being, Ground and Play in Heidegger." *Man and World* 3
   (1970):26-48.
----------. *Heidegger and Aquinas: An Essay on Overcoming Metaphysics*.
   Bronx, NY: Fordham University Press, 1982.
----------. *The Mystical Element in Heidegger's Thought*. Athens: Ohio Uni-
   versity Press, 1978.
----------. "The Poverty of Thought: A Reflection on Heidegger and   Eck-
   hart." In *Heidegger: The Man and the Thinker*. Ed. T. Sheehan. 209-215.
----------. "'Supposing Truth to be a Woman ...': Heidegger, Nietzsche,
   Derrida." In *The Thought of Martin Heidegger*. Ed. M. Zimmerman. Tulane
   Studies in Philosophy, vol. XXXII. New Orleans: Tulane University, 1984.
   1-11.
----------. "The Thought of Being and the Conversation of Mankind: The
   Case of Heidegger and Rorty." *Review of Metaphysics* 36 (1983):661-685.
Danner, Helmut. *Das Göttliche und der Gott bei Heidegger*. Meisenheim:
   Anton Hain, 1971.

Durchblicke: Martin Heidegger zum 80. Geburtstage. Frankfurt: Klostermann, 1970.

Fédier, Francois. "Heidegger et Dieu."In *Heidegger et la Question de Dieu*. Ed. R. Kearney and J. O'Leary. 37-45.

Feick, Hildegaard. *Index zu "Sein und Zeit"*. 2., verbesserte Auflage. Tübingen: Niemeyer, 1968.

Frings, Manfred, ed. *Heidegger and the Quest for Truth*. Chicago: Triangle, 1968.

Fu, Charles Wei-hsun. "Heidegger and Zen on Being and Nothingness." In *Buddhist and Western Philosophy: A Critical Comparative Study*. Ed. Nathan Katz. New Dehli: Sterling, 1981. 172-201.

----------. "The Trans-onto-theo-logical Foundations of Language in Heidegger and Taoism." *The Journal of Chinese Philosophy* 5 (1978):301-333.

Gadamer, Hans-Georg. "Hegel and Heidegger." In *Hegel's Dialectic*. Trans. P. Christopher Smith. New Haven: Yale University Press, 1976. 100-116.

----------. "Heidegger and Marburg Theology." In Gadamer, *Philosophical Hermeneutics*. Trans. and ed. David E. Linge. Berkeley: University of California Press, 1976. 198-212.

----------. "Heidegger's Later Philosophy." In *Philosophical Hermeneutics*. 213-228.

----------. "The Religious Dimension in Heidegger." In *Transcendence and the Sacred*. Ed. Alan Olson and Leroy Rouner. Boston University Studies in Philosophy and Religion, vol. 2. Notre Dame: University of Notre Dame Press, 1981. 193-207.

----------. "Sein, Geist, Gott." In Gadamer, ed. *Heidegger: Freiburger Universitätsvorträge zu seinem Gedenken*. 2. Auflage. Freiburg/München: Karl Alber, 1979. 43-62.

Gall, Robert S. "Beyond Theodicy: The Divine in Heidegger and Tragedy," *Philosophy Today* 29 (1985):110-120.

----------. "Heidegger, Tragedy and Ethical Reflection." (unpublished)

----------. "The Inside and the Outside: Religious Experience and Religious Thought." *Auslegung* 12 (1986):122-133.

----------. "Mysticism and Ontology: A Heideggerian Critique of Caputo." *The Southern Journal of Philosophy* 24 (1986):463-478.

Gelven, Michael. "From Heidegger to Nietzsche: A Critical Review of Heidegger's Works on Nietzsche." *Philosophy Today* 25 (1981):68-80.

----------. "Heidegger and Tragedy." In *Martin Heidegger and the Question of Literature*. Ed. William V. Spanos. 215-228.

Gethmann-Siefert, Annemarie. *Das Verhältnis von Philosophie und Theologie in Denken Martin Heideggers*. Freiburg/München: Karl Alber, 1974.

Gründer, Karlfried. "Heidegger's Critique of Science in Its Historical Background." Trans. William Kramer. *Philosophy Today* 7 (1963):15-32.

Harries, Karsten. "Heidegger's Conception of the Holy." *The Personalist*. 47 (1966):169-184.

----------. "Meta-Criticism and Meta-Poetry: A Critique of Theoretical Anarchy." In *Studies in Phenomenology and the Human Sciences*. Ed. John Sallis. Atlantic Highlands, N.J.: Humanities Press, 1979. 54-73.

Heftrich, Eckhard. "Nietzsche in Denken Heideggers." In *Durchblicke*. 331-349.

Heine, Steven. *Existential and Ontological Dimensions of Time in Heidegger and Dōgen*. Albany: State University of New York Press, 1985.

Hofstadter, Albert. "Enownment." In *Martin Heidegger and the Question of Literature*. Ed. William V. Spanos. 17-37.

Hoy, David Couzons. "Forgetting the Text: Derrida's Critique of Heidegger." *Boundary 2* 8 (Fall 1979):223-235.

Jäger, Alfred. *Gott. Nochmals Martin Heidegger*. Tübingen: Mohr, 1978.

Jonas, Hans. "Heidegger and Theology." *Review of Metaphysics* 18 (1964): 207-233.

Kearney, Richard, and O'Leary, Joseph Stephen, eds. *Heidegger et la Question de Dieu*. Paris: Bernard Grasset, 1980.

Kelkel, Arion L. *La légende de l'être. Langage et poésie chez Heidegger*. Paris: Vrin, 1980.

Kisiel, Theodore. "Heidegger and the New Images of Science." *Research in Phenomenology* 7 (1977):162-181.

Kockelmans, Joseph J., ed. and trans. *On Heidegger and Language*. Evanston: Northwestern University Press, 1972.

----------. *On the Truth of Being: Reflections on Heidegger's Later Philosophy*. Bloomington: Indiana University Press, 1984.

----------. "Ontological Difference, Hermeneutics and Language." In *On Heidegger and Language*. 195-234.

----------. "Thanks-giving: The Completion of Thought." In *Heidegger and the Quest for Truth*. Ed. Manfred Frings. 39-52.

Krell, David Farrell. "Death and Interpretation." In *Heidegger's Existential Analytic*. Ed. Frederick Elliston. The Hague: Mouton, 1978. 247-255.

----------. "Nietzsche and the Task of Thinking: Heidegger's Reading of Nietzsche." Diss. Duquesne University, 1971.

----------. "Nietzsche in Heidegger's *Kehre*." *The Southern Journal of Philosophy* 13 (1975):197-204.

----------. "Results." *The Monist* 64 (1981):467-480.

----------. "*Schlag der Liebe, Schlag des Todes*: On a Theme in Heidegger and Trakl." *Research in Phenomenology* 7 (1977):238-258.

----------. "Work Sessions With Heidegger." *Philosophy Today* 26 (1982): 126-138.

Lampert, Lawrence. "Heidegger's Nietzsche Interpretation." *Man and World* 7 (1974):353-378.

Lovitt, William. "A 'Gesprach' with Heidegger on Technology." *Man and World* 6 (1973):44-62.

Löwith, Karl. *Heidegger: Denker in dürftiger Zeit*. 2., erweitere Auflage. Gottingen: Vandenhoeck and Ruprecht, 1960.

Malik, Charles H. "A Christian Reflection on Martin Heidegger." *The Thomist* 41 (1977):1-61.

Marx, Werner. *Heidegger and the Tradition*. Trans. Theodore Kisiel and Murray Green. Evanston: Northwestern University Press, 1971.

----------. "The World in Another Beginning: Poetic Dwelling and the Role of the Poet." In *On Heidegger and Language*. Ed. J.J. Kockelmans. 235-59.

Masson, Robert. "Rahner and Heidegger: Being, Hearing, God." *The Thomist* 37 (1973):455-480.

McCumber, John. "Language and Appropriation: The Nature of Heideggerian Dialogue." *The Personalist* 60 (1979):384-396.

Mehta, J.L. "Heidegger and Vedanta: Reflections on a Questionable Theme."
    International Philosophical Quarterly 18 (1978):121-144.
----------. *Martin Heidegger: The Way and the Vision*. Honolulu: Universi-
    ty Press of Hawaii, 1976.
Murray, Michael, ed. *Heidegger and Modern Philosophy*. New Haven: Yale Uni-
    versity Press, 1978.
Orr, Robert P. *The Meaning of Transcendence: A Heideggerian Reflection*.
    American Academy of Religion Dissertation Series, no. 35. Chico, CA:
    Scholars Press, 1981.
Ott, Heinrich. "Die Bedeutung von Martin Heideggers für die Methode der
    Theologie." In *Durchblicke*. 27-38.
----------. *Denken und Sein: Der Weg Martin Heideggers und der Weg Theolo-
    gie*. Zollikon: Evangelischen, 1959.
----------. "Hermeneutic and Personal Structure." In *On Heidegger and Lan-
    guage*. Ed. J.J. Kockelmans. 169-193.
Perotti, James L. *Heidegger on the Divine*. Athens: Ohio University Press,
    1974.
Pöggeler, Otto. "Being as Appropriation." In *Heidegger and Modern Philoso-
    phy*. Ed. M. Murray. 84-115.
----------. *Der Denkweg Martin Heideggers*. Pfullingen: Neske, 1963.
----------. "Heideggers Begegnung mit Hölderlin." *Man and World* 10 (1977):
    13-61.
----------. "Heidegger's Topology of Being." In *On Heidegger and Language*.
    Ed. J.J. Kockelmans. 107-146.
----------. "Metaphysics and Topology of Being in Heidegger." Trans.
    Parvis Emad. *Man and World* 8 (1975):3-27.
Richardson, William J. "Heidegger and God -- and Professor Jonas." *Thought*
    40 (1965):13-40.
----------. *Heidegger: From Phenomenology to Thought*. The Hague: Martinus
    Nijhoff, 1963.
Robinson, James M. "The German Discussion of the Later Heidegger." In *The
    Later Heidegger and Theology*. Ed. James M. Robinson and John B. Cobb,
    Jr. 3-76.
Robinson, James M., and Cobb, John B., Jr., eds. *The Later Heidegger and
    Theology*. New York: Harper & Row, 1963.
Rorty, Richard. "Overcoming the Tradition: Heidegger and Dewey." In *Heid-
    egger and Modern Philosophy*. Ed. M. Murray. 239-258.
Rouse, Joseph. "Heidegger's Later Philosophy of Science." *The Southern
    Journal of Philosophy* 33 (1985):75-92.
----------. "Kuhn, Heidegger and Scientific Realism." *Man and World* 14
    (1981):269-290.
Sallis, John, ed. *Heidegger and the Path of Thinking*. Pittsburgh: Duquesne
    University Press, 1970.
Schrey, Heinz-Horst. "Die Bedeutung der Philosophie Martin Heideggers für
    die Theologie." In *Martin Heideggers Einfluss auf die Wissenschaften aus
    Anlass seines 60. Geburtstag*. Bern: Franke, 1949. 9-21.
Schufrieder, Gregory. "Heidegger on Community." *Man and World* 14 (1981):
    25-54.
Schürmann, Reiner. *L'principe d'anarchie. Heidegger et la question de
    l'ägir*. Paris: Seuil, 1982.

----------. "Questioning the Foundations of Practical Philosophy." In *Phenomenology: Dialogues and Bridges*. Ed. Ronald Bruzina and Bruce Wilshire. Albany: State University of New York Press, 1982. 11-21.

Schuwer, André. "Nature and the Holy: On Heidegger's Interpretation of Hölderlin's Hymn 'Wie Wenn Am Feiertage'." *Research in Phenomenology* 7 (1977):225-237.

Sheehan, Thomas, ed. *Heidegger: The Man and the Thinker*. Chicago: Precedent, 1981.

----------. "Heidegger's 'Introduction to the Phenomenology of Religion' 1920-21." *The Personalist* 60 (1979):312-324.

----------. "Introduction: Heidegger, the Project and the Fulfillment." In *Heidegger: The Man and the Thinker*. 3-19.

Silverman, Hugh J., and Ihde, Don, eds. *Hermeneutics and Deconstruction*. Albany: State University of New York Press, 1985.

Smith, F. Joseph. "In-the-World and On-the-Earth." In *Heidegger and the Quest for Truth*. Ed. M. Frings. 184-203.

Spanos, William V., ed. *Martin Heidegger and the Question of Literature*. 1976; rpt. Bloomington: Indiana University Press, 1979.

Steiner, George. *Martin Heidegger*. New York: Viking, 1978.

Steiner, Kenneth. "Appropriation, Belonging-Together and Being-in-the-World." *Journal of the British Society for Phenomenology* 10 (May 1979): 130-133.

Vycinas, Vincent. *Earth and Gods: An Introduction to the Philosophy of Martin Heidegger*. The Hague: Martinus Nijhoff, 1961.

Welte, Bernard. "God in Heidegger's Thought." *Philosophy Today* 26 (1982): 85-100.

Williams, John R. *Martin Heidegger's Philosophy of Religion*. Canadian Corporation for Studies in Religion. Waterloo, Ontario: Wilfrid Laurier University Press, 1977.

Wisser, Richard, ed. *Martin Heidegger in Conversation*. Trans. B. Srinivasu Murthy. New Dehli: Arnold-Heinemann, 1977.

Zimmerman, Michael E. "A Comparison of Nietzsche's Overman and Heidegger's Authentic Self." *The Southern Journal of Philosophy* 14 (1976):213-231.

----------. *Eclipse of the Self: The Development of Heidegger's Concept of Authenticity*. Athens: Ohio University Press, 1981.

III. OTHER WORKS

Altizer, Thomas J.J. "History as Apocalypse." In *Deconstruction and Theology*. 147-177.

----------, et. al. *Deconstruction and Theology*. New York: Crossroad, 1982.

Barbour, John D. *Tragedy as a Critique of Virtue: The Novel and Ethical Reflection*. Chico, CA: Scholars Press, 1984.

Barrett, William. *The Illusion of Technique*. Garden City, NY: Anchor Press /Doubleday, 1979.

Berger, Peter D. *The Heretical Imperative: Contemporary Possibilities of Religious Affirmation*. Garden City, NY: Anchor Press/Doubleday, 1980.

Blackham, H.J. *Six Existentialist Thinkers*. New York: Harper Torchbooks, 1959.

Buber, Martin. *The Eclipse of God*. New York: Harper & Row, 1952.

Bultmann, Rudolf. "Die Geschichtlichkeit des Daseins und der Glaube. Ant-
wort an G. Kuhlmann." In *Heidegger und Theologie*. Ed. Gerhard Noller.
München: Chr. Kaiser, 1967.
Derrida, Jacques. "Différance." In *Speech and Phenomena and Other Essays
on Husserl's Theory of Signs*. Trans. David B. Allison. Evanston: North-
western University Press, 1973. 129-160.
----------. *Of Grammatology*. Trans. G.C. Spivak. Baltimore: Johns Hopkins
University Press, 1976.
----------. *Positions*. Trans. Alan Bass. Chicago: University of Chicago
Press, 1981.
----------. *Spurs: Nietzsche's Style*. Trans. Barbara Harlow. Chicago: Uni-
versity of Chicago Press, 1978.
Dreyfus, Hubert L. "Holism and Hermeneutics." *Review of Metaphysics* 34
(1980):3-23.
Eliade, Mircea. *The Myth of the Eternal Return or, Cosmos and History*.
Trans. Willard Trask. Bollington Series XLVI. 1954; rpt. Princeton:
Princeton University Press, 1971.
----------. *Patterns in Comparative Religions*. Trans. Rosemary Sheed.
1958; rpt. New York: New American Library, 1974.
Eliot, T.S. *The Complete Poems and Plays: 1909-1950*. New York: Harcourt,
Brace and World, 1971.
Feyerabend, Paul. *Against Method*. 1975; rpt. London: Verso, 1978.
Grene, Marjorie. *Philosophy In and Out of Europe*. Berkeley: University of
California Press, 1976.
Heller, Erich, and Thoreby, Anthony. "Idealism and Religious Vision in the
Poetry of Hölderlin." *Quarterly Review of Literature* X (1959). 23-40.
Hick, John. *God and the Universe of Faiths: Essays in the Philosophy of
Religion*. New York: Macmillan, 1973.
----------. *Philosophy of Religion*. 2nd ed. Englewood Cliffs, NJ: Pren-
tice-Hall, 1973.
----------, ed. *Truth and Dialogue in World Religions: Conflicting Truth
Claims*. Philadelphia: Westminster Press, 1974.
Hölderlin, Friedrich. *Poems and Fragments*. Trans. Michael Hamburger. Bi-
lingual ed. Ann Arbor: University of Michigan Press, 1967.
Kaufmann, Gordon D. "Theology as Imaginative Construction." *The Journal of
the American Academy of Religion* 50 (1982):73-79.
Kaufmann, Walter. *Religion in Four Dimensions*. New York: Reader's Digest
Press, 1976.
Kuhn, Thomas. *The Structure of Scientific Revolutions*. *2nd, enlarged ed.
Chicago: University of Chicago Press, 1970.*
MacIntyre, Alasdair, and Ricoeur, Paul. *The Religious Significance of
Atheism*. New York: Columbia University Press, 1969.
Martland, T.R. "To Glorify: The Essence of Poetry and Religion." *Religious
Studies* 16 (1980):413-423.
Nietzsche, Friedrich. *Basic Writings of Nietzsche*. Trans. and ed. Walter
Kaufmann. New York: Random House/Modern Library, 1968.
----------. *The Portable Nietzsche*. Trans. and ed. Walter Kaufmann. New
York: Viking, 1954.
----------. *The Will to Power*. Trans. Walter Kaufmann and R. J. Holling-
dale. Ed. Walter Kaufmann. New York: Random House/Vintage Books, 1968.

O'Leary, Joseph S. *Questioning Back: The Overcoming of Metaphysics in Christian Tradition*. Minneapolis: Winston/Seabury, 1985.

Otto, Walter F. *Homeric Gods*. Trans. Moses Hades. 1954; rpt. New York: Thames and Hudson, 1979.

----------. "Die Zeit und das Sein." In *Anteile: Martin Heidegger zum 60. Geburtstag*. Frankfurt: Klostermann, 1950. 7-28.

Raschke, Carl A. *The Alchemy of the Word: Language and the End of Theology*. American Academy of Religion Studies in Religion, no. 20. Missoula, Montana: Scholars Press, 1979.

----------. "The Deconstruction of God." In *Deconstruction and Theology*. 1-33.

----------. "The New Cosmology and Overcoming Metaphysics." *Philosophy Today* 24 (1980):375-387.

----------. "Religious Pluralism and Truth: From Theology to a Hermeneutical Dialogy." *The Journal of the American Academy of Religion* 50 (1982): 35-48.

Ricoeur, Paul. *The Conflict of Interpretations*. Ed. Don Ihde. Evanston: Northwestern University Press, 1974.

----------. "The Critique of Religion." In *The Philosophy of Paul Ricoeur: An Anthology of His Work*. Ed. Charles E. Reagan and David Stewart. Boston: Beacon Press, 1978. 213-222.

----------. *Interpretation Theory: Discourse and the Surplus of Meaning*. Fort Worth: Texas Christian University Press, 1976.

Schuon, Frithjof. *The Transcendent Unity of Religions*. Trans. Peter Townsend. New York: Harper & Row, 1975.

Smart, Ninian. "Truth and Religions." In *Truth and Dialogue in World Religions*. Ed. John Hick.

Smith, Huston. *Forgotten Truth*. New York: Harper & Row, 1976.

Smith, Wilfred Cantwell. *Faith and Belief*. Princeton: Princeton University Press, 1979.

----------. *The Meaning and End of Religion*. New York: Macmillan, 1963.

----------. *Towards a World Theology*. New York: Macmillan, 1981.

Taylor, Mark C. "Text as Victim." In *Deconstruction and Theology*. 58-78.

----------. *Erring: A Postmodern A/theology*. Chicago: University of Chicago Press, 1984.

INDICES

INDEX OF NAMES

170   INDEX

INDEX OF SUBJECTS